THE ANGLERS' ENCYCLOPAEDIA

THE ANGLERS' ENCYCLOPAEDIA

COLIN WILLOCK

ODHAMS PRESS LIMITED

LONG ACRE, LONDON

FOR THE TWINS

First published 1960
Reprinted July, 1960
Reprinted November, 1960
Reprinted March, 1961
Reprinted July, 1962
Reprinted February, 1963
Reprinted February, 1964

Made and printed in Great Britain by
C. Tinling & Co., Ltd.,
Liverpool, London and Prescot

S.264.R6.PQ.

List of Photographs

Acknowledgements

THE author and the publishers are grateful to the undermentioned sources for co-operation and assistance rendered with reference material and/or illustrations for this book.

British Museum of Natural History (Fish Section); Margaret Butterworth, author of *Now Cook me The Fish* (Country Life); *The Field*; F. G. Goddard & Co. Ltd. ("Efgeeco"), London, S.W.12; Hardy Bros. Ltd., Alnwick; B. James & Son, London, W.13; W. Martin James, Ltd., Redditch; Millard Bros. Ltd., London N.17; Ogden Smiths Ltd., London, W.1; Pegley-Davies, Ltd., Walton-on-Thames; To the River Boards mentioned in the Appendix, for permission to reproduce extracts from their Fishery Bye-laws; The Royal Belgian Institute of Natural Sciences; W. Weymouth, Brentford, Middx.; and to Capt. Norton Bracy, Angling Holidays Ltd.

The photographs are reproduced by courtesy of the following: R. A. P. Dexter (facing p.144); Fox Photos (facing p.65); Ronald Goodearl (facing p.128); P. A.-Reuter (facing p.129); John Tarlton (facing p.32, 33, 64, 145).

Introduction

IN a long, long history of angling books this is the first A–Z encyclopaedia that embraces coarse, sea, game, and big-game fishing. In compiling it I have had two thoughts uppermost. (1) To keep it simple. (2) To remember that anglers do not want merely to know about fish; they want to know how to catch them.

There are more than 600 entries in this book. Undoubtedly I could have doubled that number. For example, it would have been possible to give every single pattern of trout fly an entry of its own: and this in itself would have brought the total of separate headings to close on 1,000. Then there could have been an intricate system of cross-referencing. But nothing, in my view, is more infuriating than a continual exhortation to look under another heading for a piece of information. I have kept such references to a minimum.

In the attempt to keep the book simple I have tried to choose obvious headings. For instance: to take the question of flies. Basically, there are two kinds of fly—the natural flies, and the imitations that the angler ties. In this encyclopaedia, all the live insects which figure in angling are grouped under NATURAL FLIES, and the information about fishermen's imitations is under ARTIFICIAL FLIES. Where, however, a specialist term occurs in one of these main sections I have given it a separate short entry to itself, so that it can be checked upon if need be. In ARTIFICIAL FLIES, for example, the terms 'dun' and 'spinner' are used without detailed explanation. Consequently both 'dun' and 'spinner' appear under their respective entries.

Now about the encyclopaedia's use in helping the angler to catch fish. Wherever a species occurs which can be said to demand a special angling technique or techniques, it receives double treatment. BARBEL, for example, is followed by BARBEL-FISHING, BASS by BASS-FISHING, and so on.

I hope that these dual entries in each case will tell the reader, who may be starting from scratch, what tackle he needs, what baits or methods to employ, the habits of the fish concerned, where it is likely to be found—

in fact enough to go out, properly equipped, and catch it. Thus, the freshwater man setting out on a seaside holiday will be able not only to discover how to catch bass, but also to judge how far he can adapt his existing tackle.

The mention of tackle brings me to another important point. I have made separate entries for rods and reels, and for sea and big-game rods, but I have not dealt at length under these headings with alternative equipments for various species. Tackle, in the main, is dealt with in conjunction with the fish concerned. Thus, recommendations for mackerel tackle will be found under the heading of MACKEREL-FISHING, following the one on the mackerel itself.

Finally, where I have felt that the reader may need more detailed and specialist knowledge I have not hesitated to suggest further reading.

C. W.

 A

ACHILL: island off the west coast of Ireland connected to the mainland by a bridge. Off this coast big game fish abound, including porbeagle, blue and possibly mako and thresher sharks. Big fish of all species are caught here and in Clew Bay centred on Westport, County Mayo, an admirable fishing centre.

ADIPOSE FIN: the small gristly appendage common to all the *salmonidae*, occurring on the ridge of the back just in front of the tail. Function unknown, maybe vestigial, but possibly has some 'aquadynamic' effect when the fish is in motion.

ADMIRALTY CHARTS: both these and Tide Tables can be bought from Messrs. J. D. Potter, Admiralty Chart Agents, 140, The Minories, London, E.C.3. Charts give invaluable offshore information as to depths and nature of bottom. Tide Tables are calculated in full for all important centres round the coast.

"AERIAL" TACKLE: a spinning flight for use with deadbait. A barbed lead is pushed down the mouth of the bait, a double and two treble hooks are stuck into it, being attached to the head of the bait by wire. The tackle gives the bait a wobbling action.

ALASTICUM: proprietary brand of fine wire used for making traces in pike fishing, both spinning and live-baiting. Available in various breaking-strains.

ALDER: a valuable fly for the trout angler. It is a member of the *Sialidae*. The nymphs, which look like those of the may-fly but have one tail instead of three, are carnivorous to a large extent. Unlike those of the may-fly family, the

alder nymphs climb out of the water on the stems of water plants to hatch. The fly is a brown insect with smooth, veined, and sloping wings that fold backwards. See NATURAL FLIES.

ALDERMAN: slang name for chub.

ALEVIN: the young of salmon and trout, and a term more properly applied to salmon during the first week or two of their lives. At this stage the alevins carry a yolk sac beneath their bodies which contains the nourishment to sustain them in this first critical period. Soon, this sac is absorbed and disappears.

ALGAE: otherwise phytoplankton. Minute vegetable organisms of different colours that form in water, encouraged by the action of sunlight. They are probably not eaten by fish but they do form food for the animal plankton (zooplankton) on which most fish feed either directly or indirectly.

ALL-ENGLAND CHAMPIONSHIP: Correct name—National Federation of Anglers' Annual Championship. This is the most important event of the match-fisher's year, one thousand and more fishermen taking part. Clubs competing must all be affiliated to the N.F.A. A different club is chosen each year to organize the event, and the venue is changed yearly. Team prizes for top weights are given but the most sought after award is that for top individual weight caught by any angler taking part. To show what can be done: in 1955, the winning team, Sheffield Amalgamated, landed 136lb. 15½oz. of fish from the Huntspill River. In 1936, the

A* 9

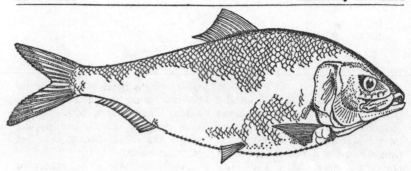

ALLIS SHAD. *A silvery marine fish found 'mostly in the waters of south-west Britain. It ascends esturies at spawning time.*

individual champion weighed in 35lb. from the Thurne at Potter Heigham.

ALLIS SHAD: *Alosa alosa,* family *Clupeidae.* A silvery sea fish with forked tail, that comes into estuaries to spawn. Grows to a greater size (up to 8 lb. at least) than its relative the twaite shad, and lacks the flank spots above the lateral line often seen in the twaite. Has extremely long, fine anal fin. Mid-April is the time the fish come into the rivers to spawn. They drop their eggs which are only just heavier than water. These sink to the bottom and wash about with the tide for about four days. They then hatch out, the fry taking to the shallows. West Country estuaries are most favoured by allis shad.

AMADOU: spongy fungus used by dry-fly fishermen for drying waterlogged flies.

AMERICAN BROOK TROUT: truly a char, *Salvelinus fontinalis,* a beautifully marked, mottled fish that was introduced to British waters some 50 years ago but did not thrive.

AMPHIPODS: invertebrates (hoppers) found in tidal pools and undoubtedly eaten by sea fish.

ANAL FIN: the rear under fin of a fish placed just behind the vent.

Important as a means of identification between chub and dace. That of the chub is convex at the trailing edge and that of the dace concave.

ANATOMY OF FISHES: the clearest divisions into which the external anatomy of a fish can be divided are: head, body, fins. The head extends as far as the rear of the gill-cover or operculum. The body stretches between this and the tail, or caudal, fin. The remaining fins are: pectorals (a pair, one either side, just behind the gill-cover), ventrals (or belly fins), dorsal (which in certain fishes, such as the perch in freshwater and many sea fishes, is in two portions) occurring on the ridge of the back, the adipose (a gristly appendage just forward of the tail and appearing only in the *salmonidae*), and the anal fin on the lower surface of the fish just behind the vent. The pectoral and ventral fins correspond to the limbs of vertebrates.

Now to deal with some of the major external features starting at the snout. The mouth is described as superior, inferior, or terminal, according to the placing of the jaws. To give examples: the rudd's mouth is superior in that the lower jaw overlaps the upper, because the fish feeds primarily on the surface.

A roach, on the other hand, has an inferior mouth, while the predatory fish such as the perch and the salmon family have terminal mouths where the lips meet equally.

Round the mouth in many species are found barbules or barbels. These are feelers, usually attached to the lower jaw, and which assist the fish in finding food: fish so equipped often have poorly developed eyesight.

The body of a fish is covered with skin in which the scales are bedded. Some fish, such as the leather carp, have practically no scales, but here compensation is often given with an extra heavy coating of natural slime: the function of this slime in all species is to act as a barrier against infection and to reduce friction with the water. The scales are laid on in tile fashion, one overlapping another. As the fish grows, so do the scales grow by the process of adding to their outer surface. From this method of growth the naturalist is able to assess the age of the fish, for scale growth is marked by a series of rings similar to the annular rings of a tree. The rings can be clearly seen and counted by the expert, while black marks indicate spawning periods and times of lean feeding. The further the rings apart, then the more rapid the rate of growth.

Along the flanks of a fish is a line of scales distinguished by a black mark or sometimes a notch. This line, known as the lateral line, is the centre of the nervous system by which the fish detects changes of pressure in the water, probably also atmospheric changes, and also the presence of other fish nearby. The latter is particularly evident with the pike which almost certainly detects the whereabouts of wounded or incapacitated fish, that will make an easy meal, by means of vibrations felt at the lateral line. The line makes a convenient point at which to count scales, both along the line and in a transverse line between the lateral line and dorsal fin. In many cases this count assists in identification of doubtful species. In very few cases, alas, does such a count provide positive identification on its own.

The colouring of a fish is produced by the colour cells or chromatophores, which make use of only four different kinds of cells—black, yellow, red, and iridescent. All colour combinations are produced by permutations of these four. It is further thought that colour adaptation to environment in fishes is controlled automatically by the eye.

The fins act as power-plant, stabilizers, and rudder. They correspond to the engines as well as to all the control surfaces of an aircraft. The ventrals and pectorals serve as brakes, being used in turning as a sculler uses his oars. The anal and dorsal fins serve much as does the fin of an aircraft or the keel of a yacht, preventing sideslipping on the turns. The caudal fin together with the muscles of the body provides the propulsion in the way that an oar sculled over the stern of a dinghy drives it through the water. The fins themselves, with the exception of the gristly adipose fin, are supported and operated on a series of rays. The rays are either jointed or unjointed in which latter case they are known as 'soft' rays. The soft variety usually spread out towards their tips, being known in consequence as 'branched' rays: to distinguish them, the jointed kind are called 'simple' rays.

So much for the external characteristics. Next, the main features of the skeleton. In general the skeleton resembles that of the vertebrates, except for the fact that there is no neck region between head and backbone, and ventral and pectoral fins replace limbs. The backbone consists of articulated vertebrae. The spinal chord runs the entire length of the body. The muscular structure of the fish lies on either side of the backbone, the muscular segments being arranged one behind the other, and fitting into each other, like a stack of discs. From the interaction of these comes the powerful body thrust that drives the fish through the water.

The head is built upon and round a complicated structure of bones, of which the main elements are: the cranium, the solid bone centre of the head; the visceral skeleton which includes jaws, tongue and gills. In the visceral skeleton are a number of bones, the most important of which are the premaxilla and maxilla of the upper jaw. The front bone of the lower jaw is called the dentary and the rear one the articular. At the rear of the head come the opercular bones that form the gill-cover.

The gills themselves are branched flaps of tissue filled with blood vessels, whose function is to extract oxygen from the water in the same way that lungs extract it from the air. They are fixed to the gill bars in the gill cavity, there being four bars on each side. On the bars are pointed gill-rakers whose job is to protect the delicate gills by filtering debris and foreign matter from the water.

The teeth of different species vary in number, type and placing very considerably. Besides being sited on the obvious and natural places such as the jawbones (the premaxilla and maxilla for example), they occur on the roof of the mouth (on the vomer and palatine), and also on the

pharyngeals and even on certain parts of the gill bars. Those species, notably the *cyprinids*, having pharyngeal teeth are colloquially said to have 'throat teeth'. These are used to crush the food against a bony palate well down in the throat. These pharyngeals often provide positive identification in cases where the fish can be dissected for examination. Notably predatory fish such as the pike and perch are largely furnished with seizing and holding teeth.

The mouths of fish have cells which secrete a mucus to lubricate food so that it slips easily down the gullet. Digestion proper starts in the stomach or intestines where powerful digestive juices, secreted mainly by the liver, go to work. It should be noted that the predators are equipped with a stomach proper in which whole fish, gorged intact by the eater, are gradually broken down, sometimes over a period of days. This, in the case of the pike, accounts partially for the fact that pike after 'going mad' in a certain water then pass through a dormant period as far as feeding is concerned. It does not, of course, explain why the fish 'go mad' at the same time.

The throat-teeth species, the *cyprinids*, have no real stomach. Here digestion takes place in the intestines where milder digestive juices come into play. A man who has had his stomach removed by surgery can exist on his intestines provided he eats a little and often and his food has been chopped up small for him. Here is a direct parallel with the *cyprinids*—carp, roach, chub, etc., who crush up their food with their pharyngeals and feed sparingly several times in twenty-four hours, a fact for which the angler can be thankful.

All save the bottom-living fishes make important use of the swim-bladder. This air or gas sac is really a continuation of the oseophagus. This elongated organ has the function of equalizing pressure inside and outside the fish as it varies its depth. It accounts for the fact that a fish pulled too suddenly to the surface from a great depth, as in a net, sometimes has its inner organs blown out through its mouth

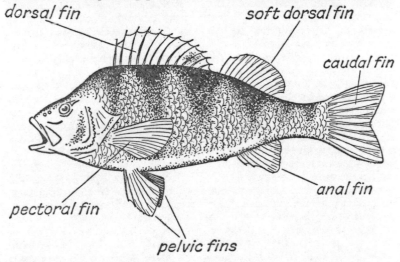

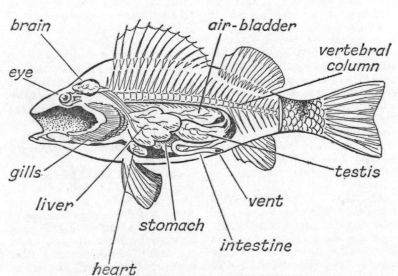

ANATOMY OF FISH. (*Above*) *The external features of a perch, and the names applied to the fins. The pelvic fins are known also as ventral fins.* (*Below*) *The nature and location of its internal organs.*

13

by pressure change. It has not had time to adjust to its changed environment by means of altering pressures in its swim-bladder. When diving deeply the fish is unable to take in enough air to fill its swim-bladder, so a special mechanism that enables gas from the blood vessels to be transferred to the swim-bladder takes over.

In many varieties of fish the young are born with dual sets of reproductive equipment, male and female, development in one direction taking place later: occasionally hermaphrodite fish are found. The roes hard and soft in adult fish generally end in the oviducts through which they are shed at spawning time at the vent. The salmon family, however, have no such ducts, the eggs lying simply in the body cavity. Fish can therefore be stripped of eggs and spawn for breeding purposes by gentle stroking of the flanks, a treatment that does them no harm. An interesting point about the shedding of the male's milt in spawning is that it has to do its work remarkably quickly. The male sperms in the milt do not become active until they reach water. Thereafter they have anything from twenty-three seconds in the case of a brown trout to five minutes in the case of a carp, to find a female egg and fertilize it.

Recommended reading on this subject: *Guide to Freshwater Fishes* by Otto Schindler (Thames & Hudson).

ANGLERS' CO-OPERATIVE ASSOCIATION: probably the most important single body in fishing today. Founded in 1947 by John Eastwood, its function is to fight water pollution cases on behalf of its members. It does so by virtue of a rule of Common Law which says that any man through whose land water flows is entitled to enjoy a purity of water similar to that of his upstream neighbour. This clause enables the A.C.A. to take action in many cases where the complicated mechanism of a River Board is handicapped. The A.C.A. has won many hundreds of cases for large and small angling societies and has acted both for the game and coarse fisherman, though probably far more often for the latter. Its most notable victory was when it fought the case of the Pride of Derby Angling Association for pollution of the Derwent against Derby Corporation, the British Electricity Authority, and British Celanese, and won.

ANGLER FISH: *Lophius piscatorius*, family *Pediculati*. Sometimes caught by accident by boat fishermen, notably off the Devon and Cornwall coasts. An ugly brute of a fish, which perhaps accounts for its unpopularity. The interesting thing about the creature is that the forward spines of its dorsal fin are fish lures, and the first spine of all is rod, line and bait combined. The angler fish uses the soft filament of skin at the tip of this spine to entice its prey within reach of its large mouth. Fry, and sometimes large fish, are attracted by the bait the angler waves about, and are grabbed as they swim towards it.

ANNELIDS: the worm family, marine or land.

ANTENNA FLOAT: float with long fine wand attached to the top. Used for fishing in windy and rough conditions when the float is weighted so that only the wand projects, periscope fashion, above the water surface, offering little resistance to the wind. See FLOATS.

ANTI-KINK DEVICES: these take many forms though their function is always the same—to prevent the rotary action of different baits from twisting the line to which it is attached. Perhaps the simplest and most effective of all anti-kink devices is the ball-bearing swivel. Fixed between reel line and spinning trace, this prevents any twist being communicated to the line. A plain metal swivel invariably has to be assisted by an anti-kink gadget. The simplest of these are small weights that depend, usually from the top eye of the topmost swivel. Spiral leads and half-moon leads attached to the line above the swivel also serve quite well. For light spinning a semicircular plastic vane fixed on or about the highest swivel can be most efficient.

ARCHER TACKLE: spinning device consisting of vanes and a combination of two double hooks and one treble hook. The vanes are hinged to clip into a deadbait and the two double hooks have prongs for a similar purpose. A long needle leading from the hinge of the vanes is stuck into the centre of the bait which may further be secured by fine wire or thread. Used for pike and for some sea fish.

ARLESEY BOMB: a patent leger weight invented by Richard Walker. Its main virtue is that it is fitted with a swivel through which the line runs. This tends to give minimum resistance to a taking fish. See LEADS.

ARTIFICIAL FLIES: imitations of insects, larvae or small fish made by tying silk, tinsel, fur, raffia, feathers and other materials to the shank of the hook. The patterns of fly are almost beyond number. In actual fact, however, the angler in any one district—effective patterns vary from area to area—can get by usually with half-a-dozen patterns at the outside. At the end of this section a representative list of pat-

terns will be given: it is by no means exhaustive but gives some idea of what is available. The different types of fly and their functions are as follows:

Dry-flies: these are flies tied to float on the surface where in the main they represent aquatic insects that have just hatched out, are returning to the water to lay their eggs, or have fallen on the water having laid them. They are known respectively in these three instances as 'duns', 'spinners' or 'spent spinners'. They also represent certain land flies blown on to the water by accident. More than any other type of fly, the floater is designed to imitate exactly a certain insect. This is particularly true of the natural chalk-stream flies which float slowly and majestically over the trout's head. However, the majority of dryflies are approximate imitations, and when you come to fish on the rougher streams the recommended pattern bears little apparent resemblance to natural insects.

The secret of the dry-fly's buoyancy lies in its hackle—the long thin feather wound round the hook to give the fly its bristly appearance at the head. These hackle points not only serve to imitate wings, thorax and legs but also, if chosen correctly, keep the fly afloat. The hackles for a dry-fly come from the neck of a cock, preferably a gamecock. They are stiff, shiny, and narrow in the fibre, quite the opposite of the soft, wider hen hackles used for wet or sunken flies. Small variations in the actual tying of dry-flies are found. Some tyers prefer hackled patterns, that is to say flies tied without wings. Others attach wings made from segments of the primary feathers of various birds. The main virtue of the wings is that they assist somewhat in giving the fly a gentle parachute-like descent on the water.

Wet-flies: these flies are designed to sink below the surface where they represent either aquatic insects rising to hatch, drowned aquatic or land insects, or the young of fish. In the case of sea-trout flies they can scarcely be said to imitate anything beyond a bright, flashing, colourful lure that may possibly have some resemblance to a small fish. The wet-fly is tied to give what is called a 'narrow entry' into the water: that is to say, its frontal aspect when attached to the cast offers little resistance to the water. This is achieved by using soft hen hackles whose fibres also have the advantage that they move in the water to give the fly life; by tying the fly sparsely; by keeping the wings thin, close together, sloping back over the body, and immediately above the hook shank. Sunken flies are used mostly in swift-flowing streams where most titbits become submerged.

Nymphs: a nymph is the fisherman's name for the last larval stage of a true aquatic fly when it rises to the surface to split its skin and emerge as a dun. When nymphs are moving, the fish can often be seen cruising across the stream intercepting them on their way to the surface, and taking them just sub-surface with what is termed a 'bulge', a name derived from the humped appearance of the surface at that point. The fly-tyer can imitate the best-known types of nymph by sparse tying without wings, and with little or no hackle beyond that necessary to indicate the true insect's wing-cases. Nymphs are cast upstream and fished sunken.

Sea trout flies: these more correctly could be called lures, for they imitate no insect in nature. They are all largish, bright, and frequently have bodies that are wound with silver tinsel. Though sea trout can be caught from time to time on small dry-flies, the true sea trout fly is fished below the surface, often two or three to a cast.

Salmon flies: the word fly is quite inappropriate here. Salmon flies are large gaudy affairs that bear no resemblance—as far as the human eye can tell, at least—to anything found in water. Yet they take salmon. What is more strange is that only local patterns work in many salmon rivers. It pays, as always, to seek local advice. Normally the salmon lure is richly and generously dressed. There is a subdivision of the species, however, in which the dressing is extremely light, so light in fact that it might be described as a mere decoration of the bare hook. Such lures are designed for fishing with a floating line—'greased-lining' it is sometimes called—when rivers are low during a hot summer.

Minor variations exist in the method of tying some of the larger flies. Among the terms used to describe these are 'hair-winged' flies and 'streamer-flies'. In the first case the wing of the fly is tied with hair rather than a section of feather: streamer flies have an extremely long, swept-back wing made of one or more feathers. These are often well marked and very large cock's hackles. The streamer, because of the action of this feather in the water, gives the impression of being a small fish, probably a minnow.

It would be impossible to give a full list of the patterns available. Would-be fly-dressers are recommended to John Veniard's *Fly-Dresser's Guide* and Roger Woolley's *Modern Trout Fly Dressing*.

The schedule of suggested flies that follows is taken from the excellent *Flyfisher's Illustrated Reference Book* produced by Ogden

SALMON FLIES   SEA FISHING FLY

Butcher

Orange Parson

*Bass & Mackerel
bait*

Thunder & Lightning

Silver Blue

TROUT FLIES (DRY)

Hackled dry fly

Olive Dun

Coachman

TROUT FLIES (WET)

Wickham's Fancy

May-fly Nymph

Golden Olive

ARTIFICIAL FLIES. *Some representative patterns showing the nature and variety of the numerous creations used by fly fishermen.*

17

Smiths, the well-known tackle firm. *North of England:* Black Gnat, Blue Dun, Greenwell's Glory, Hare's Ear and Woodcock, March Brown, Olive Dun, Partridge and Orange, Red Spinner, Snipe and Purple, Soldier Palmer, Stone Fly, Zulu. Sizes: dry, oo-1; wet, o-3.

North-east: Blue Upright, Driffield Dun, Greenwell's Glory, Olive Quill, Partridge and Orange, Pheasant Tail, Red Quill, Red Spinner, Red Tag, Treacle Parkin, Tup, Waterhen Boa. Sizes: dry, oo-2; wet, oo-2.

East: Alder, Black Gnat, Blue Varient, Brown Palmer, Coachman, Coch y Bondhu, Dark Olive Dun, March Brown, Red Tag, Red Varient, Wickham's Fancy. Sizes: dry, oo-3; wet, o-4.

South: Alder, Black Gnat, Blue Quill, Ginger Quill, Greenwell's Glory, Hare's Ear, Iron Blue Dun, Olive Quill, Red Spinner, Sherry Spinner, Silver Sedge, Wickham's Fancy. Sizes: oo-3.

South-west: Black Spider, Blue Upright, Coch y Bondhu, Greenwell's Glory, Half Stone, Hare's Ear, March Brown, Olive Quill, Red Spinner, Red Upright, Tup, Wickham's Fancy. Sizes: dry, oo-2; wet, o-3.

North-west: Black Spider, Blue Dun, Butcher, Cinnamon Sedge, March Brown, Olive Dun, Partridge and Orange, Partridge and Yellow, Red Spider, Snipe and Purple, Stone Fly, Zulu. Sizes: dry, oo-2; wet, o-3.

North Wales: Alder, Blue Upright, Butcher, Coch y Bondhu, Greenwell's Glory, March Brown and Silver, Olive Quill, Partridge and Orange, Peter Ross, Red Spinner, Teal Blue and Silver, Zulu. Sizes: oo-2.

South Wales: Black Gnat, Blue Upright, Coachman, Feather Duster, Greenwell's Glory, Hereford Alder, March Brown (Female), Partridge and Orange, Pheasant Tail, Teal and Blue, Teal and Red, Wickham's Fancy. Sizes: dry, oo-2; wet, 1-3; sea trout, 3-7.

Scotland, North: Alexandra, Black Pennell, Blue Zulu, Green Shiner, Grouse and Claret, Kingfisher, Mallard and Silver, Mallard and Claret, March Brown and Purple, Peter Ross, Teal Blue and Silver, Teal and Green. Sizes: brown trout, 1-5; sea trout, 5-7; all wet flies.

Scotland, East: Blue Quill, Butcher, Greenwell's Glory, Grouse and Orange, Hare's Ear, Mallard and Silver, March Brown, Peter Ross, Professor, Red Quill, Tup, Zulu. Sizes: brown trout, o-3; sea trout, 3-5.

Scotland, West: Alexandra, Black and Blue, Blue Zulu, Butcher, Greenwell's Glory, March Brown and Purple, Peter Ross, Silver Victor, Teal Blue and Silver, Teal and Red, Watsons Fancy, Woodcock and Yellow. Sizes: brown trout, 1-5; sea trout, 4-7.

Scotland, South: Alexandra, Black Spider, Blue Dun, Butcher, Coachman, Greenwell's Glory, Grouse and Claret, Hare's Ear and Woodcock, March Brown female, Olive Dun, Woodcock and Yellow. Sizes: dry, o-4; brown trout, o-5; sea trout, 5-7.

Here are some of the better-known patterns of salmon flies. Local advice should always be sought before buying salmon flies.

Black Doctor, Black Dose, Blue Charm, Butcher, Durham Ranger, Dusty Miller, Gordon, Green Highlander, Jock Scott, Silver Doctor, Silver Wilkinson, Thunder and Lightning, White Doctor, Yellow Torrish.

 B

BABBING: method of catching eels at night. Worms are threaded on coarse wool. The eels catch their teeth in the thread and, provided the line is pulled up softly, cannot escape.

BACKING: old but sound, or cheap, line put on the reel beneath the actual fishing line. The object is to build up the line on the reel and to give the angler a safety margin should a big fish take out a great length. A common example is seen in fly-fishing where the tapered line is perhaps only thirty yards long. There exists the possibility, therefore, of a big trout or sea trout taking twice this distance in his first run. In which case the backing comes into play. Backing can be of flax or anything you like provided it is sound. It should be spliced to the reel line rather than knotted, as a knot lying on the reel drum can easily cause a tangle and a break at a crucial moment.

BACKLASH: This is what happens when a drum reel is allowed to overrun while casting. The result is invariably a tangle of line on the reel usually called a 'bird's-nest'.

BAILIFF: the officer appointed by the owner of a fishery or his fishing tenant (a club, for example), or a River Board to enforce the bye-laws applying to the water. River Board bailiffs have considerable powers by virtue of the Salmon and Freshwater Fisheries Act, 1923 (this Act applies only to England and Wales. For Scotland and Northern Ireland there is separate legislation which differs substantially in details). They are given the powers of constables and they may, for ex-ample, demand licences, search nets, boats, baskets, and creels, and examine tackle. They may also seize both the fish and the instruments used in catching fish, i.e. rod, line, hooks and net, but *not* creel, haver-sack or seat. Any angler who ob-structs a River Board bailiff is guilty of an offence under the Act, and the bailiff need only produce his authority to enforce his powers. All bailiffs must carry credentials for this purpose.

In the case of a private fishery the owner should equip his bailiff with a letter of authority, and this applies equally to a fishing club renting the water from a landowner.

Should a private bailiff discover an angler fishing without proper per-mission in daytime he can confiscate the instruments used in catching fish but he cannot take any fish that the angler may have caught. He must make the seizure on his em-ployer's territory, and, having made it, no further action can be taken for damages or penalty, although the offender may be removed if he is trespassing. At night the picture is different. A bailiff can arrest with-out warrant anyone found illegally taking fish after sunset and before sunrise.

BAIT-CASTING: a term usu-ally applied to the method of throwing a spinning bait with a multiplying reel mounted on top of a special short rod. For pike spinning this outfit is fished with plug baits. It is, however, also used by the beach fisherman when surf-casting. The freshwater bait-casting rod is commonly only five feet in length and has a one-piece top screwing

into a special butt with an off-set
reel seat: the latter allows the reel to
be mounted on top and so that the
line leaves the spool directly in line
with the butt ring. Surf-casting
outfits are built in the same style
but here the rod is often about
eight feet in length.

BAITED SPOON: a highly
successful method of fishing for
flatfish, also, on occasions, bass,
pollack, eels and other species. The
secret of the baited spoon is simply
that it combines attraction with
succulence. Flatfish will frequently
follow a spinning lure only to turn
away when they catch up with it.
The presence of bait on the tail
hook of the spoon seems to hold
their attention and to make them
grab where they might otherwise
hesitate. Though rotating spoons can
be used, the bait at the tail tends
to limit their action. Wobbling
spoons are to be preferred.

Spoons for this type of fishing
can be made up quite easily by
removing the conventional triangle
and substituting a single long-
shanked hook. This hook should
completely clear the rear of the
spoon, shank and all, and, to give
it the necessary clearance, a chain of
swivels leading from the head of
the spoon and connected by split-
rings may have to be devised. Just
clear of the spoon, and at the
beginning of the shank of the big
single hook, a small hook should be
mounted—it can be connected to
the same split-ring as the long-
shanked hook. The point of this
should lie in the opposite direction
to that of the main hook, its function
being simply to hold the head of the
bait in position.

For flatfish, the hooks should be
baited either with rag- or lugworm:
for bass and pollack a strip of
mackerel will do better. Ideally the

BAITED SPOON. *Popular form of
spinning bait used by sea-anglers,
especially for flatfish.*

baited spoon should be fished over
a level sandy bottom. When spinning, the lure is cast out and allowed
to sink to the bottom. It is then
retrieved just fast enough to keep it
clear of the sand. For bass and
pollack the spoon needs to be spun
or trailed at a higher level.

BAIT-FISHING, Freshwater:
this term applies most correctly to
angling in which the bait is something other than a live fish or a
spinning lure, also an artificial fly.
Baits that will or on rare occasions
can catch fish are almost too numerous to list. The main ones, anyway,
will be found in the sections appropriate to the different species fished
for. Here is a resumé of some of the
possibilities when it comes to hook
baits, together with the fish that
they will attract. The first three are
the great universal baits. Those
species starred are not likely to be
caught often on the bait named.

Bread, paste or flake: barbel, bleak, bream, carp, chub, dace, gudgeon, roach, rudd, tench.

Maggots: barbel, bleak, bream, carp,* chub, dace, eel,* grayling, gudgeon, perch,* roach, rudd, tench, trout.

Worms: barbel, bream, carp, chub, dace, eel, grayling, gudgeon, perch, small pike, roach, rudd, salmon, sea trout, tench, trout.

Caddis: barbel,* bream, carp, chub, dace, grayling, gudgeon, perch,* roach, rudd, trout.

Raw meat: barbel.

Hemp: barbel (hemp paste), dace, roach.

Silkweed: barbel, chub, dace, roach.

Crayfish: chub.

Green peas: carp.

Potatoes: carp.

Wasp grubs: chub, roach, rudd.

Dead fish: eels, pike.

Bullock's pith: chub.

Banana: chub.

Frog: chub.

Cheese paste: barbel, chub.

Caterpillar: chub.

Grasshopper: chub.

Macaroni: chub.

Slugs: chub.

Elderberries: barbel,* chub, dace, roach.

Wheat: chub, dace, roach.

BAITING NEEDLE: long, fine needle with broad eye for threading wire traces through deadbaits for spinning, or legering in sea and fresh water.

BAITING-UP: another term used to describe groundbaiting a pitch before fishing.

BALANCED BAIT: a bread bait designed so that its specific gravity is only just greater than that of water. In other words, so that it sinks, but only very slowly. This can be achieved by making the bait half of crust and half of crumb,

and gauging its sinking qualities by trial and error. The balanced bait is valuable when fishing with large baits—as for carp—on a bottom covered with weed.

BALLYCOTTON: famous big fish centre in Eire situated in County Cork. Bream, pollack, ling, conger, bass, flounder, skate and halibut are caught in great numbers and of specimen size. The best fishing is from a boat.

BARBEL: *Barbus barbus*; family, *Cyprinidae.* Largest rod-caught weight (out of season): 16¼ lb. by Roy Beddington on the Hampshire Avon. Record: 14 lb. 6 oz. jointly shared by the Hampshire Avon (twice) and Thames. A new Avon record of 16 lb. was claimed in March, 1960 but turned down as the fish was foul-hooked

The barbel looks similar to a giant gudgeon, except that it has four barbels, or barbules, two at either side of its upper jaw. The colouring is bronze to green with all shades in between. The snout is pointed for rooting in the bottom for its feed, a task in which the sensitive fleshy barbules also assist. The top of the fish's head is flattened slightly and inclines quite steeply in a forward direction. This streamlining probably helps the barbel to hold the bottom in the powerful waters of weirpools which it haunts. The barbel is essentially a fish of pure, well-aerated water and it is for this reason that it has practically vanished from the Trent, once its greatest stronghold. An attempt has been made to rehabilitate it there. The Thames has always been a good barbel river, and, though there is some indication that the size of fish is falling, there are still plenty to be caught, even as far down as Kingston. The most famous barbel fishery in England is the Royalty

on the Hampshire Avon at Christchurch, and a ten-pound fish taken
there is hardly anything to get
excited about. The barbel have made
this river their home during the past
50 years for the Avon fish are
descendants of the barbel introduced into the Dorset Stour at the
turn of the century. Other barbel-
holding rivers include: The Kennet,
Severn (recently stocked), many of the
Yorkshire rivers including the Ure.

Habits: In the early part of the
season, barbel can usually be found
in the weirpools. They appear to
suffer heavily at spawning time and

Once hooked, their fight is dogged
and powerful, showing lightning
rushes and disconcerting rolling
tactics. They take a great deal of
holding, the more so since the spots
they inhabit are usually well-
equipped with underwater snags.
As summer dies, the fish are apt to
move into quieter quarters, when
they can often be found at the tails
of weirpools and even in the slower
deeps. They certainly feed at night.
Barbel are a great angling asset to
any river and should always be
returned since they are quite useless
for eating. Indeed, their roe is

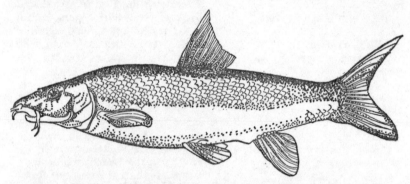

BARBEL. *The four barbules projecting from the mouth assist the barbel in its
probing for food on the river-bed. The Hampshire Avon is a notable haunt of
specimen-weight barbel.*

become badly infested with para-
sites. Leaping and rolling barbel are
common sights during June when
the fish are probably trying to free
themselves of lice. They come back
into condition fairly early, however,
and are soon in best fighting form,
which is something very considerable. Their feeding habits range
widely. Insects, larvae, molluscs all
go down well. They will undoubtedly occasionally take small fry,
especially early in the year, and
they will eat silkweed from weir
aprons as well as other aquatic
plants rooted from the bottom.

poisonous and near spawning time
is even said to make the flesh of the
lower and rear portions of their body
poisonous also.

BARBEL-FISHING: As can be
seen from the foregoing entry, barbel, even small ones, cannot be taken
on light tackle, at least not regularly,
though there is on record the case
of a Birmingham match angler, Mr.
A. Price, landing a 5 lb. 2¼ oz. fish
on a No. 16 hook to 6X gut.

Suggested tackle: an Avon rod—
nothing less than first-class split-
cane will do. A good centre-pin
reel rather than a fixed-spool one:

barbel fishing is the kind of angling in which you need the positive, direct pressure given by a centrepin reel. Line, certainly never less than 8-lb. b.s. Hook should be tied, to eliminate unnecessary weakness, direct to the nylon reel-line: sizes will vary with the bait used but will seldom be smaller than No. 10. Landing-net needs to be capacious and of great depth.

Most barbel are taken on leger tackle. The leger weight can be of the flat coffin variety designed to hold its position in a powerful current. Better by far, however, is the technique of the rolling leger. Fished over a clear bottom as often occurs at the tail of weirs or in many parts of the Royalty Fishery, the rolling bait can then be paraded before any barbel lying in the swim, provided the cast is varied at each throw and the lead is allowed to trundle along the bottom until it hangs below the angler before being retrieved. For this type of fishing a bored bullet or an Arlesey Bomb type of swivel lead gives best results.

Float fishing for barbel is best done from a boat. Because of the heavy nature of the stream, the tackle will need to be well-shotted, and this in turn means a big float. A good big cork-and-quill Thames float supporting perhaps 14 or more shot, or one small bored bullet, is a fair example of the type of rig needed.

Baits for barbel fishing are varied, not surprising really when one considers the natural feeding range of the fish. In order of usefulness the main ones are: worms, a bunch of gentles, cheese-paste (Avon particularly), bread crust, silkweed (weirpools, summer), caddis grubs, hempseed, elderberry, meat fat including bacon (use close to houseboat moorings), sausage rusk.

Groundbait, as for all fishing, should be a less attractive form of the hookbait. The most important thing to remember is that it must be heavily weighted down to hold the bottom of a typical barbel swim. Some anglers mix it with clay; others sink it in weighted paper bags. The old recipe for 1,000 lobworms is no longer practical. Cost, alone, rules out such lavishness. It is extremely doubtful if this mass groundbaiting paid dividends. True, big catches were made but there were more fish about in those days. There is some support for the suggestion that worms on this scale tempted half-hearted fish to feed.

A word of warning: when legering for barbel and the fish are on the take, never rest the rod. If a big one grabs hold you'll certainly lose the fish and you may even lose your rod.

BARBULE: or barbel, a small feeler usually occuring on the lower jaw of a fish and used, apparently, in its search for food. Fish having barbules tend to have poor eyesight. Some scientists believe that the barbule is an organ of taste rather than touch. In freshwater, the barbel is the obvious example of a fish equipped with these feelers. Many of the cod family, the *Gadidae*, have barbules on their lower jaws.

BASKING SHARK: large, harmless member of the shark family, a plankton eater of no sporting but some commercial value. Caught off the west coast of Ireland.

BASS: *Morone labrax*, family, *Serranidae*. Sometimes called the sea perch, this beautiful and sporting sea fish is very close to its freshwater relative. The fish is bright silver with a black lateral line. The scales are small and, as in the perch, most firmly attached to the skin. The tail is forked and there are two dorsal fins, the first one sharply spined. There are also spines on the gill-covers, and at the start of the dorsal, pelvic, and anal fins. For this reason the fish should be handled with care. Big shoals of smallish bass are often found together feeding along the shore line. Known as 'school bass', these seldom exceed two to two-and-a-half pounds in weight.

The school bass come in towards the end of the spring, stay throughout the summer, and sometimes linger on far into the winter. They seldom remain long in one place, however. Having cleaned up a feeding ground, they move on. The larger fish are far more cautious. Generally speaking they are taken in the autumn from rocks and piers, as well as from the shore. Big bass do fall for the shore fisher's bait even in high summer, however, particularly after storm periods when the seas are falling, the fish are hungry, and there is a wealth of feeding stuff along the beach turned up by the surf. The bass is a voracious predator. He has a large mouth that opens Gladstone-bag fashion, like his relation the perch. He will take small live fish, sand eels, crab, worm, strips of fish last, and, of course, artificial spinning baits. The bass is excellent eating.

BASS-FISHING: the bass offers more variations in technique than any other sea species. To begin with it can be taken spinning from shore, rocks, pier, or boat. To make spinning worthwhile and successful the angler must be sure that the bass are in. Better still if he can actually spot the shoals. 'Chuck-and-chance' methods along the shore will be found hard work and will, usually, bring fairly meagre bags.

It must be remembered that sea fish tend to seek their food at one level, therefore if results are not being produced at one spinning depth, try another. Bass like a fast bright spin, and, if in the mood, will slash quickly at a bait dropped across their noses. There is rarely any need to strike them. Many spinning lures will take them, from silver and blue Devon minnows, to spoons, deadbait on Archer or Aerial flights, sand eels on spinning flights, plugs, rubber sand-eels, Porosand strips, and even worms. To get the most of the splendid fight the bass can give, light tackle should be used. Fish with bait-casting rod and multiplier, or a seven-foot spinner with fixed-spool reel: line of five- to six-pounds breaking strain will usually be about right, heavier line makes casting with light baits difficult.

Ground-fishing from the shore can also prove productive. Here the angler should remember that bass seldom forage far out. At night particularly they come almost literally on to the beach. In daylight they will probably be between the third and fourth breakers, which may mean a casting distance of barely 25 yards. In ground-fishing, the sea angler is up against two things: surf and the danger of weed. The latter is usually purely a seasonal or temporary obstacle, large quantities being washed inshore at certain periods of the year after storms. The surf can be coped with by fishing with a weight sufficiently heavy to hold the bottom. This may need to be anything between two ounces and half-a-pound. Rod and line consequently should be correspondingly strong to cast it. Twenty-pound line for this type of fishing is a fair average. The weight is placed at the end of the trace (which should be of slightly lower breaking strain than the line), and two hooks are tied on paternoster fashion (preferably with monofilament links) about a foot and eighteen inches above this. Bait may be fish strip, worm, soft- or peeler-crab, mussel, or any combination of these and other baits. The main purpose of the two hooks is to allow two alternative baits to be fished. Having cast out, the angler holds his rod point well up to keep the line clear of the wave tops. It is far better to

of fishing. Weights and floats will settle themselves according to tide conditions: anything from a quarter-ounce to a one-ounce sinker may be necessary. When rock fishing, groundbaiting may help. This should take the form of chopped-up mackerel, herring or pilchard, both dropped into the water and left on the rocks where the waves can wash at the pieces, allowing the enticing

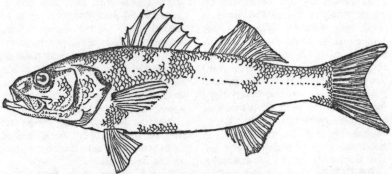

BASS. *Sometimes known as the sea perch, is related to the freshwater fish of that name. The spines of its front dorsal fin have very sharp points.*

hold the rod than rest it, for the take of a big bass will be sudden and surprising. A strap-on type rod-butt rest is an advantage. Bass like a moving bait and under some gentle surf conditions it may pay to use a lighter weight and to let the tide roll the bait back in a half circle round the angler towards the shore. When fishing with heavier weights it never hurts to move the tackle back occasionally. For one thing the baits may have become buried in the sand.

Float-fishing with fish or worm bait, mussel or crab, from rocks or pier, but especially rocks, will often produce big bass. Bass are shy fish and will keep away if the angler shows himself. A nine-foot rod with about a two to two-and-a-half pound test curve will do well for this kind

oils to trickle back into the sea.

Fly-fishing for bass is successful and exciting when the shoals can actually be spotted and rowed to. A sea trout or light salmon rod will do fine. Line should be tar-treated Cuttyhunk rather than expensive silk or Terylene fly-line. A level six-foot nylon cast will serve admirably. Flies should be of the flashy, fry-imitating sort. Sometimes sea trout or salmon flies will take fish, particularly those with silver elements. However, gaudier and larger streamer or hair flies are best. They may be simply tied with silver-foil wound bodies, and four or five good long cock's hackles, white, barred, or dyed, tied in at the head.

Bass may also be taken by *drift-lining* from an anchored boat and by trailing a bait behind a moving boat. When drift-lining a lively rod but a strong one, say a double-handed spinner, is necessary to cope with the strain of fish, weight—which may be anything up to two ounces—and bait. Baits may be worm, fish, crab, or livebait, especially live sand-eels in estuary fishing.

Pier fishing for bass perhaps deserves a special word. Bass normally keep away from crowded piers during daylight hours, but on warm summer nights the story is often very different. When hooked, a pier bass is likely to make a dash for the piles. A longish rod and strongish line is required to keep the bass under control. As a general rule 2/0 hooks will be found right for bass fishing with most kinds of bait. The record is 18 lb. 2 oz., caught from Felixtowe beach. A good bass may be reckoned at 6 lb., and a specimen at 10 lb. and over.

BATTING: 'batting the reel', a term used to describe the action of recovering line by spinning a centre-pin reel, with the check released, with the palm of the hand in a series of quick-striking, or 'batting', movements.

BEACHES, Sea Fishing From: the type of surface, the slope and other topographical features of a beach have a considerable effect upon the species of fish that frequent and feed on it.

Sandy, flat, firm, usually ridged beaches are rich in all forms of fish food, especially where muddy sand is exposed at low tide. Crustaceans, molluscs, worms, small fish of all descriptions in puddles left by the receding tide all encourage bass, flounders, mullet, etc.

Shingle beaches usually shelve steeply. Fish can often be found in the deep water off shingle spits. The most famous example is probably Chesil Beach, which joins Portland

with the mainland. Bass, codling, pollack are all taken off Chesil. The shingle itself is invariably barren of fish food.

Coarse sand and gravelly beaches support a poor supply of fish food except sand fleas and hoppers. If they fine out into good sand lower down they will frequently provide good flatfish grounds.

In estuarial waters, where fresh water mixes with salt, eels, mullet (sometimes) and flounders may be looked for. At the river mouth, where salt predominates, eels, flounders, migratory trout and salmon, slob trout, bass, mullet, pollack, and mackerel occasionally will be caught. Bass fishing usually gets better as you approach the sea.

Muddy harbours and creeks are rich in food supply. Bass, mullet, flounders, and eels can be caught on the flood tide.

Rocky shores such as those of Cornwall support a rich and varied menu for fish of all sorts. Fishing from the rocks you can often find conger, pollack, cod, wrasse, bass, sea trout, etc.

BEACHING A FISH: a tactic to be employed when landing-net or gaff is not to hand. This applies equally to salt or freshwater. When beaching, the fish must be played to a point of exhaustion far beyond that required when conventional landing tactics are used. The fish, especially if of any size, must be played until it comes in quietly, preferably on its side. When river fishing the angler caught without net or gaff should look for likely beaching points as he fishes. At any moment may come the take of a big fish that will require beaching. A flat stony or gravel shallows is ideal. Having played the fish to a standstill, bring it in calmly over the shallows, keeping the rod tip

26

well up and the reel hand ready to deal with a sudden last-minute rush away. Provided you bring the fish in head-first its struggles to escape will usually only bring it further into shallow water. Once it is ashore, waste no time in picking it up and getting it well above high-water mark or away from the river. In freshwater fishing, you should, of course, never be caught without landing gear.

BERYLLIUM COPPER: a material used in rod construction, at the moment of writing, principally in America. The metal, an alloy, was developed for vehicle wireless aerials during the Second World War. Apart from flexibility and strength, it has the quality of being practically non-corrosive. This makes it of great value to sea anglers.

BIG - GAME FISHING: in British waters true big-game fishing can be said to be confined to fishing for tunny, porbeagle, thresher, mako and blue sharks. However, many anglers feel that any fish that tops the 100-lb. mark might be admitted to the big-game class. This lets in: several species of skate and also halibut. Pleas have been made to allow the title also to conger.

Tunny fishing enjoys a limited season from the end of July until the end of September, is expensive, and is consequently tried by very few anglers. Tunny were discovered moving off Scarborough in the mid-'twenties. It was reported that they haunted the herring drifters, and that when the nets were hauled, tunny hovered round to feed on the pickings. In 1929, two big-game men, Lt.-Col. Stapleton-Cotton and L. Mitchell Henry set out in keel boats to fish near the herring fleet. Stapleton-Cotton hooked but lost two fish, while the next season

Mitchell Henry landed a tunny of 560 lb., the first rod-caught specimen from British waters. In 1932, the British Tunny Club was founded at Scarborough. Technique developed fast and in 1933 Mitchell Henry set a British record of 851 lb. Fishing grounds at Scarborough lie anything from seven to 100 miles offshore. Anglers go out either in 30-ft. seaworthy Yorkshire cobles or keel-boats of from 15- to 20-tons. Tunny are often spotted by herring-boat skippers at night moving about below and seen as semi-luminous shapes. The actual fishing is done from a small rowing boat as the tunny will frequently tow the angler for a great distance and he must be free to manoeuvre against it. Only once has a tunny been caught from the deck of the parent boat.

Shark fishing has been greatly opened up in British waters as a result of the work of the Shark Fishing Club of Great Britain based on Looe, Cornwall. Shark exist in many of the warm water channels round the coast during the summer months and do great damage to fishermen's nets, particularly those of the Cornish pilchard fleet. At Looe, most of the sharks are blues, with some mako and thresher species. Shark fishing has also recently been tried successfully off the South Coast in the region of Brighton and Littlehampton where big porbeagle have been caught and thresher seen. The record porbeagle to date, however, was taken off the coast of County Mayo, Eire, but was shot dead with a Luger pistol in the closing stages of the fight.

The best method of fishing is to drift with a whole dead fish as bait beneath a large float set at a depth of between fifteen and twenty feet. Groundbaiting is done by means of a 'rubby-dubby' bag, an old sprout sack or something similar filled with chopped pilchard or herring. This lays a trail of oil which the shark are able to detect and home on, until they find the bait. Line of 100-lb. breaking strain is used, and 300 yards is needed to be on the safe side. Specially tempered steel hooks attached to a 15-yard trace—to combat the shark's scaly body—are necessary. Rods do not need to be exceptionally heavy for blue shark, at least. A strong boat-rod should suffice. Runs of 200 yards can be expected.

The fight with a big skate is usually dour rather than exciting, the fish sticking to the bottom and requiring great strength and a long pumping battle if they are to be beaten. The Common Skate which is found in deep water all round our coasts—and occasionally close to certain beaches—often goes to 100 lb. and has been caught as high as 221 lb. off Ballycotton, Eire. Two hundred yards of 40-lb. line is advisable, fished on a big drum, say 7-in., reel. A four-foot trace of 30-lb. wire with a 10 hook is needed if whole fish are to be used as bait, and it should be attached to the reel line by a swivel. Above the latter is fitted a large leger weight of anything from 6-8 oz. The bait can be fished slap on the bottom. On being hooked the skate frequently buries itself in the sand. If this happens, brute strength and patience will be needed: on the other hand it may be possible to annoy the fish into shifting by line movement. Skate should always be landed with a gaff. They can cut or sting very seriously. Because they cover the bait to take it, skate are often foul-hooked.

Halibut are caught in deep water, and few are taken on rod and line. They are fished for generally just off the bottom with a live fish hooked through the lips. Line needs to be of 30-lb. breaking strain with a wire trace and swivels fished from a heavy boat-rod.

Conger abound on rocky bottoms and round wrecks. Usually they feed at night but in deeper water they give daytime sport. An 84-pounder was caught off Dungeness in 1933. Baits should be fresh and tackle should be 100 yards of 30-lb. line leading to a well-swivelled wire trace about four feet long. Conger hooks must be well-tempered and about 3–4 in. long. Conger take the bait gently as do freshwater eels, and should not be struck until they begin to run off with it. Once hooked, conger fight like demons. They should be gaffed through the head, pulled into the boat and stunned with a blow on the tail from a lump of pipe or other suitable bludgeon. To be on the safe side the spinal column should be severed with a sheath knife as soon as possible. A lashing conger can inflict unpleasant wounds, apart from biting through boots and toes.

BIG-GAME TACKLE (Britain): rods are usually short, about five feet, and are of split-cane, split-cane and hickory combined, steel or fibre-glass. Commonly they have pulleys instead of conventional rings as line-guides, and the winch fitting is of a screw- or bolt-on type with various locking devices.

Reels need a very large line capacity. Fish of over 100 lb. have frequently been played on Nottingham reels of seven inches or so, but with hard-fighting, quick-running fish the damage done to the angler's hands by the rapidly revolving handles can be considerable. Most big-game reels are therefore exaggerated multipliers equipped with powerful star-drags and with about

2½:1 gearing for recovery. Sizes of sea fishing reels are sometimes described by a number system starting at 1/0 for the smallest and going up to 16/0. However, the method isn't yet standard, and individual makers apply different numberings. The numbers relate to the line capacity of the reel: in one range a 4/0, for example, will take 325 yards of 15-thread line while a 14/0 holds 625 of 54-thread.

Lines are usually of cuttyhunk, hard-twisted. The last fifteen feet or so of line is usually doubled. Traces are about fifteen feet in length, equipped with special big-game swivels and of rustless wire. Hooks again are specially forged. Harness is used in order to permit the angler to exert his full weight when fighting a big fish. The harness is in the form of a skeleton leather waistcoat which connects to two lugs on the reel. In case the reel jams, there is a quick-release device which eliminates the risk of the fish dragging the angler overboard.

Gaffs are usually made with a detachable hook to which is fixed a length of rope. If the gaff handle breaks as a result of the struggles of the fish, the point still remains operational.

Since, obviously, more credit attaches to killing a big-game fish on light tackle than simply wearing it down with ultra-heavy gear, several attempts have been made to standardize gear so that light tackle feats can be properly recognized. Largely as a result of the efforts of

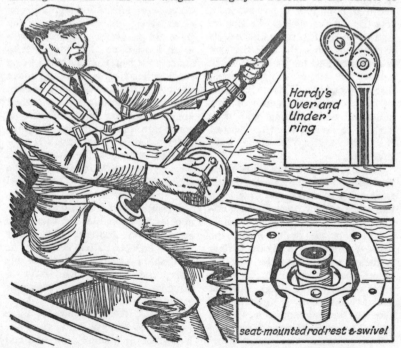

Hardy's 'Over and Under' ring

seat-mounted rod-rest & swivel

BIG-GAME TACKLE. *A special harness and rod-rest are a standard part of the big-game fisherman's equipment. Often a pulley-type fitting is used on his rod instead of the conventional top ring.*

29

the Catalina Club of California standard descriptions of light, medium and heavy tackle are universally recognized in big-game circles: the figures to denote these three classes are 3/6, 4/6 and 6/9 tackle. The classes set down maximum rod length, butt length, tip length, tip weight, maximum number of threads to the line, maximum wet breaking-strain of line, test curve of rod. 3/6 tackle for example is respectively: 6 ft., 12 in., 5 ft., 4 oz., 6 threads, 18 lb., 2½ lb., while 6/9 calls for: 6ft., 18 in., 5 ft., 6 oz., 9 threads, 27 lb., 7 lb.

BILLET: a term used to describe the young coalfish and pollack.

BITE-ALARM: a fairly recent introduction since the development of night-fishing for carp. Usually the alarm is built into the rod-rest. A fine trigger lies against the line so that when the fish takes and begins to move off with the bait the line is oscillated and makes an electrical contact that sets off a high-pitched, intermittent buzz. This gadget considerably lessens the strain of long hours of night fishing and does nothing to detract from the skill of the carp angler, as some have suggested.

BITES, Freshwater Fish: these vary in type from species to species, from water to water, and even from bait to bait. However, certain guiding principles can be laid down.

There is no doubt about the decisive thump of a taking barbel. A bream usually lays the float flat before taking it under. A tiny bleak gives a sharp bob. Carp, when at last they do make up their minds, take up the bait and run with it. Chub, once their natural sense of self-preservation has been overcome, make a gluttonous slash at the bait. Dace give a quick darting bite. Eels pick it up and run a

little way, rest to turn the bait for swallowing, and run again. Grayling give a quick bite on float tackle. Gudgeon bob the float, sometimes taking it under and cruising with it submerged. Perch suck the bait in and blow it out again several times. The resulting action of the float is a succession of bobs and curtseys before it goes under and away. Pike on live-bait take the bait and run with it, resting after some time to turn and swallow. Roach usually give a sharp indication, though sometimes barely move the float. Rudd give a definite sharp tug. Tench bob and shift the float, sometimes raising it before gliding away with it.

The kind of water in which the fish takes has a marked influence on the sort of bite it makes. Strong clear rivers usually produce shy bites. In a murky stream you will often have more time in which to strike your fish, the exception being roach which frequently simply move the float a fraction sideways or even raise it in the water. It is a practised angler who can spot this sort of roach bite consistently and act on it. Baits, too, produce variations. Hempseed is notorious for making fish dart quickly at the bait, giving it a sharp tweak that must be spotted and acted upon at once.

Despite the confusion that is apparently possible between one species and another, the angler should be able to tell what fish he is striking at. He will know his river, the sort of fish likely to inhabit his swim, and what his groundbait will attract.

BLACK BASS: there are three varieties of these sporting fish—the large-mouthed, small-mouthed, and spotted bass. They are a great quarry of the American angler on bait, spinner and fly. Though there seems no particular reason why they should not settle down in English waters, few attempts have been made to acclimatize them. One attempt made at Send in Surrey, in a large disused gravel-pit, was partially successful at least, and large-mouthed bass are still caught there from time to time. The fish is a relative of the perch and has a catholic and carnivorous appetite taking anything from fish, to larvae, and quite large frogs. The record large-mouth is 22¼ lb. caught in Montgomery Lake, Georgia. The characteristic of the large-mouth is that the maxillary or upper jawbone extends beyond the eye, while in the small-mouth it ends level with the pupil. The spotted variety has distinctive diamond-shaped markings.

BLACK-SPOT: a fairly harmless disease attacking freshwater fish, notably roach. The spots are caused by the larvae of a worm called a *trematode*. The larvae known at this stage of their development as *cercaria*, penetrate the skin of the fish and become embedded in a cyst—the well-known black-spot. Affected fish seem to lose little in condition, and the disease usually disappears after a while.

BLADDER WRACK: common species of seaweed (*Fucus vesiculosus*), recognizable by small air bladders on its flat, brown, blade-like surface.

BLEAK: *Alburnus alburnus*, family *Cyprinidae*. No one seriously bothers about the bleak record. The fish weighs only a few ounces and rarely grows over six inches in length. In appearance the bleak is bright silver with a greenish tinge to the ridge of the back. Bleak are sometimes mistaken for small dace, but the give-away is the anal fin. That of the bleak is far longer than the fin of the dace. Bleak are shoal fish,

feeding usually on or near the surface. In the summer they can be seen rising freely to smuts and other small insects, sometimes leaping clear to take a fly. In the main they inhabit rivers of slow to medium flow. The Thames, Nene and similar rivers are over-run with them. Almost the only person who rejoices in this fact is the match-angler who frequently finds that they swell his aggregate weight conveniently, being easy to catch. To serious specimen hunters they are a nuisance. The

BLEAK. *The small fish that is found, in rivers, in shoals of varying extent at or near surface level.*

conventional way of getting rid of a swarm of bleak is to throw them some floating crust which they then follow downstream and out of harm's way. Unfortunately there is invariably another shoal close behind. Bleak are taken avidly by large perch and small pike, but they make indifferent livebaits being hard to keep alive either in the bait-can or on livebait tackle. They spawn in early summer and, like most of their family of fishes, lay eggs that stick to the stems of water plants. Preserved in formalin they make attractive pike spinning baits. They are fair eating when fried crisp like sprats.

BLEAK-FISHING: As has been said, few people fish specially for bleak. However the match-angler or the man who is after spinning baits will catch as many as he wants on light float tackle. A shoal can be easily collected in summer by light and frequent groundbaiting either with cloud or with maggots. The hook bait should be cast in among the free feed as it sinks. A light quill float and the fewest possible number of shots are usually the right rig. Bites will be quick, and, for this reason, it pays to submerge all but the tip of the quill as this promotes quick striking. A slow-sinking bait may sometimes pay off, in which case the shot should be attached directly under the float to make it self-cocking. The angler has, of course, to find the depth at which the fish are feeding. This, in summer, is likely to be anything from one foot to four feet. Excellent sport can be had with bleak on the fly. Hooks size oo are advisable. Any small bright dry-fly will take bleak. A hackled black gnat also works extremely well.

BLENNIES: family *Blenniidae*. This group of small fishes is of interest to the sea angler purely as bait. There are many varieties, some being found in rock pools at low tides and others being caught well off-shore. Among the former include the butterfish or gunnel, an eel-like creature with long dorsal fin with black, gold-encircled spots along its base; also the shanny, found in rock pools during the warm weather, and being yellow or green in colour. The shanny has no scales but is covered with black spots. It has yellow fins and makes good conger bait, as does the butterfish, which is also used for pollack. The tompot, largest of blennies found round Britain, is taken in deep water, usually in crab-pots. Other blennies include: the butterfly, the viviparous blenny, Montague's blenny.

BLACK BREAM: *Spondyliosoma cantharus*, family *Sparidae*. A much sought-after sea fish that comes inshore during the summer. Some of the most famous black bream fishing

is off Littlehampton. The fish has the characteristic deep thin look of all bream, is black to blue-grey with gold fleckings and is exceptionally good to eat. A two-pounder is a nice fish, and the record, from the Menai Straits, stands at 6 lb. 5 oz. Unlike the freshwater bream it is an extremely tough fighter and gives a tremendous battle all the way to the net.

BLOOD-KNOT, BLOOD LOOP: the most secure of knots an angler can tie in gut or nylon (see KNOTS). The former is the castmaker's knot, used for joining lengths of different sized gut in tapered casts: the latter is useful for tying line on droppers, etc.

BLOODWORMS: true name *chironomus*, the larvae of tiny flies usually called gnats or midges. In fact, these flies can't bite or sting. The worms, which can often be found near the surface of water butts, like to live deep in ooze. Fish undoubtedly love bloodworms and tench bubbles are probably caused by these fish searching head down in the mud for them. Generally, they are rather too small to hook as bait successfully. Some of the larger specimens can be persuaded on to a No. 20 hook if the point is put in through the segment nearest to the bloodworm's head.

BOATS: the main requirements of any fishing boat are stability and convenience, and the truth is that design both for freshwater and salt must vary to suit the conditions peculiar to the district concerned. For inland fishing on small lakes where squalls are no serious risk, and on rivers, the ideal boat can quite safely be described. It should be sufficiently beamy to allow the anglers to stand up when gaffing or playing fish. It should be sufficiently roomy for two people to fish without

The Royalty Fishery on the Hampshire Avon at Christchurch

A fine 36-lb. ling taken off Falmouth, Cornwall.

getting in each other's way. Floorboards must be easily removable for recovering dropped tackle, and even fish. Livebait tanks fed by the water in which the boat floats are essential. Oars should be of the type secured by a single upright wooden pin passing through the shaft rather than of the conventional rowlock mounted variety. The oars can then be left to trail without fear of them drifting away. Shelter in the shape of a partial foredeck should be supplied for keeping both bait and food in eatable condition, and the gunwhales should be bored to take movable rod-rests. The boat should be fitted with plenty of cleats at bow, stern and amidships so that anchors may be lowered from any point and secured. Some sort of shelving is extremely useful for holding tackle, bait tins, etc. Ideally the boat should be easily transportable on a trailer and light enough for two anglers to carry and launch. It even may be an advantage if the boat can be carried safely on the roof of a car. The nearest approach to this ideal yet produced is the "Angler's Dinghy" supplied, either in kit form or complete, from the Bell Woodworking Company, Leicester.

B.O.D.: an abbreviation standing for Biological Oxygen Demand. A term used by biologists and chemists in estimating the amount of oxygen taken from any water in a given time in order to cope with the organisms, both living and dead, within it. This term occurs time and again in pollution cases, since one of the major factors in the mass slaughter of fish is the absorption of vital oxygen. Usually this oxygen is taken so that bacteria present in the water can deal with, and break down, organic polluting matter. The fish consequently suffocate in a badly polluted river, quite apart from any direct poisoning caused by polluting substances.

BOOTLACE WEED: *Chorda filum*, a fine green seaweed that grows in thin streamers attached to pebbles and shells in the shallows. Sometimes the streamers are several feet in length with the result that the flooding tide lifts an apparently flat weed and makes it a green thicket inches and maybe feet high above the bottom. Though the sea angler will seldom lose tackle in this weed, since a sharp pull will usually wrench it free from its moorings, it renders spinning practically impossible, even with 'weedless' spoons of the type that have a spring wire protector mounted over the hook.

BOTTOM: term usually applied to the end of fishing tackle; to the trace, cast, or even hook-link. Thus: 'a 6x nylon bottom'.

BRANCHED RAYS: a term describing the rays in a fin that

BRANCHED RAYS. *The rays, or spines, of a fin that spread out towards their extremities.*

spread outwards towards the top, as opposed to single or simple rays.

BRANDLING: a kind of small redworm whose body is circled with yellowish bands; found especially in compost heaps. Extremely active and giving off a yellow fluid and offensive smell when punctured, the brandling will lure many fish including perch and trout.

BREAKING STRAIN: term denoting the deadweight load a fishing line will take. Usually this is calculated for the line when both wet and dry. When given on the spool, it denotes wet breaking strain. Unfortunately, the issue is somewhat clouded by other methods of describing line strengths. These are sometimes indicated by diameter measurements, and at others the method associated with the gut casts of fly-fishermen is used—namely, the X system.

A comparable table showing diameters, breaking strain and X's for lines and casts commonly used in coarse and game fishing is shown below:

Diameter in inches	Breaking strain in lb.	X's
·004	1½	8X
·006	2¼	5X
·008	4	2X
·009	5	1X
·010	6	X
·014	11	
·016	14	

It must be added that nylon line loses strength when wet, and that at least a quarter of the total breaking strain is sacrificed by most knots, and 10 per cent by the best of knots.

BREAM: there are two kinds of bream in British waters. First the silver bream, *Blicca bjoernka*. Second, the common or bronze bream, *Abramis brama*. Both are of the family *Cyprinidae*. The silver bream, 'tinplate' or 'bream-flat', is when adult bright silver in colour and can hardly be mistaken. In the smaller sizes it can easily be confused with the common type. The differences are: the anal fin of the silver is shorter—it has 19–24 branched rays while the common bream's anal fin has 23–29. Moreover, there are 8–11 scales in a transverse line between dorsal fin and lateral line in the silver bream, and 11–15 in the common variety. From this it can be seen that the silver fish has larger scales. To the

angler, the 'tinplate' is a fish of little consequence, since it rarely grows over the pound mark, the record being only 4 lb. 8 oz. from Totworth Lake, Gloucestershire. The common bream is a much weightier specimen, the record fish from Chiddingstone Castle Lake scaling 13 lb. 8 oz.

In appearance both bream are thin, deep fish with a sail-like dorsal fin and a markedly forked tail. The common bream, particularly, is covered in a thick mucous that comes off only too readily on tackle, boat, and clothes. As a fighter it is of not much value, though a big bream hooked in a powerful stream in winter can give a fairly good account of itself. Bream tend to stay in deep, slow water where they forage in shoals, raising clouds of bubbles and sometimes mud. They also exhibit a peculiar phenomenon known as 'rolling', when they come to the surface in great numbers and tumble about. Some say this is a prelude to feeding, but I have never found it so. The best bream waters are the drains of East Anglia, the Norfolk Broads and rivers, the Huntspill River and King Sedgemoor Drain, Somerset, the upper Thames in the area of Pangbourne, and the Bedford Ouse.

Being a bottom feeder, the bream will take almost any aquatic insect and can therefore be caught on worm or gentles. Bread paste is greatly liked also. To feed, bream stand on their noses, and, having picked up the food, then return to an even keel, this fact accounting for the laying flat of the angler's float as the bream raises the weights on the cast. Spawning time is late April, May and early June. Often, at the opening of the season, bream can be seen cleaning themselves in shoals on the shallows.

BREAM-FISHING: Bream are the one fish whose feeding level can be confidently predicted. Though I have taken rare bream on gentles or breadcrust trotted down for roach, for all practical purposes bream forage on the bottom. I don't think bream, once on the feed, are shy fish, and they certainly aren't strong fighters. Medium tackle will do for most occasions, and I would say that all except the really big fish can pursuit, especially on a summer's evening by still water. The peculiar bite of the bream (the meaning of which has been explained in the entry BITES) adds much to the enchantment. The slow, lifting, tipping over, and sliding under of the float is a fascinating sight. Floats will tend to be light because the water inhabited by bream is likely to be slow and deep. Many bream fishermen prefer the leger, however,

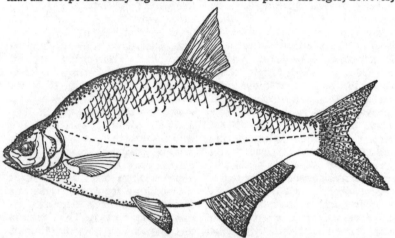

BREAM. *A deep-bodied freshwater fish usually found in the slow and deep runs of a river and in still waters.*

safely be handled by most anglers on a 3-lb. line and hook link to suit. It's not worth going down to a ridiculous number of X's on the cast or hook link. Most bream wouldn't be put off by 3X nylon.

Suggested tackle: any good bottom fishing rod. A tip-action match rod will handle bream up to 3 lb.; above that an Avon rod can't be bettered. Above all, avoid the horrible, short, stiff rods which are used by some anglers for legering. These give a fish of low sporting quality absolutely no chance to show its paces. Float-fishing for bream is an extremely pleasant or even a combination of leger and float. About this form of fishing there is little to be added beyond that already said in discussing LEGERING in general. The bream needs to be able to pick up the bait without feeling any check: as with all legering, therefore, the line should pass freely through the hole in, or loop attached to, the leger weight.

Bream commonly move about in great shoals. It is quite possible when spinning for pike, and finding yourself in the middle of a bream shoal, to foul-hook fish on successive casts until the bream move on. The bream angler's problem, therefore, is to find the bream and hold them in his swim, or, failing that, to entice them to his swim and hold them there. Despite their roving characteristics, bream do have favourite feeding places, usually in deep holes where food collects. This is demonstrated almost yearly in the All-England Championship: the individual winner is usually the lucky man who draws a bream hole and is skilful enough to keep the fish there throughout the contest.

Baits for bream fishing are, in order of importance: bread paste or flake, gentles, and worm. I'd be tempted to put worm higher on the list but for the fact that it invariably attracts other unwanted species such as gudgeon and small perch. Baits should be of generous size. Bream have big mouths. When night-fishing for carp with paste nearly the size of a golf-ball I've caught bream of five pounds once or twice.

Groundbaiting will need to be heavy in quantity and quality. The staple pulped bread mixture with bran, chicken meal, or inferior hook bait additives is a good all-round standby.

Bream take freely on summer nights. Legering is the usual method, with a torch trained on the bite indicator. The favourite indicator is probably a dough-bobbin pinched on to the line.

The strike for bream should be sharp rather than heavy, bearing in mind that when float-fishing the float should be allowed to slide away. When legering the lifting of the bait will probably be signified by a sudden sagging of the bite indicator. Strike when it jerks up again.

BRILL: *Scopthalmus rhombus*, family *Pleuronectidae*. Seldom caught by sea anglers, found like most flat-fish over sandy bottoms, it browses for sand eels and crustaceans. Brill have a circular appearance, a deep-cut mouth, and a lateral line on their upper surface which curves sharply away from the gills. The biggest brill are usually taken off the Isle of Man, the record from those waters being 16 lb.: a good brill weighs 4 lb. and an exceptional one 7 or 8 lb.

BUBBLE-FLOAT: small, plastic, transparent, spherical float which is almost invisible in the water. Bubble-floats are weighted by filling them with water through a small removable plug. The virtue of this arrangement is that the water gives ample weight for casting. Once the float hits the water, however, it weighs practically nothing. Bubble-floats are useful for surface fishing with a floating bait for rudd, and for carrying paternoster gear for pike or perch. They first came into prominence when trout anglers used them on fixed-spool gear to insinuate flies into lies which a normal fly-cast wouldn't touch. Their uses in this respect are, however, limited.

BUBBLES: these are made by several species of bottom-feeding freshwater fish, notably carp, bream, and tench. There has been a great deal of discussion as to what causes these bubbles. The most important thing about bubbles, however, is that they usually indicate a feeding fish. Whether one can interest that fish in a hook-bait is another matter. My own view is that the bubbles come from gases trapped in the bottom mud, and that these are released by the burrowing activities of fish in search of bottom food such as bloodworms. However, there is little doubt that different fish do produce different sorts of bubble. Tench bubbles are smallish, appear in a longish pattern, and are often called needle bubbles. Bream bubbles, about the size of a threepenny-bit, rise in small groups. Carp on the other hand can raise bubbles the size of a small balloon. This would seem to argue, many anglers maintain, that the source of the bubbles is the fish and not the bottom mud. Perhaps the true solution is that the bubbles are composed of trapped gases which pass into the fish's respiratory system with its food and are ejected as unwanted. I have caught both bream and tench by dropping a bait ahead of the bubble path. Carp on the bubble have so far defeated even the Carp Catchers' Club. They have even given them a label—'indifferent bubblers'. Possibly these big fish have their heads too well buried in the mud to spot a bait.

BULGING: a term to describe the hump made at the surface of the water by a fish taking nymph or fly just below the surface and without breaking the surface.

BULLET, BORED: circular weights of varying sizes usually used as leger weights by the coarse angler. Suitable for rolling-leger use on a clear stream bed. In small sizes sometimes used to weight float tackle.

BULLHEAD: *Cottus gobio*, family *Cottidae*. Often called the 'Miller's Thumb' after its flat appearance (Millers' thumbs are said to get that way through feeling the quality of flour). An extremely ugly fish, dirty green and mottled from olive to black. Rarely grows more than five inches long. A sharp spine projects from either side of the head. The bullhead is found in small pebbly streams and is caught quite easily in the hand. It makes useful livebait and is eaten by trout.

BULL-HUSS: see NURSEHOUND.

BUNG: slang name for large cork float used principally when livebaiting for pike. See FLOATS.

BURBOT: *Lota lota*, family *Gadidae*. Often called the 'Eel Pout' after its long eel-like body and large mouth. The colour is dusky green with mottlings of brown to reddish brown and occasional yellow. The fish, which is the only freshwater representative of the cod family, does look remarkably eel-like, having a long, thin body with twin dorsal fins, the rearmost of which extends about half the length of the body. Its distribution is extremely local. East Coast rivers such as the Cam and Ouse have their share of burbot, as did once the Trent. The fish is seldom caught deliberately since it is a nocturnal feeder. It will take worms or livebait and has a formidable set of teeth.

 C

CADDIS: sometimes in larval form called 'stickbait'; insects of the family *Trichoptera*, known to fly-fishermen as sedge flies. For coarse fishing, caddis in the larval stage make first-class hook-baits. The peculiarity of the caddis is that the larva builds itself a protective case of sticks, small shells, or pieces of stone. These cases can often be spotted on stony shallows. Insert a pin into the thin end and ease the

CADDIS. *A first-class bait in its larval stage for the coarse fisherman. The larva builds itself a remarkable protective casing (right) for concealment.*

caddis out of its case. A deadly bait early in the season for many coarse fish. Some anglers say the yellow larvae, probably on account of their visibility, are the most effective. (Recommended reading: *The British Caddis Flies* by Martin E. Mosely, F.R.Z.S.)

CARP: all carp are members of the *Cyprinidae* family of fishes. In British waters there are three main divisions of this carp group. First, and least important from an angling viewpoint, the Crucian Carp (*Carassius carassius*). The Crucian is a compact, chubby, rather bream-shaped fish that seldom grows to any size and is seldom deliberately fished for. The record, caught at

Godalming in 1938, is only 4 lb. 11 oz. It has no barbules at the side of the mouth.

The common, or wild carp, (*Cyprinus carpio*) is a magnificent fish with a long dorsal fin like the plume of a Roman legionary's helmet and two barbules on each side of the upper jaw. It grows to a great size (the record, caught by Richard Walker of Hitchin and transferred to the London Zoo, was 44 lb. when landed), is extremely cunning, and fights like a tiger when hooked.

The remaining branch of the carp family consists of the so-called 'King' carp. These are like the common variety except for the fact that there is something unusual about their scaling. They either have a few enormous scales, in which case they are called 'mirror' carp, or else they are scale-less, when they are known as 'leather' carp. The King carp also grow to a great size, probably larger than the common, or fully-scaled, variety.

Carp are primarily inhabitants of still water, though some very big river specimens have been landed. Only quite recently the River Thames at Kingston produced one of about 16 lb. Carp settle down well when put in as stock in most lakes but there is no guarantee that they will breed. No one seems to understand what governs the breeding inclinations and capacity of the carp. The fish are most active in warm weather, and I believe that shelter plays an important part in establishing carp in a lake and persuading them to reproduce their kind. One quite small lake I know is magnificently supplied with a natural stock of carp, some of which grow over the 20-lb. mark. This water is in the centre of a wood, and, though the sun gets to it the wind does not.

The spawning season for carp, depending on the weather, is late May and early June, and the fish are best caught in July and August, and, sometimes, during a hot summet, on into September. Occasional fish are landed during the winter but by then the majority of carp have gone into semi-hibernation.

The fish are 'vegetarian' rather than predatory, though at the start of the season they will undoubtedly go for small live fish. Carp are mainly bottom-feeders taking bloodworms, larvae and aquatic vegetation. At times, though, they will take food floating on the surface, and they can often be seen half out of the water amid the lily pads, when they are probably sucking snail eggs and other small organisms from the underside of the leaves.

As far as caution goes, they are probably the most cunning of fish and are therefore the most difficult to catch. Their brain area is larger than that of other freshwater fish but not too much store should be set by this. They are still at least as stupid as the domestic hen. Two other points: (1) they do not live to a great age, although they certainly look old and tattered in the latter stages of their life. Twenty years is probably about their span and Richard Walker's 44-pounder was exactly 15 years old. (2) They can live for a remarkable time out of water. They appear to have some power to adapt their gills as partial lungs. Wrapped in moist sacking or put amongst wet foliage they can safely be transported from one water to another, even though the journey takes an hour or more. Carp, being warm-water fish, are found in decreasing quantities the farther north one travels.

Carp feed freely at night, but the question of when they feed is governed almost entirely by the temperature of the water. They are most active when the water temperature ranges from 61 to 67 degrees.

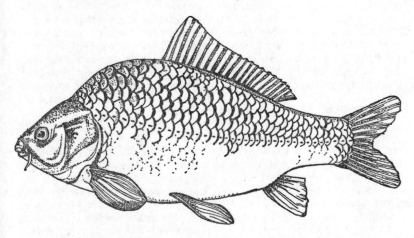

CARP. *The British record for a common carp stands at 44 lb. It was caught by Richard Walker and can be seen in the aquarium at the London Zoo.*

39

CARP-FISHING: not many years ago catching carp was thought to be impossible as a planned exercise. If you got in amongst the carp it was largely a matter of luck. The fish were said to be unpredictable and unapproachable. For a number of years the record—26 lb. from Mapperley Reservoir—stood where Albert Buckley had put it. Buckley took his fish with roach tackle in the reservoir deeps in cold or stormy weather. Lately, carp have been studied as have no fish before or since. The record has shot up and up until it stands at the present figure of 44 lb. That this improvement in the knowledge and technique of carp fishing has taken place at all has been principally the work of the man who caught the 44-pounder—Richard Walker of Hitchin. Walker is the centre of a group of fanatical carp anglers called the Carp Catchers' Club. This body exists purely to study the habits of its members' favourite quarry and to perfect new methods of outwitting it. They exchange information via a circular letter. Conditions of membership are not closely defined. You must, at least, have caught a fish of over 10 lb. to be eligible. What is much more important, you must have the proper scientific approach to carp-catching even to be considered for membership.

This, as far as the general angler is concerned, is not important. What matters to him is the information that the club has collected—information that has put carp fishing 'on' for any angler of a specimen hunting disposition and better-than-average skill at playing big fish.

The first thing to be realized about carp is that they are immensely suspicious. Their exaggerated sense of self-preservation has got to be practically anaesthetized by infinite care before you can hope to interest them in the bait, let alone persuade them to take it. Sight of the angler, or vibrations caused by the angler are likely to prove fatal to success. So is the sight of his tackle in the water or the use of an unfamiliar bait. It follows then that considerable

CARP. *The Crucian carp is a bream-shaped fish and is much smaller than the common carp.*

groundbaiting is necessary to familiarize the fish with the hook offering; that the angler must at all costs keep out of sight; that every care must be taken to make tackle unobtrusive; that tackle must be strong enough and sufficiently well prepared to meet the tremendous stresses put on it by a fighting carp. All these essentials—except perhaps the last—are the pre-requisite of any successful fishing for any species of fish; but with carp everything must be more so.

Carp, as has been said, feed only in water of the right temperature. This water must therefore be located. In the summer the fish will frequently be on the shallows, and the shallows often reach the right temperature only after sunset or as the first sun reaches the water. Dawn and dusk are usually the most productive times for fishing; these times have the added advantage that few other fishermen are about. The angler's first task, therefore, is to find where the carp will be feeding.

Groundbaiting should be done in considerable quantity. When breaking-in a new pitch at the start of the season it is not too much to bait up with a bucketful of groundbait every night for a week. If the attack is to be made at night, then I advise laying the bait in a longish carpet and marking the line with a tree or bush on the opposite bank. This will practically ensure that when casting in the dark your hookbait lands somewhere in the middle of the groundbait pattern. Bread and bran mixture with a blend of mush and lumps is as good as anything, provided paste is to be used. Potatoes on the hook—small parboiled ones—demand a mash of potatoes, obviously. Honey is sometimes mixed with the groundbait, I think to slight advantage.

Hook-baits should be large. Even a five-pound carp has an enormous mouth. A ten-pounder has one you

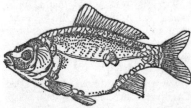

CARP. *The Mirror carp is easily distinguished from the common variety by the patches of very large scales on its otherwise scale-less body.*

can almost put your fist in. Assuming that you are not fishing purely for small carp, then nothing smaller than a golf-ball sized piece of paste should be used; a tennis-ball sized lump is certainly not too large for fish of fifteen pounds and upwards. Potatoes work well enough when the fish have been acclimatized to them

by groundbaiting. Worms catch carp, but have the disadvantage of catching practically everything else too.

Now for carp tackle: the vogue in carp fishing has produced rods designed for the purpose. Previously, one had to rely on something like a Wallis Avon rod. This type of rod can cope with carp up to ten pounds in the hands of a good fisherman. It is asking too much of it consistently to battle with bigger fish. Richard Walker has designed his own carp rod, and this cannot be bettered. Known as the Mark IV, it has a test curve of one-and-a-half pounds, should be fished with a seven- to twelve-pound line; it can throw a bait of an-ounce-and-a-half comfortably and is all power right the way down to the butt cap. Another excellent rod, though designed as a salmon spinner, is Milward's Spinversa.

The reel should without question be a fixed spool. When a carp takes, it runs fast and far with the bait. Any feeling of check will make it drop the bait. A fixed spool left with the pick-up open allows the fish a free take-off.

Line had best be monofilament which can be stained the last six feet of its length to correspond with the bottom colour of the lake (I am assuming that practically all carp fishing is done in still-water). The hook should be tied direct to the end of the reel line with a whipping knot. As to the pattern of this hook, there can be no doubt. It should be either eyed or spade-end for easy tying to the reel line, and it should be an Allcock's 'Model Perfect'. This pattern has an off-set point that not only gives improved hooking power but also aids in holding the unnaturally large bread baits used in carp fishing. Size 3 or 4 is needed, at least.

No weights of any sort are used. The bait gives the necessary weight for casting and the tackle lies on the bottom without let or hindrance to the fish. Since long waits can be expected, the rod should be supported in two rests. The first must give free play to the line should a fish take: the second, which simply supports the butt, can be of the ordinary forked stick variety. The tip of the rod when rested should point towards the fish.

When night-fishing, many carp experts use electric bite-alarms that tell them when line is being taken out. This certainly eases the strain of a long vigil, particularly if the angler has a sleeping-bag in which he can get some rest. The irritating buzz of the alarm will have him awake instantly, and, if the rod is at his elbow, he will sit up and strike in time—as Richard Walker and his colleagues have proved. Effective indicators for carp fishing can be made by pulling off a yard of line from the reel and folding a piece of white paper over it, the paper being lightly weighted by a stone. At the take, the paper will jerk out as line begins to disappear with the running fish. Even when he is dozing, the movement of the white paper cannot be missed by the angler.

So the bait is out in position, cast with a forward lob (this should be practised in daylight if fishing is to be done at night). The rod is rested, the pick-up open, the line to the bait slack, the indicator paper folded over the loop of loose line to one side of the rod. When the paper moves, pick up the rod, whip in the pick-up and jam the spool of the reel in one movement, and strike with a firm backward sweep. After that the battle begins. It only

remains to be added that a very large landing-net—a special carp net —is necessary.

Such is the general technique. Float fishing is not seriously to be thought of for carp. The line slanting from the surface almost invariably scares off these cautious fish.

There remains the business of margin-fishing, already described in a separate section. In this the fishing is done at night on the windy side of the lake. The rod is rested and the bait, usually a large section of bread crust, or crust and crumb, is attached to the hook and is allowed to float on the surface close under the bank and practically beneath the rod top. Foraging fish taking surface scraps sometimes fall for this type of bait.

Bottom weed often presents a problem to summer carp fishers. If there is danger of the bait sinking into this and disappearing from view, two ruses can be tried: (1) a balanced bait of half crust and half crumb which only just sinks in water, (2) if potato is being used, then put a flat slice on the hook which will 'shimmy' down gently through the water and settle on top of the weed.

Some terms invented by the Carp Catchers' Club: *clooping*, carp sucking in surface snacks; *smoke-screening*, carp routing the bottom, possibly for bloodworm and other larvae, and raising clouds of mud; *tenters*, fish raising the lily pads with their backs when foraging, probably for snail eggs; *margin-patrollers*, fish likely to take a margin-fished bait.

CAST: the terminal portion of the tackle between reel line and hook. This nowadays is usually of nylon. Many fly-fishermen still prefer silkworm gut because its stiffer quality makes it more suitable for casting in a wind. A cast for dry-fly fishing is usually three yards in length and tapers from thick (perhaps 1X) at the reel line end to 3X or 4X at the 'point where the fly is attached. In windy conditions, or on small streams, the cast is sometimes shortened to two yards. Wet-fly anglers use level casts of uniform thickness, since delicate presentation of the fly is not so important.

CASTING: the act of presenting bait, lure, or fly with rod and line to the fish. There are many different styles to suit varying techniques and places of fishing, the most important of which are:

(1) Nottingham style: this was originally designed for use on the River Trent in which the best fish, especially roach, often lie well out from the bank. Essentially, it was designed to give added distance when fishing with a drum reel and fairly light tackle. The cast is now widely used by anglers on all rivers. It consists of drawing from the reel one or more loops of free line and holding them away from the rod with the left hand. The free loop or loops should issue from between the bottom rings of the rod. The bait is allowed to hang free from the rod tip and is cast out with a gentle sideways flip.

When the weight of bait, float, and shot begin to exert a pull as they fly through the air, the loops of line are released, adding distance to the throw. Once the tackle has hit the water, it is checked for a second to allow the bait to sink and be swept by the stream slightly ahead of the float. Then the angler feeds line smoothly off the reel to allow the tackle to 'trot' or 'swim' evenly downstream at the pace of the current. Using a free-running centre-pin reel he may find that the pull of the river on the float is

sufficient to rotate the reel drum and pull out line smoothly. Without such a reel he will have to strip line by hand from the drum and keep feeding it out through the rod rings. By these methods he may allow his bait to swim twenty or more yards down river. At the end of his swim he stops the float and retrieves his tackle, usually by spinning the reel drum with the palm of his hand. This trick is known as 'batting'.

(2) There is a variation of this cast sometimes called the Avon cast but more often known by the name of its inventor, F. W. K. Wallis, one of the most famous of all Nottingham experts. This cast is practically impossible to describe in words, extremely difficult to do well, but, once mastered, is more accurate and more powerful as to range than the standard article. For a right-handed cast the baited hook is held loosely in the left hand. The thumb of this hand is hooked round the line close to the reel in the loop between it and the bottom rod ring. As the rod is flipped forward in the cast the left hand lets go of the baited hook, the thumb at the same time drawing line from the reel and setting the reel turning. The line thus runs out over the crook between base of thumb and first finger. The movement of the left hand is continued until the left arm is fully extended away from the rod. The spinning reel is stopped before an over-run takes place by the fingers of the right hand. *Note:* an extremely free-running reel is essential, as is a heavy float and shotting. Perhaps the best description of this cast is given in *Fine Angling For Coarse Fish* (Lonsdale Library series) by its inventor.

(3) Sheffield style: as the Nottingham cast was developed for the wide, powerful waters of the Trent

so was the Sheffield cast perfected for the shallow, slow-flowing and often gin-clear waters of the Fens and Midlands. The Sheffield angler fishes far off but he fishes fine also. This fine tackle (often down to a No. 18 hook and 8X cast) cannot be thrown far by the fairly robust methods of the Nottingham man. It has to be flicked in an overhead cast very similar to that of the fly fisherman. The rod used is very light in construction (bottom joints are often of hollow Spanish reed) and all the action is in the tip. Floats are often of matchstick size and the only weight may be a tiny half-moon lead or a couple of small shot. The chief quarry of the Sheffield-style angler is the roach, and, generally speaking, small roach. By and large the Sheffield angler is a match-angler. His rod is not built for dealing with large fish. Considerable skill, therefore, is called for in playing out a three or four pound bream that would succumb quickly to the Thames or Trent man.

(4) Thames style: this is seldom seen these days. It took its name from the roach-pole experts of the Thames and Lea. It is really fishing over a short, well groundbaited swim without paying out extra line, and simply by casting to the upstream limit and allowing the tackle to swim down to the bottom limit. Originally, of course, the line was a fixed one, at least in roach-pole fishing where no reel is used.

CATALINA CLUB: this Californian club was the foremost pioneer for standardization in sea and big-game fishing tackle.

CATFISH: *Silurus glanis*, known also as the wels. An ugly fish with enormous flat head and elongated barbules, that sometimes weighs 100 lb. Very common in many European waters and also America. The 'cat' has been introduced to at least one English water, a lake at Leighton Buzzard. Several have been caught there, and, though they give fair sport, would be a menace to other fish life if allowed to spread and grow. They eat enormous quantities of food in competition with other freshwater species.

CAUDAL FIN: the tail of a fish.

CEPHALOPODS: the squid and octopus, fantail and cuttle families.

CHALK STREAMS: these are rivers that have their origin in chalk hills. They produce some of the finest dry-fly fishing for trout in the world, and certainly the finest in the British Isles. They are rich in

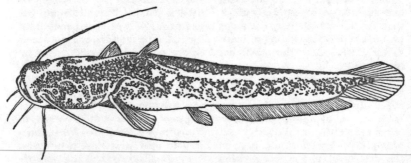

CATFISH. *An ugly flat-headed creature that inhabits many European waters but is rare, and only where introduced, in Britain.*

every form of life, the reason being that their water, by virtue of the chalk filter through which it has passed, is crystal clear and abundant in the right natural salts to stimulate life and growth. Clarity is essential to angling water in that it allows the sunlight to penetrate to the greatest possible depth. The sunlight enables green weed to grow, and the prolific weed growth supports an enormous population of nymphs and other insects which in turn feed the trout. Thus you have a perfectly established and properly balanced food chain. In a chalk river not only the trout grow large but also the coarse fish. A four-pound brown trout, a seven-pound chub, a two-and-three-quarter-pound roach, a three-pound perch, a three-pound grayling, a thirty-pound pike, a two-pound silver bream, and a fourteen-pound barbel could undoubtedly all be caught—by a miracle—in the same day's fishing in the Hampshire Avon and, having been taken, there would be plenty of similar-sized fish, or better, to take up their feeding stations for them.

It takes months for the rain falling on chalk hills to seep through to the springs that feed a true chalk water. Thus, a chalk river is never in spate or flood, unless of course it collects a great deal of surface water from non-chalk lands lying along its banks on its lower course. The most famous chalk streams are those of Hampshire. Include among them: the Avon, Test, Itchen, Wiley, and Nadder. Then there is the Dorset Stour, and in Berkshire the Lambourn and the river it feeds, the Kennet, which might be described as partially chalk. The latter certainly has most of the chalk river characteristics including big fish. Hertfordshire has a few small chalk brooks such as the Mimram, while in Yorkshire there is the solitary and famous Driffield Beck.

Chalk streams have developed dry-fly fishing to the status almost of an art. The flow of such rivers is powerful yet stately: the water is, as has been said, of an appalling clarity. Thus the big trout have no trouble in keeping station in the stream, watching every floating insect with a fastidious eye and selecting exactly what they want to eat, rising in a fairly leisurely manner, and taking the insect without fuss. To compete with them, the angler has to present his imitation with perfect skill. It must alight like a real fly, and, what is more, look like a real fly. A great deal has been written about artificial flies for chalk streams. You could probably carry one hundred patterns and still not have exhausted the possible repertoire. On the other hand you could undoubtedly get by with half-a-dozen.

Most chalk stream flies are of the *Ephemerid* family—the olives, pale wateries, blue-winged olive, iron blue, mayfly, etc., with sedges (*Trichoptera*), for evening, thrown in. A chalk stream angler's basic artificials are therefore such flies as Greenwell, Tup, Olive Dun, Sherry Spinner, Ginger Quill, Red Quill, Hare's Ear, usually in sizes oo–1. G. E. M. Skues perfected the technique of fishing the sunken nymph cast upstream and across to fish feeding on larvae, but this is as near to sunken fly fishing as anyone on a chalk stream dare go. The rules invariably say: dry-fly only. The reason for this is a fairly good one—namely that dry-fly fishing for these trout provides the maximum entertainment, test of skill, and sport. There is no object, therefore, in aiming lower than a well-presented dry-fly. Chalk stream trout are as greedy as any other trout, and they would fall just as readily for wet-fly, spinner, live-bait, or even worm.

Grayling provide excellent chalk stream sport, though most trout fishing societies wish to extract them by electrical fishing and netting from their water, simply because they live in direct competition with the trout and take their food. Trout experts have the same view of coarse fish, and coarse fishing societies can frequently arrange with chalk stream clubs to take away coarse fish for stocking their own waters.

Coarse fishing in chalk streams is better than anywhere else, and again, because of the clarity of the water, and the abundance of natural food, the fish are not easy to catch. Long-trotting or legering takes most fish. Floats need to be very large—probably cork and porcupine quill is best—and able to support a small leger bullet or up to sixteen shots. Midland anglers fishing chalk streams should abandon all thought of small hooks and light tackle. They will not serve.

In general, it must be added that chalk stream fishing is for the well-to-do, although small clubs do manage to exist on these much sought-after streams, and often issue tickets. The best approach is to find the local club in a town adjacent to a chalk stream and seek information and help there. At the same time, magnificent fishing—at probably the finest mixed fishery in the world—can be had for a few shillings per day at the Royalty Fishery, Christchurch, Hants. The river runs right through the town and enquiries should be made at Fishery House to the Head Bailiff.

Recommended reading: *Fly-Fishing* by Lord Grey of Falloden; *Minor Tactics of a Chalk Stream* by G. E. M. Skues; *A Summer on the Test* by John Walter Mills.

CHANNELLED WRACK: *Pelvetia canaliculata*, the seaweed with fronds curled up at the sides, found on the upper part of the shore. The name derives from the fact that the curls look something like gutters or channels.

CHAR: a member of the salmon and trout family showing considerable colour differences when compared with trout. Here is William Gilpin's description of the fish taken from his *The Lakes of Cumberland and Westmorland*, first published somewhere about 1750:

"It is nearly twice the size of a herring. Its back is of an olive-green; its belly of a light vermilion: softening in some parts into white; and changing into a deep red, at the insertion of the fins. A parcel of char, just caught and thrown together into the luggage-pool of a boat, makes a pleasant harmony of colouring. The green-olive tint prevails; to which a spirit is here and there given by a light blush of vermilion; and by a strong touch of red if a fin happen to appear. These pleasing colours are assisted by the bright silvery lights, which play over the whole; and which nothing reflects more beautifully than the scales of these fish . . ."

Char haven't altered a great deal since Gilpin's day; in fact, they have altered little since the Ice Age that probably isolated them in a few of our lakes thousands of years ago. In the first place it is likely that all char were of the migratory species *Salvelinus alpinus* which ascend Arctic rivers to spawn. Trapped in land-locked waters they have, however, developed their own characteristics and minute colour differences. The lakes in which they live all have one thing in common: they contain pockets of extremely deep water. Here the fish usually are caught by a very deeply trailed bait, though sometimes during summer they can be caught at the surface with a fly. Char leave the deeps to spawn in shallows and in the side-streams feeding the lake. They are not particularly sporting fish.

Here are some of the species found in Britain, together with the Latin names given to them. It is stressed that there is little actual difference morphologically or in appearance.

Willoughby's Char or Windermere Char (*Salvelinus alpinus willughbii*). Apart from Windermere, is found in other Lake District meres, also in Scottish lochs Grannoch, Dungeon, Doon, and Builg. Possibly other Scottish lochs, too.

The Torgoch (*Salvelinus alpinus perisii*): is found in Lake Bodlyn and in the Llanberis district.

Struan Char (*Salvelinus alpinus struanensis*): found in Loch Rannoch, Perthshire.

Lonsdale's Char (*Salvelinus alpinus lonsdalii*): is found in Haweswater.

The Haddy (*Salvelinus alpinus killinensis*): found in Loch Killin, Inverness-shire. Darker than other char.

Large-mouthed Char (*Salvelinus alpinus maxillaris*): is found in Ben Hope, Sutherlandshire.

Orkney Char (*Salvelinus alpinus inframundus*): probably extinct, once found on Hoy Island.

Malloch's Char (*Salvelinus alpinus mallochii*): found in Loch Scourie, Sutherlandshire.

Shetland Char (*Salvelinus alpinus gracillimus*): from Loch Girlsta in the Shetlands.

There are in addition six Irish char: Cole's, Gray's, Trevelyan's, the Coomasaham, Scharr's and the Bluntnose Irish Char. They differ little from those of Britain.

One of the most beautiful of all char was introduced here at the turn of the century from America. This is what the Americans call the 'brook trout' but is in fact *Salvelinus fontinalis*. The American Dolly Varden 'trout' is also a char.

CHECK: spring-and-pawl device built into practically all reels to prevent the drum spinning wildly on the take of a fast-moving fish. In most types of reel the check is optional: it can be applied or released by means of a movable stud. In a fly-reel, however, which is never required to be free-running, the check is permanently on. Audible checks are now incorporated in many fixed-spool reels, the reason being that the click of the working check is often the first indication that a fish has taken the bait: this is particularly true when legering at night when movements of the line and rod top cannot easily be seen. The check on a drum reel also prevents the drum from rotating, causing slack line when legering. One of the most exciting sounds to an angler is the scream of a racing check. It invariably means 'big fish on'.

CHEVIN: an old name for chub, also 'chavender'.

CHIRONOMIDS: small gnatlike insects that develop from the larvae commonly called bloodworms.

CHUB: *Squalius cephalus*, family *Cyprinidae*, sometimes called chevin or chavender (Old English), alderman, loggerhead, or skelly. The record is 10½ lb. taken from the River Annan, a sea trout and salmon river debouching on the Solway Firth, by Dr Cameron of Dumfries. The fish fell for a fly. Previously, the record had been held at two pounds under this weight by a fish from the River Rother, Sussex. Other notable chub waters include: Hants Avon, Bristol Avon, Wye, Severn, Ouse, and upper Thames.

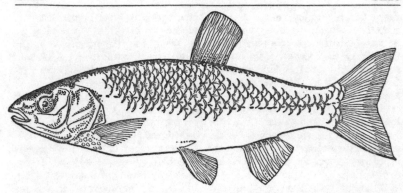

CHUB. *Described by Izaak Walton as the 'fearfullest of fishes' because of its shy nature. Small chub are sometimes mistakenly identified as big roach.*

In appearance the chub is silvery with a red or brownish tinge to the fins. It is all too frequently confused with the roach, and many a club competition has been won with a two-pound 'roach' that was in reality a smallish chub. In fact, the chub should be immediately recognizable by virtue of its block head, white leathery lips, gold-flecked eyes, and paddled-shaped anal fin with rounded, or convex, edge. Experience proves, however, that none of these recognition points is good enough in the field. A scale count is unfortunately not conclusive. The number of scales a chub has along its lateral line is from 42 to 49: a roach has from 40–46, and a rudd 39–43. Perhaps the only sure test is to dismember the fish and examine the pharyngeal or throat teeth—which few anglers will wish to do. Other details which may help you to confirm your chub are the numbers of rays in the fins. The branched rays in the dorsal number 7–9, and the same in the anal fin. Scales counted transversely from root of dorsal to lateral line are 7–8.

The feeding habits of the chub are varied, to say the least. Almost any bait will take it, from a cherry to an elderberry, from greaves to a frog, from a slug to an exquisitely tied dry-fly. The chub is an extraordinary mixture of wild gluttony and almost ridiculous caution. It will rush at a caterpillar skilfully dapped on the surface, but will sink from sight, as if scuttled, at the sound of a footfall.

Chub are river fish, liking a fair pure stream and rarely taking to still water except in the case of some stream-fed lakes. Spawning takes place mainly in May and June, the female laying an astonishing number of eggs. During the early part of the season the bigger fish are partial to live meals, not excluding their own fry. Chub are generally shoal fish, fifteen or so similarly sized chub swimming together. The really big specimens of five pounds and upwards become solitaries, however and prefer to forage for themselves without competition.

Chub, as do all fish, change their stations according to temperature and pace of stream. During the summer they will frequently be found under trees or bushes waiting for insects to fall on the surface, or between weed beds foraging for larvae and similar tit-bits. In winter they are taken legering or long-trotting in quieter lay-byes and in the deeps. Walton described chub as 'the fearfullest of fishes' and was not far wrong. They must be approached with great care if success is to be chalked up regularly. As a fighter the chub has little staying power. Once hooked, a big chub will make a spirited dash for its hole. After that, if the angler can retain the initiative, the battle is over fairly quickly. But the first rush is very impressive.

CHUB-FISHING: big chub are not easy fish to catch. By 'big chub' I mean anything from four pounds upwards. The chub is an extremely greedy fish, but also a very shy one. The slightest hint of angler, rod, shadow of angler or of rod, and the big chub and his attendant shoal of lesser chub sink from sight. Chub are practically omnivorous. They will eat anything from a slug to a cherry. Yet, baits on which they can regularly be taken can be narrowed down to very few. They divide themselves between surface and sunken baits. First, however, for chub tackle.

A small chub can be taken on any tackle you like, just as can any small fish. A tradition has sprung up, however, that chub are spiritless fish and can be wound in to the landing-net without fight. Chub of three pounds and above, make no mistake about it, are capable of plenty of fight during the opening few seconds of the engagement and can quite easily break the tackle, especially during their first panic dive. The man who caught the current record—10¼ lb. from the River Annan—reported that the chub gave no struggle worth the name. But this was a Scot, and Scots despise all coarse fish. More-

over, Dr Cameron of Dumfries who caught this monster was fishing for sea trout and no doubt was quite unwilling to give a word of praise to his unexpected catch. In fact, having landed the fish he gave it to the cats. Thus does the confirmed game fisherman regard chub, but this does not mean to say that the reputation is warranted. When fishing for big chub the weakest link in the tackle should not be below 4-lb. breaking-strain, and this may prove too flimsy. By the same token, the rod must be capable of dealing with the first rush of a big powerful fish. An Avon-type rod can hardly be bettered. Hooks should certainly not be smaller than No. 10.

The first requirement of the chub fisher is that he remain out of sight of his quarry. If he intends to catch his chub on the surface he must therefore creep and crawl and make use of all natural cover.

Surface feeding chub are caught in the summer, usually beneath trees and bushes where they would expect to find a regular supply of falling insects. A fly-rod is excellent for chub catching and the fly should be good and bushy and a nondescript pattern that gives the impression of bulk and imitates, if anything, a large furry caterpillar. Palmer flies in large sizes are fine, as is a big Sedge or Coachman. I have caught plenty of chub on home-made cork beetles and ladybirds.

The alternative method of taking surface feeders is by dapping. Here a genuine insect should be used whenever possible, either being impaled on the hook or else attached to one of the spring-grip hooks for holding live flies. Grasshoppers, beetles, caterpillars, woodlice all do well. When dapping, a longish rod is needed for insinuating between bushes. A weight must be fixed about eighteen inches above the bait to take it down, and the lure is simply lowered to the surface while the angler remains hidden. Once the fish takes, as it often does, with a mighty swirl, the angler can stand up and fight it out, for it is practically certain that once a chub hole is disturbed you will get no more fish out of it.

Chub also, particularly at the start of the season soon after spawning, feed on live fish. Small fry, gudgeon and minnows fished on paternoster tackle, or, better still, swum down to the chub on float gear will often take good-sized specimens. It follows, then, that chub will fall for small spinners imitating these fish. I have taken large chub on wooden plugs right up into December, though I fancy this is the exception to the usual rule.

Chub will fall for leger tackle, particularly that baited with cheese, or cheese-paste. In this case the ground bait should be flakes of cheese thrown into the swim at intervals. A useful variation of the technique is that of the rolling leger, where the tackle is allowed to run along the river bed with the current. Leger weights for this purpose should be sufficiently light for the stream to work them, and be preferably of the bored bullet or Arlesey Bomb pattern. By carefully regulating casts, the whole of the river bed downstream of the angler can be systematically searched.

In summer, chub will take silk-weed from weirpools in the manner already described in a separate section.

Perhaps most chub are taken by long-trotting. This is certainly true of the Hampshire Avon and the Thames, and similar rivers. Big floats and well-weighted tackle are required for this, and the bait on the hook should be bread cubes, cheese-paste, or maggots.

CHUMMING: an American word of obscure derivation meaning to groundbait.

CLAMS: one of the largest of the molluscs found burrowing on the seashore. The biggest of the tribe is the gaper (*Mya arenaria*) which sometimes reaches a foot in length. When opened and cut up it makes tolerable bait in deep water for the bigger fish such as rays, cod, skates, etc.

CLAYBALLS: used sometimes in fishing for barbel. The worm bait is imbedded in a small ball of clay, other fragments of worm being included. Groundbaiting is done with further clayballs. The theory is that the barbel get used to finding food in the clay. Eventually a fish noses the baited ball and picks out the worm with the hook in it. The balls have the added advantage that they keep the bait in front of the fish in the swift currents in which barbel are usually found.

CLOSED SEASONS: these are laid down for England and Wales in the Salmon and Freshwater Fisheries Act, 1923:

(1) Salmon: 'The close season for rods shall be in any place the period which has been fixed in that behalf by a bye-law under this or any other Act, or, if there is no such bye-law, the period between the thirty-first day of October and the first day of February following.'

There are, however, so many variations to this rule where the run of fish begins earlier or later than the statutory date of 1 February that enquiries should be made locally. In any case, the rod licence which must be bought before fishing for salmon will give the dates imposed by the local River Board.

(2) Trout: the statutory close

season for brown trout and sea trout is between 30 September and 1 March. Here again there are local exceptions.

(3) Coarse fish (described in the Act as 'Freshwater Fish'): the statutory close season is between 14 March and 16 June. Again there are several local exceptions. For instance: Hull and East Yorkshire and Yorkshire Ouse River Board areas (27 February–1 June); East Suffolk and Norfolk River Board area (7 March–16 June). Some river boards impose a close season for pike that lasts until 1 October, among them: Essex, Great Ouse, Nene and Welland. East Sussex River Board extends its close season for pike from 16 June until 15 July. There is also the much-disputed 'truce' period on the Norfolk Broads to allow coarse fishing during the Easter and Whitsun holidays for all species except pike and perch.

In most rivers there are provisions for taking fish for scientific purposes, or for livebait where trout are known to exist—as in the Thames. Unfortunately, some anglers abuse this privilege.

The Salmon and Freshwater Fisheries Act, 1923, applies only to England and Wales. But Scotland has legislation for the same purpose under which the close season varies from district to district. Northern Ireland also has its own legislation.

CLOUDBAIT: fine groundbait used to attract rather than satisfy fish. Made of several ingredients, the main one of which is usually finely ground breadcrumbs. Silver sand is sometimes added. The main thing is that the bait on hitting the water should give out a 'milky' cloud which brings the fish round but does not give them anything substantial to get hold of.

The theory is that having collected they will then be more likely to spot and take the hook bait.

COALFISH: *Gadus virens*, family *Gadidae*. Sometimes called saithe. A fish very similar in appearance to, and often confused with, pollack. Though the coalfish tends to be darker in appearance, this is in itself no certain means of identification. The lateral line of the coalfish is straight while that of the pollack curves over the pectoral fin. Moreover the jaw of the pollack is inferior, or undershot, whereas that of the coalfish is level, the lower jaw being equipped with a small barbule. The coalfish is caught mainly by northern sea anglers. The coalfish grows to greater size than the pollack and is a better fighter. Methods that will take pollack, will certainly catch coalfish. The record is 23½ lb.

COARSE FISH: all those British freshwater fish that are not members of the *Salmonidae* group of fishes. A possible exception is the grayling which, though a true *salmonid*, spawns in late spring with the coarse fish. However, it cannot truly be considered a coarse fish. The origin of the term 'coarse' is obscure. It has been suggested that it refers to the texture of the flesh, and even to its taste. It seems much more likely that 'coarse' is applied to the scaling of this group of fishes, for most, in contrast to the trout, have large 'coarse' scales. An exception is the tench which has scales at least as fine as those of the trout. However there is nothing clear or consistent in the derivation of this term. Coarse fish, sometimes referred to in legislation as 'freshwater fish', have their own protected close season. The actual period varies slightly from district to district: generally speaking, the fence dates are 14 March to 16 June.

COCKLE: a burrowing bivalve found on the shore. It digs in with a muscular foot and both feeds and breathes through two slender siphons raised to the surface. The presence of cockles can be spotted by means of the two little holes made by the siphons and by the slight discoloration of the sand. They make good bait when placed two or three at a time on the hook for dabs, plaice, whiting and wrasse. Family *Cardiidae*. Common cockle, *Cardium edule*.

COD: *Gadus callarias*, family *Gadidae*. The record cod is 32 lb. and it was caught in deep water. The big fish of this tribe seldom come inshore. The young cod, called by the angler 'codling', are nothing like so cautious, however. What weight of fish constitutes a codling as opposed to cod has never been officially ruled. A consensus of sea anglers' views would probably fix the dividing line at five pounds. The cod is easily identified among the rest of its family—the whiting, haddock, pollack, etc.—by its white lateral line curving upwards over the pectoral fins. It is usually spotted and has three dorsal fins and a barbule below the lower jaw. It has an all-round taste in food and will take almost anything the angler offers provided that the bait is large enough: a bunch of marine worms, crab, lumps of fish, mussels, preserved limpets—all these will catch cod.

Cod is primarily a winter quarry. The codling come inshore from late autumn and stay until February. They are to be caught by hardy anglers from beaches, rocks, and piers. Once hooked the fight is not spectacular except for the peculiar dog-like head shaking with which the fish tries to throw the hook. The only answer to this tactic is to keep a very tight line. When on the feed they will take the bait in any conditions; rough weather and inshore weed does not put them off. Because of the winter conditions and the ground over which codling are sought, tackle has to be strong. A four-ounce weight will probably be needed to hold the bottom. Perhaps the best all-round gear is the old-fashioned wire-boomed paternoster with two hooks. Line should not be less than 20-lb. breaking-strain and 100 yards at least should be put on a big drum reel. A strong beach-casting rod or boat-rod is needed to cope with tackle and winter conditions. When boat fishing, cod can also be persuaded to fall for trailed feather lures.

COFFIN - LEAD: flat, bored leger weight designed for holding the bottom rather than rolling along the bed of a powerful river. Shaped like a coffin.

COLORADO: type of spoon

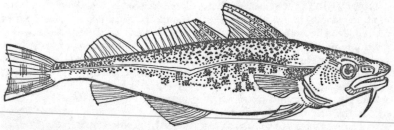

COD. *The larger specimens are found only in deep water; small ones are known as codling. They forage inshore during the winter months.*

revolving about a central wire axis and having spinning vanes attached to the head of the bait. Armed with a triangle. Useful for pike, perch, and some sea fish.

CONGER: *Conger conger*, family *Muraenidae*. Conger frequent rocky ground and wrecks. In colour they

big-game fishing, although the battle with a conger is more likely to be dour than full of second-to-second thrills; those come, quite frequently, when the big eel is lifted into the boat. Whole fish baits take conger best, although at night they will go for smaller offerings. It is always said that conger baits should be fresh but plenty of successes have been scored with stinking fish heads and far-from-fresh herrings. Whole whiting, herring or mackerel, squids, in fact any fish up to six inches in

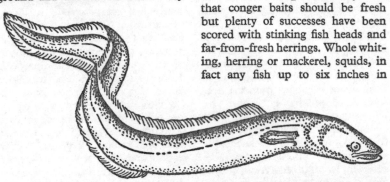

CONGER. *The best sport is obtained from conger at night during warm summer months. Its powerful writhing body and sharp teeth make it a formidable quarry.*

vary from grey to blue-black, being very adaptable to their background. They are not close relatives of freshwater eels and almost certainly do not follow the same migratory spawning habits. The female far outgrows the male. The record is 84 lb. but there are certainly conger of 100 lb. and upwards waiting to be caught on rod and line. There is an account of a conger that weighed 160 lb. being caught in 1940 but there is no real evidence to back up this story. As in freshwater eel-fishing the best sport is had at night, and particularly on warm thundery nights in summer. Then the eels are likely to come inshore, and may even be seen on or near the surface. Conger are formidably armed with teeth and can give a dangerous bite to the unwary angler.

CONGER-FISHING: round the coasts of Britain this sport has almost won for itself the status of

length is ideal for conger fishing Despite its size and strength, the first offers of a conger eel are tentative and shy. He will nose at the bait first, and only when the rod has trembled and trembled for some time, will he make his run. Let the eel take the bait until there comes the sharp tug that means that he has definitely decided to swallow it, then hit him hard. Once the conger is on, the trick is to get him away from the bottom as swiftly as possible. If the eel once gets his powerful tail round a rock or part of a wreck nothing will move him— except extreme luck and brute force. Once you've got him away, pump him up as fast as you dare. Be prepared for sudden dives that may drag the rod top into the water. You will probably need help to gaff a big conger. The head is possibly the best spot at which to find a gaff hold. Once the eel is in the boat stun his nerve centres with a heavy blow on the tail, aft of the vent. This will quieten the eel, but severance of the backbone with a knife, taking great care of the fingers the while, is probably the only sure way of dealing with him. It's best to break off the hook and trace and recover it later when the eel is dead beyond doubt.

Conger can be taken by drift-lining and by ground-fishing, preferably with paternoster. When drift-lining the bait should be allowed to hang about a fathom from the bottom. Strong wire is needed on paternoster gear to foil the eel's teeth. Piano wire does nicely, failing that, two strands of Alasticum of about 15 lb. twisted together give sufficient strength. Above all, conger gear needs to be liberally equipped with swivels. Hooks must be well tempered, about three inches long and one-and-a-quarter inches in the gape. The lead should be attached to the tackle with weaker line than the rest of the tackle—an elementary precaution to save loss of gear. The rod for conger work needs to be a tough boat-rod and the reel, a big drum-type with at least 100 yards of high breaking strain—say 30 lb. line. At night when the conger are near the surface, float-fishing in harbours or close to jetties gives good sport. The same rod and line will do with the bait fished close to the surface. Ground-baiting under such conditions can prove helpful with chopped herrings or other oily fish thrown into the water above known conger haunts in sheltered position, such as alongside jetties.

CONTROLLER FLOAT: celluloid or wooden float the function of which is to provide weight in order to cast a light bait in surface fishing. A bubble-float performs much the same task. The line is attached to both ends of the controller which lies flat on the surface.

COOKING FRESHWATER FISH: most coarse anglers look upon the killing of fish as unsporting or unethical, particularly if they are wanted for the pot. In fact, most coarse fish are practically inedible, though many Continental countries disprove this belief. In France, for example, practically every species is eaten, while in middle-European countries freshwater fish farming is carried on on a huge scale. In Czechoslovakia are vast lakes which are manured and drained so that fish may be fattened and netted: fish are treated like any other agricultural crop, the main harvests being carp, pike, and pike-perch.

Game fish—trout, salmon, grayling, and sea trout—are magnificent eating of course. Generally speaking, the more simply game fish are cooked the better. Salmon and sea trout can hardly be beaten when poached or boiled. As to coarse fish, roach and dace are, in the view of the writer, just about edible if fried with bacon. Chub are untouchable however treated. Barbel should be left alone, especially since the roe is thought to be poisonous. Bream don't bear thinking of as food, although I have known people eat them from choice. Bleak can be treated as sprats, as can gudgeon. The latter are very good when freshly caught and fried crisp in very hot fat, being sprinkled with lemon juice and red pepper. Rudd are best left alone, but tench can be very good when baked slowly. Carp are a delicacy among Europeans and also among the Chinese, though the writer has yet to try one. Pike can be very good according to the water from which they come. Perch are without doubt magnificent eating, giving beautiful white firm flesh that is quite as succulent as that of trout, but perhaps not so flavoursome. Ruffe are good, too. Eels make first-class fare, either jellied or cooked in eel pie. Freshwater crayfish boiled are a meal not to be scorned. A fry-up of minnows is said to taste very much like whitebait though few streams these days produce minnows in sufficient quantity. Some recipes for freshwater fish follow:

Recommended reading: *Now Cook Me The Fish* by Margaret Butterworth.

Jellied eels. Place two to three pounds of eels, cut into fairly short lengths, in a saucepan with two or three small carrots, a couple of onions and—if liked—small pieces of celery and green peppers (sliced very finely), also a *bouquet garni* (parsley, thyme and bay leaf). Season well with salt and pepper, cover with white wine (or cider) and then cook very gently for an hour or so. When the eels are quite tender, arrange them in a fairly deep dish, straining the cooking liquor over them to set. If difficulty is experienced in getting the liquor to jell, a little gelatine is advisable before the liquid grows cold.

Eel-pie Island pie. Skin, clean and bone two eels and cut them into pieces. Chop a couple of small shallots and fry them in butter or margarine for five minutes, then adding to this a little parsley chopped, with nutmeg, pepper, salt and one or two glasses of sherry. Place the eels in the midst of this, add enough water to cover them, and then boil the lot slowly. When boiling point is reached the pieces of eel are then taken out and arranged in a pie-dish. Thicken the sauce, in the meantime, by adding two ounces of butter kneaded with

two ounces of flour, stirring it constantly over the heat for two or three minutes. Add the juice of one lemon and pour it over the pieces of eel in the pie-dish. If desired, slices of hard-boiled egg may be arranged on the top. Cover the whole with puff or flaky pastry and then bake for an hour.

Fried gudgeon with herbs. Clean the little fish, roll them in seasoned flour, and fry them in boiling oil with a little shallot (finely minced), clove of garlic, parsley, thyme and bay leaf. Arrange the gudgeon on a dish, pour the oil and herbs over them. Serve hot or cold.

Perch in butter. Put two or three ounces of butter or margarine seasoned with minced shallot into a saucepan and add some skinned and sliced tomatoes. Clean and prepare the perch, and season with lemon juice and salt (and garlic if liked) and place them in the saucepan with some chopped parsley and basil. Place the saucepan over a very low heat without any water, and simmer slowly until cooked. Then take out the fish and arrange them on a hot dish. Make a sauce with the remaining liquid and pour it over the fish.

Perch à la meuniere with mushrooms. Roll some fairly small perch in flour well seasoned with salt and pepper, and fry them in very hot butter. When the fish are golden on each side, take them out, arrange them on a serving dish and keep them hot. Put a little more butter into the pan in which the fish were cooked and add some very finely chopped mushrooms. As soon as the butter is slightly browned pour the contents of the pan over the perch, sprinkle them with chopped parsley, capers and a little lemon juice, and serve immediately on a warmed dish or plate.

Roasting a stuffed pike. Izaak Walton wrote:

'I am certain this direction how to roast him when he is caught, is choicely good, for I have tried it, and it is somewhat the better for not being common; but with my direction you must take this caution, that your pike must not be a small one, that is, it must be more than half a yard, and should be bigger.

'First, open your pike at the gills, and if need be, cut also a little slit towards the belly; out of these take his guts and keep his liver, which you are to shred very small with thyme, sweet marjoram, and a little winter savory; to these put some pickled oysters, and some anchovies, two or three, both these last whole; for the anchovies will melt, and the oysters should not; to these you must also add a pound of sweet butter which you are to mix with the herbs that are shred, and let them all be well salted; if the pike be more than a yard long, then you may put into these herbs more than a pound, or if he be less, then less butter will suffice. These, being thus mixed with a blade or two of mace, must be put into the pike's belly, and then his belly so sewed up as to keep all the butter in his belly, if it is possible: if not, then as much of it as you possibly can; but take not off the scales: then you are to thrust the spit through his mouth out at his tail; and then take four, or five, or six split sticks, and a convenient quantity of tape; these sticks are tied round the pike's body from his head to his tail, and the tape tied somewhat thick to prevent his breaking or falling off the spit.

'Let him be roasted very leisurely, and often basted with claret wine and anchovies and butter mixed together, and also with what moisture falls from him into the pan: when you have roasted him sufficiently, you are to hold under him, when you unwind or cut the tapes that bind him, such a dish as you propose to eat him out of; and let him fall into it with the sauce that is roasted in his belly; and by this means the pike will be kept unbroken and complete: then, to the sauce which was within, and also that sauce in the pan, you are to add a fit quantity of the best butter, and to squeeze the juice of three or four oranges: lastly, you may either put into the pike with the oysters two cloves of garlick, and take them whole out, when the pike is cut off the spit; or to give the spice a *haut-gout* let the dish into which you let the pike fall, be rubbed with it; the using or not using of this garlick is left to your discretion.

'This dish of meat is too good for any but anglers, or very honest men; and I trust you will prove both, and therefore I have trusted you with this secret.'

Baked stuffed pike. Wash and clean a medium-sized pike and stuff with veal forcemeat. Lay it on a bed of chopped, partly cooked mushrooms in a dish that has been rubbed with garlic. Season with salt and pepper and place a large nut of butter or margarine on the fish. Add a wineglassful of red wine, and bake it for about forty-five minutes, at Regulo 5 (390 deg. F.) basting well with butter. Serve it with the wine and butter as sauce.

Pike with egg and lemon sauce. A two- to three-pound pike is needed, two tablespoonfuls of oil, two onions, chopped parsley, salt, pepper, egg and lemon sauce.

Cut up the fish into fairly small pieces. Peel and slice onions. Put the oil in a saucepan, add the onions and fry very gently till just coloured; then lay in the fish, season with salt and pepper and pour over sufficient water just to cover. Cook very gently till the fish is done. Lift out the fish on to a serving dish, pour over the egg and lemon sauce, and serve cold sprinkled with chopped parsley.

Pike and potato salad. Separate the flesh of a cold cooked pike into small flakes. Rub a salad bowl with garlic. Put the fish in the bowl together with twice the quantity of thickly sliced, cold boiled potatoes, a tablespoonful each of chopped parsley, chives, tarragon, capers and grated raw cabbage. Season with salt, pepper and a pinch of sugar if liked. Mix well together with a little mayonnaise and put the salad in the refrigerator for an hour or two.

Before serving cover with thick mayonnaise, and scatter the top with chopped herbs and surround with crisp lettuce hearts quartered, watercress, sliced red peppers, and hard-boiled eggs cut in halves and filled with the yolks mixed with *maitre d'hotel* butter.

Fried tench à la provençale. Prepare some small tench, dust them with well-seasoned flour, and then fry them in a little olive oil and butter, adding a little minced leek, shallot (or small piece of garlic) a little chopped parsley, and some breadcrumbs. All this should now be served, as hot as possible, in a shallow dish.

Trout au bleu. Clean the fish by the gills; trim it but do not scale or wash it. Then sprinkle the fish with boiling vinegar, then put it quickly into a *court-bouillon* of vinegar and salted water. The fish should be well covered with the liquid. Simmer gently until the fish is done. If the trout is a fairly large one the *court-bouillon* should be hot but not boiling. Small fish should be put into the *court-bouillon* while it is boiling.

When the fish is cooked arrange on a napkin and surround with fresh parsley or fennel. The fish should be a bright blue in colour. Serve with boiled or steamed potatoes, and melted butter or Hollandaise sauce. If the trout is to be served cold, serve with tartar sauce.

Fried trout. Clean, wash and dry the trout, season well with salt, roll each fish in rather coarse oatmeal, and fry them in butter. Serve with herb sauce, or Bearnaise sauce.

Once more may I give acknowledgement to Margaret Butterworth's *Now Cook Me The Fish* (Country Life), easily the most complete guide to this sort of cooking.

CORROSION: salt water tackle is particularly susceptible to this trouble. The time-honoured recipe is to wash reels and all metal fittings after each sea-fishing expedition, ending with a coat of Vaseline. Hard-chromed rings of stainless steel or nickel alloy are proof against corrosion, though more expensive. Sea fishing reels suffer greatly from rusting: they can be bought in entirely non-corroding metals. If any doubt exists they should be washed and oiled punctiliously.

CRAYFISH: *Astacus*, the largest British freshwater invertebrate and

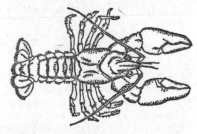

CRAYFISH. *A small freshwater crustacean related to the lobster is favoured by predatory fish.*

a close relation of the lobster. In the natural state the colouring is olive to dark green but when boiled (it is very good to eat) it goes the traditional lobster red. The crayfish lives only in pure, fast-running streams and delights in the chalk waters. It lives in holes in the bank and can be caught with a baited drop-net. There is no doubt it forms an important part of the diet of freshwater predators. Trout thrive on it. It is found in the stomachs of perch and pike, and big chub sometimes fall for crayfish tail used as bait.

CREEL: wicker-work basket slung from the shoulder and carried at one time mostly by trout anglers. In fact, the creel is going out of fashion, most fly fishermen these days preferring to carry haversacks. The use of wicker baskets is much more common now among coarse anglers. In their case the creel takes the form of a strong rectangular wicker basket, usually on short legs, which can be carried on a sling. This, known as a Sheffield basket or sometimes as a seat creel, carries all the multitudinous gadgets of the float angler. It does not, as did the old-fashioned creel of the trout angler, have a slot in the lid through which the catch can be slid.

CREEPER: angler's name for the larvae of the stone-fly, the largest member of the *Perlidae*, or stone-fly family, and the 'may-fly' of the rough moorland streams. The stone-fly comes on in April and May, at which time the creepers are about to leave the river bed to crawl to the bank and into the air to hatch— a process quite different from that of the ephemerid flies. Creepers can be gathered by shifting stones in the shallows. Ideally a small muslin-covered net should be held down-stream of the shifted stone, for the creeper moves fast when disturbed. The larva itself is an ugly looking creepy-crawly about an inch to an inch-and-a-quarter long. The bait can be either put on a spring hook designed for holding live insects or impaled carefully on a No. 14 or even 16 hook, or else tied to the hook with silk—a tricky performance. The creepers should be kept in a bait tin in damp moss.

To fish the creeper, the angler starts at the bottom of the water and works up, casting ahead of him with an underswing. For this purpose he can use a wet-fly rod, as when fishing the upstream worm, or a roach or Avon coarse rod with fixed-spool reel and monofilament line of about 4-lb. breaking strain. The vital thing, as in upsteam worming, is to let the bait wash back naturally in the current. A small lead shot may be necessary to take the bait down and hold it there. As when may-fly fishing, trout taken on the creeper tend to be large.

CUTTLE-FISH: the *Cephalopods*, to which group the cuttles belong, are the most highly developed of the molluscs. They have a head, eyes, beak, and long sucker-equipped arms. The common cuttle (*Sepia officinalis*) is about a foot long, has a continuous fin round its body, ten arms, two of which are knobbed. Cuttle, either whole or cut up, is a good bait for conger, haddock, bass, etc.

CUTTYHUNK: the name given to twisted flax sea fishing lines, after Cuttyhunk Island on the Massachusetts coast where they were first used. They are cheap, should be washed periodically in fresh water and then hung up to dry. A season is usually their maximum useful and safe life.

 **D**

DAB: *Limanda limanda,* family *Pleuronectidae.* This small flatfish is the happy stand-by of small boys since it bites freely when nothing else will take. The fish is light brown, the scales are rough, except between the eyes which are on the right side of the head. It is often spotted but the spots are smaller and darker than those of the plaice. The fish feeds freely on almost anything and can be taken with paternoster from shore or boat. A pounder is a specimen.

DACE: *Leuciscus leuciscus,* family *Cyprinidae.* Sometimes called the dart (Old English). Bright silver in colour with yellow or greenish tinge to the fins; small, neat, streamlined in appearance without the block-headed aspect of the chub with which it is often confused. Usually has a dark greenish stripe along the ridge of the back. Eye yellow-flecked. The record dace was taken by R. W. Humphrey in 1932 from a Hampshire Avon tributary. It weighed 1 lb. 8 oz. 5 drams. The classic means of telling chub from dace is by the curve of the trailing edge of the anal fin. In the chub this is convex or outwardly rounded; in the dace the same fin is concave at the edge, and looks as though a shallow bite has been taken from it. The dace has 47–54 scales along the lateral line to the chub's 42–49 and the 40–46 of the roach. This can be of some help in determining species since the dace only overlaps by two scales with the chub and does not come in the same range at all as the roach. Ray counts in the fins are not so conclusive, but, for the record, the dace has 7–8 branched rays in the dorsal and 7–9 in the anal fin.

The dace is a shoal fish and thrives only in a clear, well-oxygenated stream. Thames dace are poor specimens these days whereas all the south country chalk streams

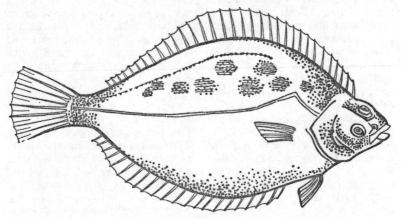

DAB. *A flatfish frequently caught by beach and pier anglers.*

59

produce beautiful specimen fish. So do the chalk or part-chalk rivers of Bedfordshire and Herts. The Ivel and the Beane are both fine dace streams. The fish will never be found in still water. Evenlode, Gipping, Kennet, Medway, Bedford Ouse, Soar, Dorset and Suffolk Stour (the latter is probably the best dace river in the country), Swale, Tees and Tone have all produced good fish in recent years.

Dace fight splendidly, rather like a miniature sea trout, though without the spectacular leaps. It would be a crime, therefore, to fish for them with heavy tackle. A light roach rod, Avon rod, or even match rod will give good results. Line should be monofilament of not more than 3-lb. breaking strain, floats should be smallish quills carrying few shot, and hooks size 10–14. Personally I do not believe

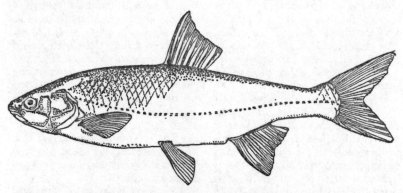

DACE. *The best specimens are found in the clear waters of chalk streams. In the Thames and similar rivers a 12-oz. fish would be exceptionally good.*

The fish feed at all levels from surface to bottom. The bite is exceptionally fast, quicker even than that of a trout taking surface fly.

In Lancashire and Cheshire dace are sometimes called 'graining'. There is no support for the theory that these fish are of a different species. They are just dace by another title. The fighting quality of dace is superb for their size.

DACE-FISHING: Dace can be caught anywhere from surface to bottom. At the latter level they will normally be found only during winter floods when taking shelter. At such times conventional leger tackle will catch them on worm, maggots or bread, so nothing more need be said about this.

in very small hooks for dace since the bite is so quick that one must give oneself every chance of making contact with an equally rapid strike. To catch dace with such tackle the angler must keep well down and out of sight and trot down to the fish, using gentle or a fragment of crust on the hook.

In summer, dace feed on the surface as frequently as trout. Conventional dry-fly work will take them time and again, and great sport it is. The coarse angler can also catch dace on artificial fly (or the real dead article), with fixed-spool tackle and a bubble float. With this rig, the bubble float is partly filled with water to give it casting weight, and the fly is either stuck on the hook (or, if artificial, tied on the cast) about two feet from the bubble. The whole is cast above the feeding fish, checked slightly to let fly swing downstream of bubble, and then floated down over the dace.

With a suitable downstream wind, dace can also be taken amusingly by a variation of the Irish method of blowline fishing for trout. A rod of at least 12 feet is needed, armed with monofilament of 1–2 lb. breaking strain. A fly (allow some maggots to go off in a bait tin) is attached to the hook, and the whole gear is flicked out gently so that it will waft downstream to the fish. Cover is, of course, essential for success.

DAPPING: or dibbling, a very simple manner of taking surface-feeding fish such as chub and dace, and, indeed, trout, by lowering the bait, usually an insect, on to the surface of the water within view of the fish. This is not to say that the dapper does not need considerable skill for, to approach his quarry, he must have the stealth of a Red Indian. One hint of the angler's presence, and the fish will be away. The rod used is generally a longish one. This enables the angler to stay well back from the bank. A weight sufficient to take the bait down to the fish is fixed on the line about eighteen inches above the hook. Once the fish is on there is no further need for caution and the dapper can stand up and play his quarry normally.

A further form of dapping is that practised on big Irish lakes during the may-fly season. This is sometimes called 'blowline fishing'. A very long rod with the lightest of silk lines is used from a boat. The live may-fly is attached to the hook and is allowed to blow out on the breeze to the feeding fish. Very big trout are caught in this way.

DEADBAIT FISHING: the use of dead fish as bait is a branch of angling insufficiently explored. The old-timers knew the virtues of trolling deadbait for pike; using drop-minnow tackle for perch; fixing dead roach on to spinning flights or wobbler tackle such as the Archer flight or Bromley-Pennell tackle. All these are discussed under Spinning Baits. Too few anglers today use the natural lure for pike or perch spinning: they prefer the ready-made spoon or plug, which is not necessarily any more effective.

The use of deadbait for eel fishing is less well known than it should be, and this, too, is discussed under the appropriate section.

A new branch of deadbait angling, and one that deserves every attention is when legering for big pike. Several huge specimens have been

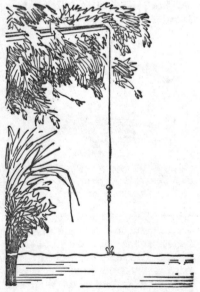

DAPPING. *A freshwater technique used in the pursuit of chub and other surface-feeding species, in which the concealment of the angler and his tackle is all-important.*

taken by deadbait enthusiasts, generally when using herring on leger tackle. The theory is that the pike has a well-developed sense of taste-smell (in a fish the two are practically identical), and is able to detect the natural oils exuded by the herring from a distance of several hundred yards. That being the case, it seems that the pike angler should certainly groundbait with herring oil, or at least with chopped-up herring. A wire trace must, of course, be used and large snap-tackle is advisable.

DEMERSAL: a word used to describe forms of life living on or near the bottom. As distinct from demersal forms are pelagic forms which live in the upper layers of water and at the surface.

DEVON MINNOW: a small metal (occasionally wood) torpedo-shaped spinning bait with vanes at the head and a flight attached to a triangle hook running through the

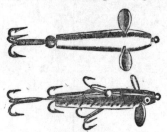

DEVON MINNOW. *Slotted (above) and unslotted patterns. Available in various colours.*

centre. The bait revolves on this wire, a small bead acting as a bearing surface at the tail end and in front of the triangle. Very deadly for salmon, sea trout, fair for perch, poor for pike: useful for some sea fish, including bass.

DIPTERA: a family of two-winged flies of great interest to the trout angler. The black gnat is one member commonly imitated. The diptera fold their wings something like a house-fly.

DISGORGER: an instrument of steel, or occasionally of wood, used for removing hooks that have lodged deep down in the throat of a fish. The commonest variety consists of a long needle-like rod with a forked end. This fork is pushed against the bend of the hook to loosen its hold. There are few better instruments for disgorging than a pair of artery forceps from the chemist. These can be left locked on to the hook should the angler need to keep both hands free.

DORSAL FIN: the back fin of a fish. Sometimes as in the case of a perch it is divided into two sections. Many sea fish have this characteristic too. The main function of the dorsal in swimming is to assist in turning and above all to maintain vertical stability. In some cases—perch, bass, etc.—the spines are sharp and can inflict quite painful wounds. This does not stop predatory fish such as pike from swallowing fish like the perch which has a well-armed dorsal fin.

DOUGH-BOBBIN: a very common device used by leger fishermen for indicating bites. A lump of dough, usually pinched from the loaf the angler is using for bait or groundbait, is squeezed on to the line between the reel and bottom rod ring. This hangs down slightly when the rod is in its rest. A taking fish is indicated by a twitch of the bobbin. Not very sensitive.

DRAG, Fly: the arch enemy of the dry-fly fisherman. It occurs when his floating fly moves sideways because of the pull of the line rather than proceeding evenly down with the current. Drag can soon be detected by the fisherman by a tiny V-shaped wake left by the fly as it moves unnaturally across the cur-

DISGORGER. *A device used for disengaging a hook from the mouth of a fish.*

rent. The fish, however, spot the deception long before the angler, and it is useless to leave a dragging fly on the water. The usual cause of drag is a faster current pulling on the line between fisherman and fly. The cure is to throw a snaky line that the fast current must first straighten before it can begin to affect the movement of the fly.

DRAG, Reel: the fitting standard to all fixed-spool reels (called in their case, a slipping clutch), to most freshwater multiplying reels and all good sea multipliers. A drag allows tension to be put on the spool to check a running fish. In sea multipliers the drag is usually of the 'star' type, the 'star' referring to the nut by which tension is applied. The drag can act as a check when trailing a bait behind a boat: when the angler is winding in a fish and the fish decides to run, the drag comes into play and slows it up without allowing it to break the line.

DRAGONET: *Callionymus hyra,* family *Callionymidae.* A fancy-looking sea fish sometimes caught in shallow water. Actually there are two varieties, the Dragonet and the Spotted Dragonet. The body is long and thin and seems to be scaleless. There are two dorsal fins, the front dorsal of the male being extraordinarily long. The female dragonet is brownish but the male is yellow with blue spots and its head is orange with blue flecks. The spotted dragonet is, naturally, covered with spots, particularly on the rear dorsal.

DRIFT-LINING: a method of sea fishing from a boat without use of float, leger, or paternoster gear. The bait, on a suitably weighted line, is allowed to stream away from the boat, down-tide, so that it is just off the bottom. Very often careful plumbing with a heavily weighted line must be done first to make sure that the correct amount of reel line has been paid out. When the bottom has been found by plumbing, the correct depth must be marked on the actual fishing line with a piece of waterproof sticking plaster. Remember to add one or two fathoms, according to the strength of the tide, for line-slant. Weights used may vary from a few ounces to half a pound or more according to the strength of the current.

DROP-NET: a large saucer-shaped net with cords at four equidistant points by which it can be lowered into the water. When baited, this can be used to catch small fish of all sorts for bait purposes.

DOUGH-BOBBIN. *A bite is indicated by the twitching of the bobbin.*

DROPPER: a wet-fly fisherman's term to describe the top flies on his cast when he is fishing what is usually called a 'leash', that is to say three flies. The dropper is attached to the cast by means of a short, about three-inch, length of gut or nylon. About eighteen inches

fibres represent the thorax, legs and sometimes wings of the live fly. But more important than this, in the case of a dry-fly, they cause it to float. Dry-fly hackles should be selected from the best game-cock necks. The feathers must be narrow and hard, as opposed to the soft,

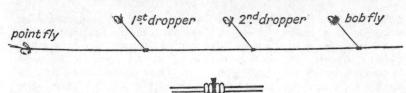

DROPPER. *Game fisherman's term for the flies attached, usually as a blood knot, to a wet-fly cast above the point fly.*

usually separates dropper from the point, or bottom, fly. The topmost of the three is sometimes called a bob fly rather than a dropper and is fished just on the surface while the other two are sunken. Sometimes four wet flies—point, first and second dropper, and bob fly—are used.

DRY-FLIES: dry-flies are designed to float on the surface and imitate a live insect either hatching, egg-laying, dying after egg-laying, or just in difficulties having been blown there by an unfriendly breeze. The patterns are too numerous to name. Many of them are designed to imitate members of the ephemerid family. The sedges, gnats, moths, wasps, alders, as well as many 'fancy' flies that do not imitate anything in particular, are usually tied dry. The difference between a wet- and dry-fly is largely in the tying and in the materials used. The most vital part of a floating fly is the hackle. This feather from the neck of a chicken is wound in circular fashion about the hook shank so that the fibre points stick outwards. The

broad hackle feathers of the hen. The latter are used in wet-fly tying. In addition dry-flies have to be assisted to float by treatment with special paraffin preparations, or lately with silicones. With the former the hackles are touched up with a small brush: using silicone preparations the whole fly is immersed in a spirit containing silicones. Treated thus the fly will float for an extraordinary time, as long as it is cleaned after catching a fish. Dry-flies should be cleared of surplus water either by being pressed in amadou fungus, or by false-casting in the air, or by both.

DUN: the name given to a member of the ephemerid family of flies in its penultimate stage of emergence. To the scientist the dun is known as the sub-imago. The dun is the fly as it emerges from the nymphal shuck. It is still covered by a final skin which gives it its dun appearance. Twenty-four hours or so after hatching it will shed this last skin and appear as the translucent and perfect 'spinner' or, to the scientist, imago.

Bagging salmon outside the fish-hut at Balnagown Arms, Ross and Cromarty.

Chalkstream Waters. The River Wylye, Wiltshire.

 E

EEL: *Anguilla anguilla*, family *Anguillidae*. The common eel has the most fascinating natural history of any British fish, not excluding the salmon. The eel is a true fish, having gills and minute scales. Moreover, though you hear talk of silver eels and yellow eels, there is only one kind of eel in British rivers and ponds: the varying colour denotes different phases of life, and that is all. The eel breeds in an Atlantic deep midway between the Azores and the Bahamas. Having bred, it dies, but its progeny, as minute specks of jelly at first, are carried by the Gulf Stream to the shores of all the countries which that warm water current brushes. Arrived at these coasts, the tiny eels—now known to us as elvers—swim upriver. From the river they branch out overland to colonize lakes, canals and duckponds. There they stay until the urge to reproduce turns them back to the far Atlantic again. The eels then wriggle out of their inland water, across country in wet weather or early morning when the dew is thick until they reach a river, and so to the estuary, where they wait for a period of acclimatization, and then to sea. The eel is unmistakable in appearance and voracious in appetite. It feeds on live and dead fish, besides insects and spawn. In game-fish rivers, particularly, it does enormous damage to spawning beds, far more than that accomplished by otters, herons, dabchicks, or king-fishers. There is nothing good to be said of it from the conservationist's point of view. Fortunately it can give good sport if properly fished for

and makes magnificent eating. The record is 8 lb. 8 oz.

EEL-FISHING: the object of most anglers is not to catch eels, for they not only make an appalling and usually inextricable mess of tackle, but they also take bait intended for other species. To fish for eels deliberately, the angler should use deadbait—a bleak, small roach or dace, gudgeon, or even fishmonger's sprat all make ideal baits. These should be mounted on a wire trace (Alasticum is excellent) with a baiting needle, the head hanging downwards, and a large shot pinched on above the vent to stop the eel ejecting the bait. A very large hook (eel hooks are made specially: failing that, large sea hooks do well) is pulled home into the mouth of the bait. The dead fish is pressed to squeeze air from its swim bladder so that it will hold the bottom, and cast out without further addition of weight.

Eels take most freely at night. The start of thundery weather often seems to put them on the feed. When the bait is taken, the angler should ignore the first few movements of the line. Allow the eel to pouch the bait and start to run before hitting it. Once on the bank stun quickly. A blow on the tail helps to paralyse the fish, but decapitation is almost the only way (or at least severing the backbone) of making sure an eel is dead.

To skin an eel for cooking, slit round behind the gills, fix to wooden board by banging a nail through the head and roll skin off body towards the tail, gripping with a rough cloth

c

The tastiest of eel dishes is the traditional Richmond eel pie, the recipe being as follows:

Chop two small onions and brown them in butter, adding parsley, pepper, salt, nutmeg, and two glasses of sherry. Chop up the skinned eels and put them in this, adding enough water to cover the fish. Bring to boil. Take out the eels and arrange them in a pie dish. Now add to the liquor two ounces of flour mixed with two ounces of butter. Stir this until you have a white smooth sauce, adding the juice of a lemon. Pour the sauce over the eels, adding two sliced hard-boiled eggs, bacon, mushrooms, etc. Cover with puff pastry and bake for an hour.

EEL-GRASS: *Zostera marina,* sometimes called widgeon grass. A green thin weed once beloved by wildfowl and a useful feeding zone for fishes. Now nearly extinct round the coasts of Britain.

ELDERBERRY: an excellent bait for several coarse fish, notably roach when trees along the river are in fruit. Choose a swim under a tree with ripe berries and your ground-baiting has been done for you. Use the berries impaled on a smallish hook. Chub and sometimes barbel will take this bait. In season late August.

ELECTRICAL FISHING: a method, pioneered on the Kennet and Lambourn, and now universally used by River Boards and others in conservation and restocking programmes, of catching fish by means of electrical current. The apparatus consists of a generator putting out a direct current of 250 volts, and having positive and negative electrodes. A small area of river is chosen, and, where possible, a stop-net put below the apparatus. When the current is turned on it has

the effect of lining up the fish in the immediate vicinity between the two electrodes. They then swim to the positive electrode which sometimes takes the form of a landing-net, and, if exposed long enough, the fish gradually keel over and become unconscious. Before this happens they are lifted out and transferred to storage tanks for removal or examination. No damage results to the fish. In early electrical fishing experiments, carried out largely by the Americans, the fish were shocked by a large dose of electricity and were found to suffer later. Trout fishing societies use this electrical apparatus for ridding their waters of grayling and coarse fish, which they frequently give away to coarse fishing clubs who will transport them to other waters.

ELVERS: the young of eels as they enter the rivers from the sea. In some rivers, such as the Severn, they are commercially trapped. Delicious to eat.

EPHEMERIDAE: one of the most important families of flies to the fly fisherman, and for the chalk stream fisher certainly the most important. The name suggests that they are short-lived; this is only partially true since, though they survive as flies for only a day or so, they have by this stage already spent anything from two or three years below the surface and in the bottom silt as larvae. The life cycle is a complex one which at all stages is of practical interest to the fly fisherman.

Once the mated female fly has dropped her fertile eggs on the surface they sink and find a resting place on the bottom. There they hatch out into minute larvae known to the fisherman as 'nymphs'. The nymphs grow progressively larger. Each time they feel the need to expand, they split their skins and emerge in a new coat. The fish feed greedily on these nymphs and an artificial lure tied to resemble a nymph can be very killing. After two or three years of this progress the moment comes to rise to the surface and hatch out as a fly. Trout and other fish, of course, take the nymphs as they float upwards, and take them also as they sit on the surface vulnerable in the act of emerging. To do so they again split their casing, this time appearing for the first time as winged insects, but still not perfect winged insects. They are called at this stage 'sub-imagos' by the scientist and 'duns' by the fisherman.

Once the dun has recovered sufficiently from the hatching process—this rising of nymphs to hatch is what the fly fisherman knows as a 'rise' or 'hatch'—the fly flutters away to a bush or tree for shelter. Later, usually about a day later, the skin covering the fly splits once more, and for the last time, and the perfect fly known to the scientist as the 'imago' and to the angler as a 'spinner', emerges. By comparison with the leaden dun it is a gossamer shimmering insect. The fly now performs its only role in life, namely to find a partner, mate, lay its eggs and die. The fly has no mouth or stomach.

The females can often be seen in the evening hovering up and down in the shelter of a tree waiting for the males to find them. Mated, the female instinctively flies off up river so that she shall in some measure neutralize the drift imposed on her by the stream in her earlier life. She dips to the surface to lay her eggs, and the fish are waiting for her. If she escapes she will eventually fall exhausted on the surface, wings outspread, and die. In this last stage of all the angler still has a use for her and refers to her as a 'spent spinner' or simply as a 'spent'.

The wings of the ephemerids are folded vertically above the body, the body itself having a slight up-curve, ending in whisks or *setae* which balance the insect in flight. The fly sits delicately on the water on six legs which enable it to ride out quite sharp breezes without being capsized. The folded wings act as a sail swinging the fly into the wind and out of trouble. Practically all the ephemerid family live in and on smooth-flowing, clear, alkali streams, though they appear also in smaller numbers on swift, acid brooks. Here are the various members of the family with notes on their colouring, identification and seasonal appearances.

The Olive: straw coloured to pale and quite darkish green, with two whisks at the tail. Over 50 slightly different species. Some of these hatch out throughout the season, and indeed, except in the coldest weather, throughout the year.

The Iron Blue: taken avidly by trout, described in colour by its name. Appears first in May.

The March Brown: second largest of the tribe. Light to darkish brown, not found on chalk rivers but in acid water. Season: throughout the fishing period for trout.

The May-fly: largest and most noble of the ephemerids, hatching often in great numbers during the first two weeks of June, and sometimes later: rarely in May. Trout feed on it ravenously because of its size. Has three tails.

The Pale Watery: rather like a small, very pale olive, at times almost transparent. Appears often in the evening.

The Blue-Winged Olive: has smoky wings and is confined to a definite season, usually late in July.

The only ephemerid, other than the may-fly, to have three tails.

Fly anglers have special names for various stages of development of these flies apart from the general application of the words 'dun', 'spinner', etc.

For example: May-fly spinners, male and female, are known respectively as 'grey-' and 'green-drakes'. The Iron Blue spinner is called a 'jenny spinner'. Blue-winged olive spinners are 'sherry spinners'. Olive spinners are 'red spinners'. All very confusing. Artificial flies to imitate these will be found under that heading.

Recommended reading: *An Angler's Entomology* by J. R. Harris in the Collins' 'New Naturalist' series.

EUTROPHIC LAKE: one in which the oxygen of the lower strata of water becomes used up during the summer heat, largely due to the amount of organic matter that sinks to the depths and decays. A eutrophic lake is therefore a lake rich in surface life.

EPILIMNION: the upper stratum of warm water in a lake. See THERMOCLINE.

EVENING RISE: this all too short period of the fishing day is the dream time of every trout angler. After a hot summer's day the water is cooling and putting the fish into the mood to feed. It is becoming fresher and more oxygenated. Coupled with this is the fact that the spinners of the *ephemerid* flies now return to the river to lay their eggs. The trout are thus presented with a banquet of both spinners and spent flies, together, sometimes, with a hatch of duns. The problem then is to discover what the fish are feeding on.

Sometimes, it must be stressed, the evening rise does not take place at all. On rough streams it may scarcely ever be seen, but on the placid chalk rivers the whole surface will often explode with feeding trout. The angler's problem is to make the most of it while it lasts. Above all he must not become flurried or he will lose everything. Trout to be attacked should be singled out carefully and worked on systematically. Remember that the light is failing, so tackle must be well-ordered and flies cut to the minimum number of patterns likely to be required. Gear should be well disposed in known pockets so that every second of fishing time can be used to the utmost.

It pays to notice what has been hatching during the day, and what hatched the day before. For yesterday's duns are often tonight's spinners and the same will be true tomorrow. This in itself may give a guide to what is the correct pattern to use. At least it will give you a choice of fly on which to begin. Sedge flies should be kept in reserve for the last moments of light, when they will often take a big trout. When all light has gone success can sometimes be snatched from an otherwise lost evening rise by tying on a white moth. Swallows and swifts darting in concentrations over the water point the way to rich hordes of fly during this magic hour.

 F

FAMOUS ANGLERS:

Bazley, Jim: a great Leeds angler who was president of the N.F.A. and twice won the All-England championship. He wrote *Fine and Far Off* and several other angling books. He was also a great specimen hunter for pike and roach.

Berners, Dame Juliana: authoress of the first-known book on fishing in the English language—the *Treatysse on Anglyne* from the *Boke of St. Albans*, dated 1492. This work was illustrated and contained some surprisingly sound information, even down to the dressing of certain flies.

Bickerdyke, John: the pseudonym of a great fishing writer, author of *The Book of the All-Round Angler*. Died in mid-'twenties. His book, brought up to date, is still on sale in separate sections—notably *Coarse Fishing* and *Pike Angling*.

Buckland, Frank: a famous Victorian naturalist and Inspector of Salmon Fisheries. Much of our present knowledge of British fish and their habits stems from his work.

Buckley, Albert: for many years the unchallenged holder of the carp record with a 26-lb. fish taken on roach tackle from Mapperley Reservoir.

Chalmers, Patrick: one of the finest chroniclers of the Thames in its golden days both in verse and prose. Most notable work: *At the Tail of the Weir*.

Ensome, Ted: a great fishing writer under the pen name of 'Faddist'. An expert on roach fishing especially. Died in the early 1950's.

Fennell, Greville: author of the historic but now largely outdated *Book of the Roach*. Still worth reading.

Francis, Francis: famous angler and naturalist of the turn of the century. A boat-fishing club at Twickenham is named after him

Garvin, John: in 1920 landed the first authenticated rod-caught pike of over 50 lb. from Lough Conn, Ireland. It weighed 53 lb. and won for him the £10 reward put up by R. B. Marston, then editor of the *Fishing Gazette*. It is interesting to note that the *Daily Herald* currently offers £100 for the first rod-caught English or Welsh pike of over 40 lb.

Grey, Lord, of Falloden wrote: an immortal book on chalk stream fishing and of the Itchen in particular—*Fly Fishing*.

Halford, F. M.: author of *The Dry-Fly Man's Handbook* and originator of much new thought on fly-dressing for chalk streams. Halford's theory was to achieve exact imitation, a line now largely abandoned by fly tiers.

Hardy, E. Marshall: author of *Angling Ways*, only coarse fishing book to go into nine impressions in the writer's lifetime.

Hastings, Warren: famous Thames angler particularly noted for his knowledge of Thames trouting in its heyday.

Illingworth, A. Holden: Yorkshire woollen manufacturer who invented and patented in 1905 the first fixed-spool reel.

Jardine, Alfred: great fisherman of the turn of the century. Gave his name to, among other things, the Jardine snap-tackle. An expert on pike.

Lunn, W. J.: keeper of the Houghton club at the turn of the century, and inventor of many techniques for rearing and catching trout, which now form part of chalk stream lore.

Martin, J. W.: wrote excellent angling books under the pseudonym of 'Trent Otter'. Notable work: *Coarse Fish Angling*.

Mundella: though not an angler, this Sheffield Member of Parliament was largely responsible for promoting the first Bill to give fish protected close periods. The so-called Mundella Act became law in 1878: it has been modified many times since.

Parker, Captain L. A.: expert on the Hampshire Avon, notably as a captor of big roach.

Pennell, H. Cholmondeley: author, among other works, of *The Angler Naturalist*, published in 1863. A great man and a great angler. Gave his name to various items of tackle, notably to a deadbait spinning flight for pike.

Regan, Dr. C. Tate: the foremost authority on British freshwater fish. Though many years old, his *British Freshwater Fishes* is still a standard work of reference for icthyologists.

Sheringham, H. T.: one of the most delightful of fishing writers. Works include *An Angler's Hours*.

Skues, G. E. M.: famous chalk stream authority who invented and pioneered the science of nymph fishing for trout.

Turing, H. D.: great all-round angler whose books *Coarse Fishing* and *Trout Fishing* remain steady sellers.

Venables, Bernard: foremost fishing illustrator of today.

Vincent, Jim: was one of the best-known Broads experts. Lived on Hickling Broad, has a large spoon named after him and advocated sink-and-draw tactics with deadbait for big pike.

Walker, Richard: of Hitchin, holder of the carp record at 44 lb. Author of *Still-Water Angling*. A writer who has produced an entirely new approach to coarse fishing.

Wallis, F. W. K.: famous Nottingham angler who gave his name to the long-range centre-pin Avon cast.

Walton, Izaak: see separate entry.

Wanless, Alexander: the 'high-priest' of the fixed spool reel for salmon and trout, before it became the popular weapon it is today.

Wood, A. H. E.: pioneer of the system of low-water salmon fishing called greased-lining.

FERRULES: the metal joints by means of which a two- or three-piece rod is put together. Ferrules are almost invariably of brass and are machined to within very fine limits to ensure a perfect fit. Suction type ferrules hold firm simply by virtue of this fit. The two portions are known as male and female ferrule: the female, the receiving end of the coupling, is always on the lower joint to be connected. Some rods, fly-rods especially, have a tenon or centre-pin that fits into a socket in the base of the female ferrule. On the more expensive fly-rods, various makers have invented locking devices that eliminate the possibility of a throw-out of a top joint in casting.

Hard fitting ferrules should be eased by greasing them with a little tallow. Never rub down a tight-fitting ferrule as the metal once lost can never be replaced. When ferrules jam, give a straight pull on the joints, getting a companion to

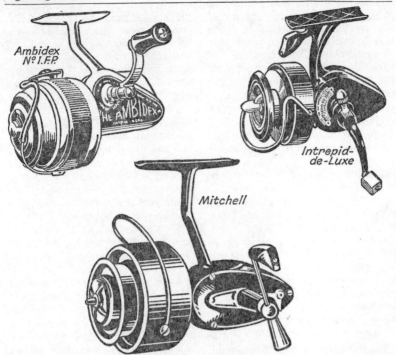

FIXED-SPOOL REEL. *This type of reel, initially devised for the benefit of the trout fisherman, is now widely used for coarse fishing. It enables lightweight tackle to be cast a considerable distance.*

hold one joint while you pull the other. In exceptional circumstances, usually in cold weather, heat carefully applied to the outside of the female ferrule sometimes frees a jam. Care must be taken not to injure the rod whippings or the cane.

FIGHTING CHAIR: the chair, fixed to the deck at the stern of a boat and able to swivel through a complete circle, from which the big-game sea angler fights such fish as marlin. His harness is usually attached to the chair.

FISHING THE WATER: trout angler's term to describe the technique of placing the fly in likely spots rather than casting to a clearly marked and feeding fish.

FIXED-SPOOL REEL: sometimes inaccurately called the 'threadline reel', and now widely used for all forms of fishing. Invented by A. Holden Illingworth in 1905, the main feature of the reel is that the axis of the drum is parallel to the rod itself rather than at right-angles to it as in the ordinary Nottingham type of centre-pin reel. This arrangement permits extremely long casting.

Imagine a cotton reel held with the end of the spool towards you. Now take hold of the loose end of the cotton and pull it gently: the cotton slips easily over the edge of the spool towards you—exactly the principle applied in casting with the fixed-spool reel. Note that the fuller the reel with cotton and the finer

71

the cotton, the easier will the thread slip over the lip of the spool. Again this is true of the fixed-spool reel. For long casting, therefore, the reel spool should always be kept full: the finer the line used, the longer the cast will be.

However, the average fixed-spool reel has many other refinements. First, there must be some method of preventing the line from spilling off the spool all the time. This device is called the 'pick-up'. As long as it is in position, the line will be held securely on the drum. To cast, the pick-up is lowered and the line held momentarily on the tip of the fore-finger, being released only as the bait is flipped forward into the air. This same pick-up flicks back into position and catches the line to pay it back onto the spool immediately the reel handle is turned to retrieve the bait. Second, to stop the recovered line from piling up in one place on the spool there is a mechanism that pushes the drum in and out as the pick-up rotates in the retrieving action: the line is thus evenly distributed over the spool. Many models also incorporate anti-backwind devices and audible checks.

There remains to be described the slipping clutch. This refinement is made necessary because of the big fish frequently played on very light lines. Tension on this clutch can be varied by means of a finger nut in the centre of the spool. If you slacken this off, then a fish is able to pull line from the spool, over the pick-up, by rotating the spool. Tighten it and the spool becomes harder to rotate, thus imposing severe strain on the fish. However, far too much has been made by some regarding the properties of this clutch. It is no substitute for angling skill. The last thing you can do in

playing a fish is to set the clutch and wind against your quarry in the hope that you will tire it out. All you are doing is to put a series of kinks into your line. Which brings us to the correct method of playing a fish with a fixed-spool reel.

Playing a fish: first the clutch should be set to a hard medium adjustment, that is to say so that line can be pulled off but with a certain amount of resistance. On striking a fish, the spool should be jammed hard by tightening it with the fingers. Once the hook is home the fish will probably run.

With a large fish, do not try to stop him. Instead, keep the tightest finger pressure consistent with safety on the rim of the spool. Let him take line but under the greatest possible restraint. Don't bother about shifting the clutch setting to vary this restraint. Play the fish with finger pressure exactly as you would on a Nottingham reel. Whenever he lets you, recover some line by winding in, but never do so against the run of the fish. If you have to try to stop him, take your courage in both hands, jam the reel with finger pressure and give him sidestrain with the rod. Supposing he goes to the bottom and sulks. So far you have played your fish with the rod upright, for all rods are designed to give maximum efficiency when the butt is at right-angles to the pull of the line. When he goes to ground, however, you must try something different. So, wind the rod down until it is almost pointing at the water, being ready to shift your position back to normal if he attempts to move off. Once the rod point is down, apply finger pressure to the spool and try to 'pump' him up by lifting the rod. If the strain becomes too much and the line is in danger, ease off. But keep trying.

Eventually, either he will shift towards you, in which case you recover valuable line, or he will up and run for it. In either event you have gained a point, for, the more he runs, the sooner he will tire. If he won't budge and nothing will shift him, relax the pressure. You may tempt him to move off by slackening the line, but be ready for lightning action. When the fish at last comes to net, remove your finger from the

FLOAT-LEGER. *A very effective technique when used in slow, deep swims.*

drum and apply it to the pick-up carrier. You can then let go of the reel handles and use the other hand for the net. If your fixed-spool reel has an anti-backwind device, so much the better.

Most good reels these days are made to take line up to about 12-lb. breaking strain, so the chance of a break on big fish is considerably lessened. Where possible, two drums, one filled with, say, 4-lb. line and one with 10-lb., should be carried. For efficient use all fixed-spool reel drums should be filled with line to the lip.

FLAKE: hook bait made at the waterside by compressing slightly the crumb of a new loaf. Its virtue is that particles are apt to flake off as an attraction to feeding fish.

FLOAT-LEGER: combination of leger gear with float. Very effective in fishing slow deep swims for bream, etc.

FLOATS: there is a world of fascination for anglers in floats. This is indicated by the fact that most fishermen have at least twice as many floats as they are ever likely to need. In tackle shops floats catch many more anglers than they will ever catch fish. A float has three roles in angling, and of these, the first is the least important as far as catching fish goes: (1), to give pleasure to the angler; many people do not enjoy floatless fishing: (2), to convey the tackle to where the fish are in moving water; (3) to indicate bites. It should be added, however, that a float is in many cases a handicap to really efficient angling. In still waters and on clear river bottoms it is generally more productive to fish with some form of leger. The reason is that a float inevitably imposes some resistance on a taking fish. It follows then that if you insist on using a float it should be as light as is consistent with the power and nature of the water being fished. There are endless varieties of floats to suit different conditions. Here are some of them:

Quill float: the simplest float of all, made from any wing quill from a bird's primary feather. At its smallest, the quill can come from a crow when it will probably support only the bait and one or two shots. At the other extreme a swan quill can be used, and, if this is not sufficiently buoyant on its own, it can be made to carry more weight by adding a balsa or cork body.

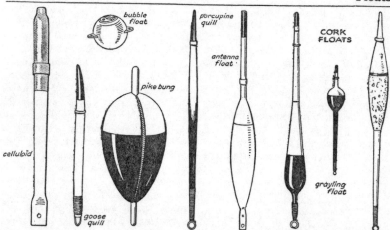

FLOATS. *At best floats are a source of resistance to a taking fish. The angler should always use the lightest possible pattern that conditions permit.*

Bubble float: a plastic sphere whose weight is provided by water poured into the body. Useful for surface-fishing and also for supporting paternoster gear.

Antenna float: this pattern has an elongated central spine, the idea being that the body can be weighted to submerge in windy weather so that only the wand at the top shows above the ripples. In this way drift by wind action is cut down.

Self-cocking float: this pattern is weighted at the bottom end so that it sits upright in the water. Useful when weightless tackle is used or in cases when the float is being used as a sliding float.

Sliding float: a type reserved for fishing water that is deeper than the length of the fisherman's rod. A stop is tied to the line at the required depth, usually a piece of bristle or a fragment of rubber band. The essential thing about the stop is that it should pass out through the rod rings freely at the cast. The sliding float is attached to the line by its rings only and can slide freely up and down. Let us assume that the angler is using a 10-ft. rod and that his swim is 15-ft. deep. He puts up his tackle and decides to use a sliding float. When the tackle is allowed to dangle from the rod top this float rests with its bottom ring on the topmost shot of the terminal tackle. Now, fifteen feet from the hook, he ties to his line the rubber stop. He casts out. When it hits the water, the weighted tackle pulls the line through the rings of the sliding float which has probably been carried beneath the surface at the moment of impact. Eventually the float rises until it meets the rubber stop at the fifteen-foot mark. The hook is now just on the bottom in the desired position. The tug of a taking fish will pull the stop against the top float ring and the float will give a normal bite indication.

Pilot float: small round float—which can easily be made from an oak apple, incidentally—fixed to the line above the big livebait float, or 'bung', when pike fishing. Its function: to keep the line afloat.

In the coloration of floats, yellow and orange are the most visible all-round colours. Black will probably prove best in the last hour of twilight.

FLOODS: these need not have a disastrous effect upon fishing. Frequently good fishing follows and can sometimes be found during flood time. In a slow, low-country water such as the Thames or Ouse, flooding puts fish off the feed in the stronger currents. Much suspended matter is brought down and the fish are sickened and irritated. However, after a time they will still want to feed. For this they will choose the quiet deep lay-bys; they will also venture out over flooded fields, and this is probably where the best fishing is to be found. When fishing a few inches below the surface over grass in a flooded meadow, all sorts of species can be found foraging for land insects and, of course, worms. The flood fisher under these conditions should know his territory well; a tumble into a flooded ditch can be very uncomfortable and even dangerous. Worms are the best bait in flood time.

However, it must be said that the best flood fishing is probably still to be found in the main river. Sheltered swims that hold fish in normal times will probably still hold them now. It pays to know your river bed.

Mountain rivers and their trout population are well used to floods, or spates as they are called. The fish feed often as the spate is clearing, as indeed happens in any river. A tremendous killing can be made as the river, slow or fast, begins to return to normal. Even the most terrifying floods do not appear to damage quite small fish. An example was the Lynmouth flood. In parts of the Barle at this time the river rose seventeen feet. Neither the small trout of this river nor the fly life were seriously disturbed as a result. The only fish that died were those caught feeding on the meadows when the water went down again.

FLOUNDER: *Pleuronectes flesus,* family *Pleuronectidae.* This flatfish is of the same general group as the plaice and the dab but has a number of marked characteristics. Though

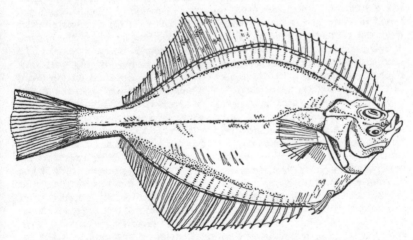

FLOUNDER. *Although it has a resemblance to the dab, the flounder has a smooth skin while that of the dab feels very rough.*

similar in outline to the dab, its skin is smooth while that of the dab feels very rough. In addition the flounder has small tubercles at the roots of the fins and a lateral line that curves markedly round the pectoral fin. The lateral line of the flounder is much straighter than that possessed by the dab. There is no absolute colour identification with most fish, but the flounder is more variable than many of its kind. It can adapt itself to any sea bed over which it swims in a very short time: perhaps it would be safest to describe the general colour of flounder as dirty brown. The belly is invariably white.

The flounder when first emerging from the egg starts off on an even keel like any normal torpedo-shaped fish. Then, gradually, it loses its swimming powers and, over a period of weeks, undergoes a transformation. It begins to tilt over on one side. Then an eye creeps round from the underside to join its fellow. The flounder retires to the bottom and becomes a fully-fledged flatfish. Unlike the other flatfish, the flounder has a liking for freshwater and is found in many rivers far upstream from the estuary. Anyone catching a two-pound flounder may congratulate himself. Though fish of five pounds undoubtedly exist, a flounder of half this weight is a specimen.

The flounder has a catholic taste when it comes to baits: worms, lug, lob, and rag; crabs, and live shrimps, limpets and herring strips will all catch fish. Flounder can be caught paternostering either from the shore or from a boat. Also by light float-fishing with the bait just tripping the bottom to stir up an enticing sand trail. But the most attractive and probably most successful method is with the baited spoon. A six-foot trace is used with a weight of about ¾ oz. at the top of it. The spoon, protected by adequate swivels, should be between 2½ and 3 inches long and either white or silver in colour. It must be of the pattern that flutters freely from the swivel at its head. A long-shanked hook, that must stand well clear of the spoon in order not to foul its action, carries the bait. It can be covered with any of the baits mentioned. The whole rig is fished from an 8-foot spinning rod with either a free-running drum or multiplying reel. The belief is that the flounder lying on the bottom sees the spoon fluttering by and, driven by curiosity, takes off after it. When he closes with it he notices the tasty morsel attached and takes a bite. Obviously, recovery must be slow enough to keep the spoon near the sea bed, preferably kicking up spurts of sand from time to time, but still moving fast enough to maintain its action. Whatever happens, the bait itself must not flutter or revolve, only the spoon.

The baited spoon can also be fished from a boat. Then the technique becomes a kind of trailing.

FLY-BOARD: a keeper's device for increasing fly-life of the ephemerid family. A board is moored by a wire to a bridge or to a post. The fly eggs are deposited on the board where they are safe from the attacks of caddis larvae. These cannot crawl along the wire mooring to eat them.

FLY-BOX: small compartmented box for holding a selection of ready-to-use flies. The best patterns are those which prevent flies being blown from the box directly it is opened. Individual compartments with separate lids are expensive but give this security. Boxes with loose-fibred fabric linings into which the points of hooks can be stuck are also satisfactory. For wet-flies, boxes with magnetic clips are extremely efficient. A good fly-box should also have a pouch in which gut casts can be stored and kept moist.

FLY-CASTING: non-fly anglers tend to be over-impressed and over-awed by the apparent miracle the fly fisherman performs each time he throws a feather-light fly to the fish. In fact, fly-casting is no miracle at all. It does not even take very long to learn to cast sufficiently well to enjoy oneself and catch fish (though it must be added that to become a first-class dry-fly caster may take a lifetime). All the novice has to grasp is that the angler throws the heavy line and not the tiny fly. The fly just goes along because the line is pulling it through the air. The art, of course, comes in putting just the right power and direction into the throw to make the fly, at the end of its gut or nylon cast, land as a natural fly would do. To do this consistently when casting under trees, among tall grass, left-handed, fore-handed, back-handed, with cliffs at one's back and bushes at one's front may well take a fishing lifetime. It is the straight-forward, and basic overhead cast that can be easily learnt.

In essence the overhead cast is the same action as that made in cracking a carriage whip, but with one vital difference. No crack must take place or the fly will be snapped off the cast. To avoid this happening a longish pause is made as the whip, or rather line, stretches out behind the angler in the back cast.

But to start at the beginning. The line is stretched out in front of the fisherman (imagine it lies on water, but for the sake of instruction it had better be on smooth grass). (1) To get the line moving, the angler draws in a foot or so with his left hand. (2) Immediately this movement

starts he picks the line up off the water with a firm but determined backward and upward movement of the rod top. (3) This quickens into a flick as the rod nears the vertical: at this point the line will start to stretch behind the angler. (4) The rod is checked at the vertical and the pause previously mentioned takes place: during this pause the line flies out behind the fisherman until it is fully extended in the air. The angler must judge the moment at which to begin the forward throw exactly. If he is too quick he may crack the fly off: if too slow, the line may drop behind him to the ground, or at least the fly may become caught up in grass or bushes to the rear. This backward throw, incidentally, should have been made in a shallow curve away from the right shoulder. The line is soon going to start its forward journey. In doing so it must follow a different path from that taken in the back cast if collisions and knots are to be avoided. (Remember the line is probably 10–20 yards long.) (5) The forward throw starts with a vigorous drive of the rod tip. If we regard the butt of the rod as though it was pivoted, the rod moves through an angle of 90 degrees. All the power for back and forward casts comes from the movement of the rod tip between the 75- and 90-degree positions. When the rod is at an angle of about 75 degrees in the forward cast the power fades away and becomes a follow-through. The line is now straightening out over the water, and if allowed to spend its force should fall, more or less extended, where it began.

There are, naturally, several refinements. You cannot, for example, start with your line extended unless you have somehow cast it that far in the first place. The method of

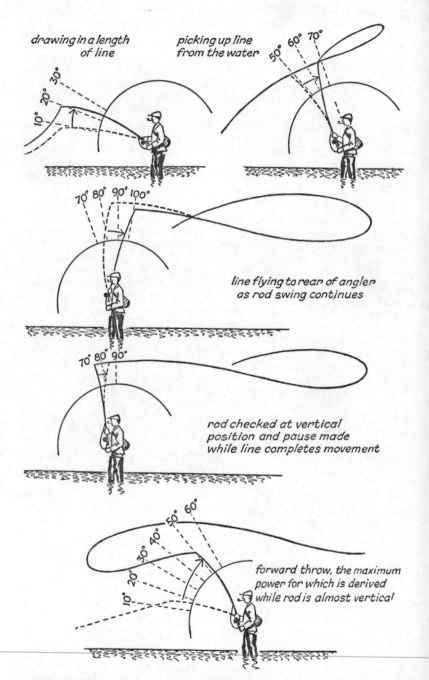

drawing in a length
of line

picking up line
from the water

50° 60° 70°

10° 20° 30°

70° 80° 90° 100°

line flying to rear of angler
as rod swing continues

70° 80° 90°

rod checked at vertical
position and pause made
while line completes movement

50° 60°
30° 40°
20°
10°

forward throw, the maximum
power for which is derived
while rod is almost vertical

FLY-CASTING. *Five stages in making a conventional overhead cast.*

getting out line when fly-casting is called 'false-casting' because the line never drops to the water: it is kept in the air. To false-cast, the fisherman pulls off a yard or two of line and flips it into the air with the rod action already described. He will find that the more line he gets out, the better will his rod work. As ten or fifteen yards of line become airborne he will feel the rod come to life, right down through the cork butt. It is seldom possible to cast a good line of less than ten yards in length. To return to false-casting: each time the back cast is made the angler pulls more line off the reel and 'shoots' it. That is to say, he feeds it up through the rod rings and into the air. Thus, six or more feet are added to the line at every false-cast. He continues doing this until he has enough line out to cover his fish—naturally he makes the false-casts well to the side of any intended quarry.

However, in most cases it would be fatal to cast a dead straight line to the fish. The pull of the differently paced currents between angler and fly would certainly tug the fly sideways in the attitude known as 'drag' and which the fish is quick to detect as a fraud: a dragging fly leaves a small, tell-tale V-shaped ripple. A snaky line can be thrown by means of several modifications to the basic cast, the two most important of which are: shooting an extra yard or two of the line as the cast expends its force in the air; taking the rod top back and forward again as the follow-through begins.

The overhead cast is not, of course, suitable to every situation in which the angler finds himself. Broadly speaking, to make this cast, the angler flicks as much line behind him as he throws in front. Any large obstacle such as a cliff or belt of trees behind the caster is liable to make the overhead throw impracticable. The following are some of the principal variations:

The steeple cast: in this the line is thrown up rather than back. The knack can be acquired quite easily by anyone who has mastered the ordinary back cast.

The backhand cast: the normal overhead cast is made except for the fact that the angler makes it across his body. Invaluable when casting to a fish under your own bank when you are facing upstream.

The left-hand cast: normal overhead throw but made with the left hand, even better in the situation just mentioned than the backhand.

The side-cast: the overhead cast made in a horizontal plane. By careful checking of the line, or alternatively shooting line, as the cast expends its energy, the angler can produce useful up- or downstream curves in the end of the line.

The roll-cast: the line is extended on the water. With a brief circular movement of the rod top in an almost horizontal plane, the fisherman makes the line roll round in the same direction as the rod top, without going more than a foot or two behind him. Quite easy to master.

The Spey-cast: this is one for experts, and was developed for fishing the River Spey where cliffs and rocks often back the fisherman. It is practically impossible to describe in words. It has something of the roll-cast about it although the angler starts with the line directly downstream of him.

The trout fisherman who wants to learn fancy casts would be well advised to spend an hour or two acquiring the necessary skill at a casting school.

FLY-FISHING: the technique of fishing with an artificial fly for those species interested in such a lure. Primarily, of course, these are trout, sea trout and salmon, although in the latter cases the imitation used bears no resemblance to an insect. There are two main methods: dry fly and wet-fly. The first is used to impersonate the arrival on the surface of the water of (1), a freshly hatched fly after it has emerged from the larva; (2), an aquatic fly returning to the water to lay its eggs; (3), a land-based insect blown onto the water by accident. Dry-fly work is at its most delicate on the south country chalk streams where the water is clear and its pace leisurely. In such circumstances the fly must be presented with great delicacy and must sit the water exactly as would a natural insect. It may even be necessary to match the natural insect that is at that moment prevalent upon the water. Of this technique more will be found under the sections on CASTING, NATURAL FLIES and ARTIFICIAL FLIES.

Wet-fly fishing is practised usually on rougher streams such as the brooks of the West Country and Wales, and the powerful Scottish and Border rivers. Here a fly has little chance to sit the water sedately. It is dashed under. The trout are therefore used to watching for their food underwater where, as a matter of fact, they can spot it farther off and see it more clearly. In wet-fly fishing the fly is tied to sink and represents (1), a natural insect rising to hatch; (2), a drowned natural insect; (3), a small fish. Whereas the dry-fly cast is usually made upstream and across and the line and fly are oiled to float, the wet-fly fisherman casts downstream and across and aims to have his line, cast and fly submerged.

He lets the cast work across stream with the current until the fly or flies—he frequently uses two or even three where the dry-fly man uses one—are directly below him. Then he works them back to him, retrieving the line by hand and gathering it for a fresh cast. The art of the wet-fly man is in knowing where the fish will lie and in working the sunken flies past them. It is also in knowing how and when to strike. A trout taking the fly under water gives little intimation beyond a 'bulge' at the surface or the flash of a turning flank beneath the surface.

A third fly-fishing method is that known as nymph fishing in which an imitation of the larval stage of the fly is thrown upstream to an individual fish seen feeding below the surface. This system was worked out for chalk streams by G. E. M. Skues. It requires great delicacy in casting and precision in the timing of the strike.

Coarse fish will also take a fly. Rudd, dace, chub and bleak are the leading examples, but roach, bream, perch (wet-fly) and pike (large wet-fly) have all fallen on occasions. Some big roach can be taken on the may-fly.

Recommended reading: *Trout Fishing* by H. D. Turing; *Trout in Troubled Waters* by F. E. Tudor; *Still-Water Fly-Fishing* by T. C. Ivens.

FLY-LINE: this is an item of equipment which it does not pay to skimp. There are two main sorts of line—level and tapered. Level, in which the line is the same diameter throughout its length, is perfectly suitable for sunken fly work where the actual casting of the fly does not need to be so accurate or subtle. For dry-fly work, tapered lines are essential. Double taper is expensive but means that your line lasts twice as long, for the taper occurs at both ends. When one end begins to wear, the line can be reversed on the drum and begun again as new. Four to six years is a fair expectation of life for such a line, well looked after. For casting short and accurate lines, special forward-taper fly lines are made. These have the effect of causing the rod to work efficiently when a minimum of line has been got out and into the air. As a general guide, thirty yards is the length of line for brown or rainbow trout, with an extra ten yards for sea trout. In either event the line should have backing in the form of old line wound on the drum beneath it. Until fairly recently all fly lines were silk dressed with oil. They became tacky when not in use and had to be hung up, powdered, during the off season. Today Terylene and other man-made fibres have moved in and provide excellent substitutes. Most of the lines used for dry-fly work need to be treated, as do flies, with grease or silicones, but the Americans have now produced lines, such as the Gladding Aerofloat, whose dressing is made microscopically, in such a manner that tiny air bubbles in it are sufficient to keep the line floating all day.

FLY-REEL: a fly-reel is a simple affair with few basic requirements. The most important of these is that it should balance the rod. Secondly, since when fly-fishing the check is permanently on, it must have a 'musical' ratchet. Thirdly, it must be able to accommodate sufficient line. Fourthly, it must be of the caged variety to prevent line slipping off when casting. See REELS.

FLY-RODS: a fly-rod has action throughout its length since its function is to drive a heavy line through the air. Its length may be anything from a minimum of seven feet for brook fishing to eleven feet for sea-trout work. For salmon, it will, of course, be longer still, perhaps thirteen feet. Longer rods than this are not these days in vogue. Fly-rods are made from three materials: split-cane, greenheart, and fibre-glass. All these materials are discussed under RODS. Good split-cane always has, and always will, make the best fly-rods. Few craftsmen can make it today and a good fly-rod in cane costs £7—£20. Greenheart gives excellent action but is these days unseasoned and likely to develop an early 'set'. Even at its best, greenheart had a nasty habit of breaking unpredictably at any period of its life. Fibre-glass is cheap, efficient, and easy to produce and will undoubtedly be the thing of the future.

Wet- and dry-fly rods differ considerably in action. The dry-fly man's rod is stiff and throws a more definite line. To the dry-fly fisher, the wet-fly man's rod feels floppy. This is because it has to have more 'give' to pick up yards of sunken line.

FLY-TYING: the art of decorating a hook with feathers, tinsel, and fur to imitate a natural insect. The subject is so large that only a brief picture of the whole can be given here. Further study should be made of the books mentioned at the end of this entry.

An artificial fly consists mainly of these parts: the whisks or tail fibres: the body; the hackle; and the wing, where used.

Whisks are usually represented by single fibres of a bird's primary wing feathers or by hackle fibres. The body can be of silk, horsehair, silk to which fur has been attached ('dubbing'), raffia, or quill. The body in turn may be 'ribbed' with tinsel or wire to give a striped effect. The hackle is invariably a hackle feather tied to the hook shank at the butt and then wound circumferentially round the shank. The wings of a fly are usually made from small segments of a bird's primaries. These, of course, are but a sample of the possible materials.

Fly-tying is fiddling work and so precise and neat tools are necessary. The principal tools are: hackle pliers in which the point of the hackle is gripped for winding; a bobbin-holder to retain the silk during winding; a dubbing needle for picking out and fluffing up bodies; a whip-finish tool for tying the whipping knot that completes the fly; a pair of sharp hackle scissors; a vice to hold the hook on to which the fly is being tied. Accessories include: beeswax with which the silk is rubbed in order to give it holding power; spirit varnish and cellulose varnish for fixing whippings and finishing the heads of completed flies.

The permutations and combinations that can be achieved with these tools and materials is endless. However, anyone keen on tying flies shouldn't be put off or confused by this fact. The books mentioned below besides telling the student how to tie flies, are also the equivalent of recipe books. In them are hundreds of recognized patterns which the fly-tyer can look up and attempt, just as a cook can look up the formula for a new dish.

Let's take one simple dry-fly, a hackled pattern without wings for simplicity's sake, and describe its tying stage by stage. We are going to tie a well-known West Country fly—a Half-Stone dry-fly of hackle pattern.

A hook is selected. For the West Country this will be fairly large, a fact that makes tying easier, anyway.

It is placed in the vice and is held somewhere in the region of the barb or just above.

Yellow tying silk is taken, the first foot or so of the spool being run several times over a knob of beeswax until the thread feels tacky. The spool is put in the bobbin-holder and threaded through ready for use.

The loose end of the silk is laid against the shank and the silk wound quickly and evenly over it. The silk is taken nearly to the eye of the hook and is then wound back quickly in the reverse direction. We are now ready to tie in the whisks—three fibres from a blue dun hackle.

These delicate fibres are laid on top of the hook shank so that they extend well out over the bend. They are held there between thumb and forefinger while the tying silk is wound back over their roots and until they are thoroughly held. They are then separated with the dubbing needle, and a turn or two is taken with the silk under the point at which they stand clear of the shank, to make them stand up. Note that tying silk can be left hanging in the bobbin-holder at any point of the operation without fear of it unravelling.

Next the silk is wound forward again down half the length of the shank and is once more allowed to hang. Here a new ingredient enters —mole's fur. A pinch or two of this fur is taken from a moleskin, rubbed between the fingers until it takes on a kind of cigar shape, then this is 'dubbed' on to the waxed tying silk left hanging below the hook. Plenty of wax should be applied first in order that the fur sticks. When the fur is firmly in position on the silk, continue to wind the silk round the body so that the mole's fur dubbing occupies the front half of the shank: leave the last section of shank, just before the hook eye, bare. If the fur looks loose or fluffy, a turn or two back through it with the tying silk will take care of the situation.

Select a suitable blue dun cock's hackle (cock's hackles for dry-flies), strip the 'flume', i.e. loose fibres, off the butt and tie this in somewhere towards the start of the dubbed body. Make sure it is secure and that the blade of the feather ends up at right-angles to the shank. Take the point of the hackle in the hackle pliers and wind it round the shank in a forward direction so that the hackle points stand out from the shank.

The job is practically done. When all the hackle is wound leave the pliers hanging down to secure it temporarily, then wind the silk forward through the hackle points taking care to work in between them so that none are tied in. When the head of the hackle is reached, tie it in with the silk, and finish off the fly with a whip-finish at the head —for ease using the whip-finish tool. A blob of clear cellulose varnish will fix the whipping.

Further reading will be found in: *Fly-dresser's Guide* by John Veniard, and *Modern Trout Fly Dressing* by Roger Woolley.

FOG-DUST: fine cloud ground-bait used extensively by Sheffield anglers.

FORMALIN: preservative useful for pickling spinning baits. One part of formalin to forty of water is a fair working percentage. Leave baits immersed for two or three days. Wash thoroughly and bottle in sugar syrup.

FOUL-HOOK: to hook a fish anywhere other than in the mouth, lips, throat or outer jaw surfaces. A foul-hooked fish will fight like a demon because the angler is unable to put any restraint on it. Foul-hook even a six-pound pike near the tail and you've got a scrap on your hands.

FOUR-SIX TACKLE: official description of medium sea tackle drawn up to international standards by the Catalina Club of California and others. The rod in this case must not be less than six feet in length, the butt not more than 18 inches. Maximum weight of line to be used 6 thread (18-lb. b.s.) and the test curve of the rod to be 2½ lb.

FREE-FISHING: there are very few free fisheries in Britain. Fishing almost always belongs to the riparian owner, that is to say the person to whom the land belongs through which the river flows. From either bank a riparian owner is held to own the river to its middle line. To fish a river, or lake for that matter, the angler usually has to pay a fee to the riparian owner. He frequently has to pay a small licence fee to the River Board as well. The only notable exception is the Thames below the Town Stone at Staines. This fishery was presented free and for all time to the citizens of London by Richard I.

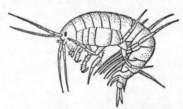

FRESHWATER SHRIMP. *A small crustacean that is almost transparent.*

FRESHWATER SHRIMP: *Gammarus pulex,* a small crustacean, transparent in appearance, found in running water and forming a valuable item of fish food. Trout that get rich shrimp feeding tend to have pink flesh.

G

GAFF: means of landing large fish which the angler, usually, does not intend to return to the water. The business end of the gaff is a large steel hook without barb. This screws, or is fitted, into a wooden handle. The usual method of gaffing a big fish like a salmon is to play it out, bring it alongside, slip the gaff over its back at the point of balance, without fouling the cast, pull the hook home into the fish's flank and, with one smooth continuous movement, lift it on to the bank well clear of the water. Coarse fishermen do not often use gaffs because it is their intention to return their catch

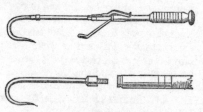

GAFF. *A short-handled telescopic pattern, above, and a detachable screw-on type which may be fitted into the socket of a landing-net handle.*

unharmed. It is quite possible to gaff a pike, however, without doing it serious damage. Simply bring the fish in head first, slip the gaff point up through the soft membrane of the lower jaw just behind the bow of the jaw. This gives an unbreakable hold. If desired the fish can be returned afterwards.

GAG: spring metal device for wedging in the jaws of a newly caught and still lively pike so that the hooks can be removed without damage to the angler's fingers.

GAME-FISHING: fishing for members of the salmon family, but principally the salmon, sea trout, brown trout and rainbow trout.

GAPER: the name given to the largest of the clam family. When cut up this makes quite useful sea fishing bait.

GARFISH: *Belone belone*, family *Scomberesocidae*. A silvery green, eel-like fish with a jaw and face like a beaked pike. If one could imagine a cross between a snipe and a pike one would have a fair idea of a garfish's head. The fish come inshore in small numbers in late spring but are caught mainly towards the end of the summer. Garfish are usually caught while anglers are fishing for something else. A pity they are not more numerous for they give a brilliant fight, skittering across the surface and frequently becoming airborne. A two-pounder is a very good fish and will give an excellent account of itself. Float tackle is the most effective for garfish. The bait, which can be strips of mackerel skin, herring, or sand-eels, is placed only a foot or two beneath the float. Occasionally, particularly close to rocks, the fish may be contacted at a depth of six feet or more, but they are usually found in the surface layer. Garfish make good eating.

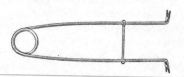

GAG. *A device for keeping open the jaws of a pike when extracting a hook.*

84

GENTLES: maggots, usually of the bluebottle fly. These can be bred easily enough—in remote areas —by hanging up a dead fish or animal carcase above a pan of sawdust. The carcase becomes fly-blown, the eggs hatch, the maggots develop and drop when ripe into the sawdust pan. Commercially, maggots are bred for bait on a large scale, the best being liver-fed maggots. They are excellent bait for enormously thick stomach wall that somewhat resembles a gizzard. It is thought that this is required to assist it in the digestion of the many molluscs it eats.

GILLIE: the hired man, usually a boatman, who acts as guide and sometimes comforter on many game fish waters in Scotland and Ireland, and occasionally in England and Wales. Gillies, like caddies, can be tremendously helpful. They can, on

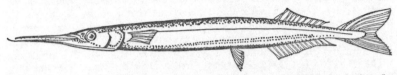

GARFISH. *They shoal near the surface around the coasts of Britain during the spring. They are caught mainly towards the end of summer.*

almost every freshwater fish with the exception of pike, eels, and carp, although all these have at times been known to take them. The poorer quality of maggots—used by match-anglers as groundbait—are generally called 'squats'. Some match men even dye their maggots for added attractiveness and dyes can be bought for this purpose. Warm maggots are the liveliest ones, though if kept too warm they quickly turn into *pupae*. These red-brown chrysalises will sometimes catch fish, especially in the early stages of turning. The development of maggots can be retarded in hot weather by keeping them in a refrigerator— if permitted. They should always be hooked by the loose skin at the blunt end. Squeeze them to puff this up as the point of the hook is applied.

GILLAROO: a large Irish lake trout found in Mask and elsewhere. Very red externally, the fish haunts rocks and dives deeply when hooked. The main difference between it and other trout is that it has an the other hand, prove a nuisance, especially when surly, critical or pursuing their own ends rather than their employer's. The fee is usually fixed. The tip is not, however. Therein lies the remedy.

GILLS: organs of respiration in fish. The gill filaments, which are soft tissue richly equipped with blood-vessels, extract dissolved oxygen from the water and pass it to the blood-stream of the fish, as is described more fully under ANATOMY.

GIMP: old-fashioned wire and flax combination once used for traces for predatory fish, notably pike. Gimp has now been superseded by single-strand rustless wire such as Alasticum. It used to rot and was horribly visible in the water.

GLYCERINE: useful for the wet-fly and nymph fisherman who is having difficulty in making his flies sink. If they are dipped in glycerine they easily penetrate the surface film. Photographic wetting agent also does the trick. For wet-fly fishing keep the casts in a glycerine-soaked damper. Glycerine damages gut.

GOBIES: family *Gobiidae*. There are several varieties of these small fish, the most interesting to rock pool hunters being the Painted and Rock Gobies. The Painted Goby (*Gobius pictus*) seldom grows to more than four inches and is found on a sandy bottom, sometimes trapped in tidal pools. The body is pale grey. There are two dorsal fins bearing bright longitudinal bands of bluish green and red: chiefly of interest to small boys. The Rock Goby (*Gobius paganellus*), found in rock pools, has a buff band at the top of the first dorsal and many soft spines on the pectoral fins.

GORGE-TACKLE: old-fashioned, and now largely illegal, method of taking pike in which the fish was permitted to swallow the bait completely so that the hooks caught in the top of the stomach. Unsporting and unnecessary. Snap-tackle more or less ensures proper hooking these days. Gorge-hooked pike can seldom be returned to the water, nor can they give fight.

GRAINING: a Lancashire and Cheshire name for dace, not a separate species of fish.

GRAYLING: *Thymallus thymallus*, family *Salmonidae*. In appearance a beautiful silver grey fish with blue, purple and greenish overtones. It is absolutely unmistakable and cannot be confused with any other member of the salmon tribe, having a large dorsal fin shaped something like an artist's palette. It has, of course, the characteristic adipose fin of all the *Salmonidae*. The extraordinary thing about the fish, though, is its refusal to spawn at the same time as the rest of its family. Whereas salmon and trout are winter spawners, the grayling chooses the same season as our coarse fish, and consequently enjoys the same fence period. This gives the fly-angler the advantage of being able to fish all the year round, for grayling will take a sunken fly even when snow is on the banks. The name grayling derives from its appearance, while its scientific tag refers to the fact that it is said, when freshly caught, to smell faintly of thyme. Few fishermen have detected this scent, though.

Grayling like fast clear streams such as the Lambourn, the Wharfe, the Hampshire Avon, Nadder, Teme and the rivers of the Welsh border country. They feed almost entirely on aquatic and surface-borne insects, and show few of the predatory instincts of the trout. Despite this, where trout and grayling occur in the same stream, the trout are likely to suffer in the fight for survival and food supply.

The grayling lies deep in the water and rises with tremendous speed to attack surface prey directly over his head. For flies spotted at longer range he has a technique of drifting up until within grasp and then pouncing. When he comes up fast through the water he frequently misses his target: hence splashy and untidy rises, and the belief in the angler that he has struck the fly out of the grayling's mouth. Usually the fish will make a second, and often third attempt. Grayling are excellent eating. The record is 7 lb. 2 oz. from the River Melgum in 1949. A two-pounder is a good fish.

GRAYLING-FISHING: grayling can be taken either on bait or fly. Let's look at bait-fishing first. Trotting tackle is needed. An Avon rod with centre-pin reel is ideal with light monofilament line terminating in a one-yard 4X hook link or cast. The float needs to be small but visible and the shotting light, though with one shot at least fairly close to the hook to take the bait down when

GRAYLING. *A silver-grey fish with purple-green overtones, is related to the salmon yet it spawns during the coarse fish period.*

slower deeps are reached. Worm or maggots are the bait. The bite shown at the float is much the same as the shy type of roach bite. The float may hesitate, move sideways, or even upwards. All these signs should be answered by a strike. The fish can also be caught in the deeper pools by sink-and-draw methods. The traditional bait for this is a mixture of green and yellow wool tied like a grub round a weighted hook shank. For some reason this bait is called a 'grasshopper', to which insect it bears little resemblance.

Fly fishermen can take grayling in all weathers. Dry-fly experts agree that the floating fly fished down and across brings the best results. Grayling have keen eyesight and are quick to detect 'drag'. When fishing downstream to them it is essential to keep enough loose line on the water to prevent the fly dragging as it passes over the fish. Because the fish are lying deep they are not so likely to see the angler clearly, provided he keeps well down. The strike needs careful timing, for, having seized the fly, grayling dive steeply. To let them turn down with the fly before pulling the hook home seems to be a good rule. In shallow water, conventional upstream and across dry-fly work will pay better than the down-river technique.

Wet-fly fishing for grayling requires no special approach. Some flies recommended are: partridge and orange, snipe and purple, zulu, treacle parkin, waterhen bloa, red tag, green insect, fog black, orange bumble, black spider. Hooks should not be too small and should be wide in the gape to assist holding.

GREASED-LINE FISHING: a technique of salmon fishing in low water invented by Arthur Wood. A sparsely dressed fly is used and the line is greased up to the cast. This causes the fly to work only just submerged. The line is 'mended' several times during a single cast: that is to say, as the current bellies it out downstream the angler lifts it bodily with the rod until the curve lies in the upstream direction. With a normal sunken line this is not possible. When a fish takes, the line is allowed to belly downstream and the salmon frequently hooks itself.

GREATER SPOTTED DOG-FISH: see NURSEHOUND.

GREAVES: the fatty refuse of candle manufacture. Once highly valued as bait and groundbait.

GREEN DRAKE: the perfectly formed female may-fly spinner: an angler's term.

GREENHEART: a wood once much used in rod-making. Gives good action, particularly for fly-rods.

GREY DRAKE: the term used to describe the imago or spinner of the male may-fly.

GRILSE: the name given to a salmon on the occasion of its first return from the sea to the river for spawning within a year of its departure from the river.

GROUNDBAITING: the practice of putting feed into the water to attract fish to the angler's hook-bait. It follows, then, that the ground-bait should at least contain elements that are similar to the hook-bait, and that these elements should be of less attractive quality both in size and succulence. For example: when fishing with maggots it is perfectly sound to 'feed' or bait the swim with other loose maggots. But those selected as free feed should be inferior in size and quality. Thus, the match fisherman using a liver-fed 'special' maggot on the hook will throw 'squats' or 'feeders'—poor stuff by comparison—into the swim. There are many methods of ground-baiting and many recipes, but certain rules remain constant. The first relates to the power and pace of the river being fished. The stronger the current flows, the further upstream will the groundbait have to be put in, at least if the angler wishes to fish the bottom immediately around him. Likewise, the faster the river, the thicker and more pudding-like must be the groundbait to hold the bottom. It may even be necessary to press stones into the centre of lumps of pulped bread mixture. This applies equally should the angler want his groundbait to remain at the bottom of a particular swim or if he wants it to break up gradually and float downstream in small particles to carry the news to fish below him. Whichever role is chosen for the groundbait—to stay put on the bottom or to break up slowly—its conduct will be decided by the consistency of the mixture. When groundbaiting still water the most urgent need is to attract the fish without making the swim dis-coloured, stale and unappetizing. For many species in still water, 'a little and often' is the golden rule. Here are some notes on methods of groundbaiting—the term is inter-preted rather widely—for different species.

Barbel: pudding is needed to hold the bottom; it may have to be artificially weighted, especially in weir pools. The classic groundbait is one thousand lobworms. Lob-worms and gentles can all be pressed into a basic pulped bread mixture.

Bream: similar, but since bream are usually found in slow water the mixture can be lighter. If paste is used on the hook, no individual lumps of groundbait should be of similar size and quality.

Carp: buckets of groundbait are often needed for carp, baiting being done at the rate of one bucket a night for a week before fishing. This, at any rate, is true at the start of a season before the fish become educated. Worms in the bait tend to be a nuisance, as do gentles: they attract too many small fry.

Chub: similar treatment to bream. Groundbait should have a tendency to break up, sending particles down-stream.

Dace: small quantities of the hook-bait thrown in loose.

Eels: fish guts, worms, smashed up lumps of dead fish.

Grayling: as for dace.

Gudgeon: stir the bottom mud with a stick. Failing that, 'cloud' bait allowed to sink to the bottom will prove effective.

Perch: these fish move about in shoals looking for prey and no true groundbaiting is profitable. Remember that they will come where small fry abound. Attract the small stuff and you will get the perch. You may therefore groundbait at one remove —by raking the bottom for gudgeon, for instance, or by feeding in 'cloud'.

Roach: light groundbaiting and often, according to the pace of the stream. Hook-bait thrown in loose or pulped bread-and-bran mixture with hook-bait additives.

Rudd: when found on the bottom, groundbait as for roach. Rudd are surface-feeders mainly. A half loaf moored just sub-surface works very well. Loose hook-bait can be thrown in.

Tench: fairly extensive groundbaiting with bread-and-bran mixture with hook-bait additives is essential for success. Raking the swim sometimes helps, since bottom organisms such as bloodworms are usually stirred up.

Note that though no groundbaiting is usually done for pike, there is a growing school of thought, however, that believes dead herring is effective for large pike. If this is so, then chopped herring can probably be used as an attractor, the rich oils dispersing and reaching the fish at a distance.

Pulped bread-and-bran mixture and also cloud have been referred to frequently in this section. They are the two basic recipes for making up groundbait. For the first, get two to four stale loaves, soak them in the kitchen sink, then squeeze as much water as you can out of them, particularly out of the crusts which will otherwise refuse to sink. Now add chicken meal or bran until you can make up dough balls of the desired consistency. If you wish, gentles or chopped worms, hempseed, or anything else you please,

can be added at this stage. For heaven's sake, clean the sink afterwards. Cloud can be bought at many tackle shops. It can also be made up from old loaves baked dry in the oven and ground up in the mincer. Silver sand can be added to make the mixture sink. The preparation should be moistened at the water and pressed into balls. Its function is to attract rather than to feed.

Some match-anglers, it should be noted, use catapults for groundbaiting at long range.

GROUND-FISHING: a sea-angler's term to describe fishing where the bait is actually on the sea bed, as when paternostering or when using a leger.

GUDGEON: *Gobio gobio,* family *Cyprinidae.* A record for gudgeon is claimed from time to time but, in the view of most serious anglers, shouldn't be considered among British records, since the fish is usually caught by accident. A good

GUDGEON. *Considering its small size the gudgeon puts up a remarkably good fight when hooked.*

gudgeon is one weighing 3 oz. In appearance the fish is somewhat like a small barbel, being brownish with the same flat top to its head. It has only two barbules at its jaws, one at each side, and its flank is often marked with a line of bluish spots. The tail is a marked fork. Gudgeon usually inhabit slow swims, often close to the bank. They feed voraciously on almost anything going, and generally on the bottom.

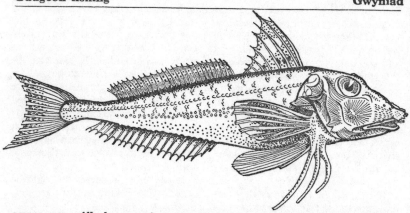

GURNARD. *All three species, grey (shown here), yellow, and red, have the same basic features, blunt head, high-set front dorsal and tapering body.*

From the angler's point of view they have two great virtues: they provide excellent livebait for perch, pike and trout; when popped into very hot fat, fried crisp, sprinkled with red pepper and lemon juice, and eaten with brown bread, they make a delightful meal. They are not very often found in still water.

GUDGEON-FISHING: few anglers fish deliberately for these little fish, unless satisfying either of the two demands last mentioned above. Any rod will do. The best bait is a small piece of redworm, failing that, gentle or a fragment of crust. A very small quill weighted until only the tip is showing is the best float to use. No groundbaiting is necessary, but raking the bottom upstream of the swim will often bring the gudgeon round.

GURNARD: family *Triglidae.* There are three varieties of gurnard likely to be caught off the coasts of Britain by sea anglers. All have basically the same appearance—blunt head and tapering body with high-set front dorsal fin and long, thin rear dorsal and anal fins. The three varieties are grey (the commonest), yellow and red, and they can be easily identified as follows. The grey is slate-coloured with white spots. The yellow gurnard has no spines to its dorsals and very large pectoral fins. The red is reddish-brown and the smallest of the three.

GUT: substance obtained from silkworms to make casts, notably for the fly fisherman. The best gut comes from Southern Spain. It arrives in England as raw material where it is 'drawn' to fine it down to the required thickness. Gut is graded in diameter by the X system. Thus 6X gut (·0052 of an inch) is the finest drawn gut, and X (·0100) as thick as is likely to be used, at least in trout fishing. Gut substitute and nylon have largely replaced gut, but, in the opinion of many dry-fly experts, gut cannot be beaten for its gentle and easy action. True gut must always be soaked before use.

GWYNIAD: *Coregonus clupeoides pennantii,* a member of the salmon family found only in Lake Bala, North Wales. The word gwyniad means 'shining' in Welsh. The fish seldom grows over a foot in length and is bright silver. It has, of course, an adipose fin.

90

H

HACKLES: the long pointed feathers taken, usually, from the neck of a chicken and used in fly-tying to represent feet and thorax of a fly and to make it float.

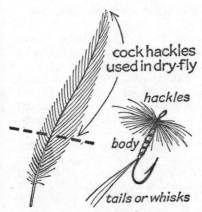

cock hackles used in dry-fly

hackles

body

tails or whisks

HACKLES. *Before using for fly-tying the soft lower fibres (below dotted line) are stripped off.*

The best hackles come from game-cocks. Hen hackles are used principally in wet-flies since the softer, broader fibres do not keep the fly afloat. Hackles are taken from many other birds for different patterns of fly, including the partridge, snipe and woodcock.

HADDOCK: *Gadus aeglefinus,* family *Gadidae.* This member of the cod family is not often rod-caught. A three-pounder is a good fish. Haddock spawn in early spring somewhere out in the deeps. The fish remain well offshore for at least a year and then move in close to feed. The really big haddock seldom comes into shallow water, however, feeding over sandy bottoms on molluscs and crustaceans. The North of England and Scotland provides the best haddock fishing during the winter months. Haddock are not unlike cod but may be told by their forked tail (that of the cod is almost straight-cut), and by the dark patch on the shoulder.

HADDY: a species of char found in Loch Killin, Inverness-shire.

HAKE: *Merluccius merluccius,* family *Merlucciidae.* Seldom caught by sea anglers. Large, powerful and fiercely predatory fish with greyish

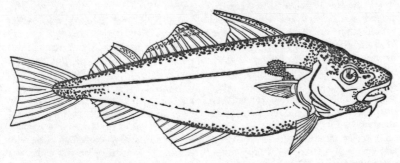

HADDOCK. *From the same family as the cod, from which it may be distinguished by its slightly forked tail and the dark patch on its shoulder.*

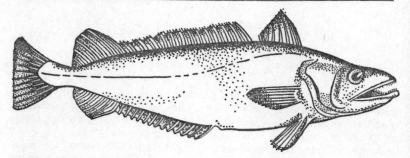

HAKE. *A fierce grey-bodied predatory marine fish which has sharp teeth.*

body, no barbule, and sharp teeth. The fins of the hake have a fringe of black to them. Hake will take quite large fish, such as pilchard, down whole, and large fish bait is the best lure for this species. The record from Penzance is 17 lb. 8 oz., but a good hake may be reckoned at 8 lb.

HALF-COCK: a float is said to be at half-cock when it is leaning over at about 30 degrees from the vertical. This occurs when part of the weight it is supporting is on the bottom. In other words when the angler is 'laying-on' the bottom. An ideal method of catching all bottom-feeding species in still or slow-moving water.

HALF-MOON LEADS: small lead sinkers or anti-kink weights that consist of two semicircular halves folded together. They can be prised apart with the fingers and pinch easily on to the line or cast.

HALIBUT: a very large member of the flatfish family having a dark olive top surface and pearly white underside. The scales are very smooth. The fish spawn from May until July and should be sought at all seasons in deep water. They are only to be caught by rod and line anglers well offshore. Whole live-baits are favoured. Young whiting, codling, wrasse and pollack will all

serve. The technique is to drift over likely grounds. Tackle needs to be strong. Record, 152 lb. 12 oz.

HAND-LINING: a useful dodge when a fish has gone to weed. By laying down the rod and pulling the line gently, or even by irritating the fish with a series of sharp tugs, the creature can sometimes be persuaded to start moving into open water. Another method is to remove all pressure from the fish. On a slack line the fish sometimes imagines it is free and moves off on its own.

HARLING: method of trailing at sea when the trail, or troll, is made back and forth across a current with a long line behind the boat. The boat drops down the tide the while. Sea trout are taken like this in estuaries and the method can be used in big rivers for salmon and sea trout.

HARNESS, Big-game: when fishing for large, strong quarry such as tunny or shark the angler needs to be able to put terrific leverage on his fish if he is to beat it. To do this he must have the rod anchored to him so that he can use both arms, and feet, to put a bend into the rod. The harness is usually in the form of a waistcoat. The reel is attached to straps on the waistcoat and the rod butt sits either in a leather socket attached to the fisherman or in a socket on his 'fighting chair'. By leaning back he is able to use his whole body via the straps connected to the reel. Most harnesses have a quick release device, for should a jam occur, a big fish could conceivably take an angler overboard. See BIG-GAME TACKLE.

HATCH-HOLE: seen usually on a chalk-stream where small feeder streams drain the water meadows. The hatch-hole is a minor sluice cutting off the drain from the main river. Good trout are sometimes found taking station by these possible sources of food supply.

HEMPSEED: this bait has collected more 'old wives' tales' about it than anything else in fishing. It is said that hemp is poisonous, drugs the fish, intoxicates them, makes them lethargic, upsets their digestive systems. All this nonsense probably derives from the fact that hemp is (a), difficult to fish successfully and the angler who masters it is thought by less skilful club members to have given himself an unfair advantage; (b), it is confused with Indian hemp, known in some forms to be a powerful drug. In fact, hemp fishing was intro-

duced here from the Continent by Belgian refugees during the First World War. Even now it is not known what the fish take hempseed for. Probably the most plausible theory is that they imagine it to be some small freshwater mollusc. Again, in elderberry season they may mistake it for ripe fruit fallen from riverside trees. Hemp needs to be used sparingly. It can be bought either bottled and prepared or you can buy the seed in its natural state and make it ready yourself. The seed should be soaked overnight and then simmered gently until the casings begin to split. Small hooks are needed, preferably ones with flattened shanks, and it may even help to paint the shank white in order to make the creamy kernel of the seed look more attractive. About a pint of seed should see you through a day's fishing, and feeding of the swim wants to be done sparingly and fairly often. In still water beware of baiting up heavily as the seed is apt to go sour on the bottom and discourage fish from the swim. Bites when 'hemping' are quick and sharp, and quick striking is essential. Shot should be avoided

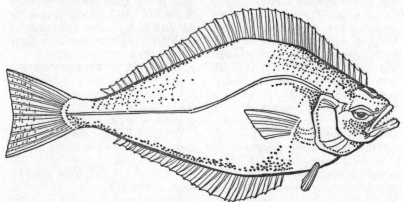

HALIBUT. *The largest of the various kinds of flatfish, usually found only in very deep water. Caught mainly off the northern coasts of Britain.*

as weights on the cast as the fish sometimes grab these in mistake for hemp. Lead wire or a small half-moon lead get round this difficulty.

HERLING: a word used in some parts to describe young sea trout.

HERRING: this fish needs no detailed description. Scientifically it is known as *Clupea harengus*, family *Clupaiedae*. For many years it was thought that herring were not a rod-and-line proposition. Then a few West Country anglers began to catch them. It was found that they could be fished for successfully on light tackle with lug or rag worm, particularly in the neighbourhood of harbour lights at night. The best rig was found to be light float tackle with two or three hooks suspended beneath the float and the whole weighted with split-shot. The two top hooks are best attached to the main trace between a foot and eighteen inches apart. Hooks should be small, somewhere in the region of No. 8. Herring fishing comes very close to normal freshwater float practice. The fish is a shy one, being easily put down by disturbance or by appearance of the angler or his gear, or even, as with many river fish, by the shadow of rod or angler on the water. The bite is a sly and very slow one. A good pause should be given before the strike is made as the herring appears to take the bait and hold it before making off. Some people say that you should count up to ten. Once hooked, the fish gives a lively account of itself. To allow it the utmost sporting chance it should be fished for on something like a light roach rod.

HONEY: sometimes used as an added flavouring for carp baits. Breadpaste is sometimes made up with honey added, or else hookbait is dipped in honey. It probably does no harm.

HOOKS: It is no accident that the majority of the fishing tackle trade is based on Redditch, in Worcestershire. Redditch, once the centre of the needle-making trade, quickly turned to the manufacture of fish hooks, since the same sort and thickness of steel was needed for both products. The system of grading hooks by size that is commonly used by coarse anglers is still called the Redditch Scale, and takes its numbers direct from the gauge numbers used in needle-making. In the Redditch Scale (sometimes called 'Old' scale), the larger the number, the smaller the hook. Thus, the smallest hook even a match fisherman is likely to use is a No. 20, and the largest any coarse fisherman will use will probably be a No. 4 (for a very large lobworm or a livebait). What makes it confusing is that trout fishermen, and some coarse anglers, know their hook sizes by a different system of numbering, and in most ways a more logical one. This is called the 'New Scale' and starts sensibly enough with small numbers for small hooks and works up from there. In fact, it even starts below zero. The 0 hook of the trout man corresponds to the No. 16 of the coarse man on the Redditch Scale. The smallest hook on which you can tie a fly is an ooo—Redditch Scale No. 18.

Apart from this basic confusion in regard to hooks there is a bewildering number of patterns. Perhaps the best thing would be to take them in order of importance.

Crystal: this pattern has a bend that is a combination of the curved and the angular. It both holds bait and hooks fish well. It is the stand-by of most coarse anglers.

Round bend: the name describes it. Its virtue is that the bend has plenty of 'gape' allowing big baits

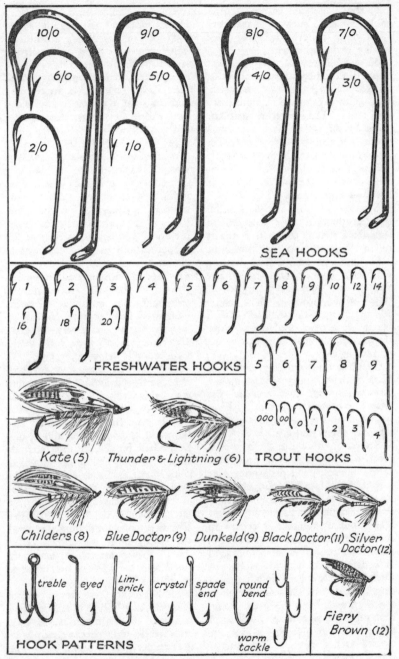

SEA HOOKS

1 2 3 4 5 6 7 8 9 10 12 14
16 18 20

FRESHWATER HOOKS

Kate (5)　Thunder & Lightning (6)

5 6 7 8 9
000 00 0 1 2 3 4

TROUT HOOKS

Childers (8)　Blue Doctor (9)　Dunkeld (9)　Black Doctor (11)　Silver Doctor (12)

treble　eyed　Limerick　crystal　spade end　round bend

worm tackle

HOOK PATTERNS

Fiery Brown (12)

HOOKS. *The lures are small salmon flies; the numbering of larger salmon hooks corresponds to that used for sea hooks.*

to be hooked, such as lobworms. Both these patterns are also used by the trout fisherman.

Model Perfect: an excellent hook, patented by Messrs. Allcocks, and particularly successful when after big-mouthed fish such as chub, carp and tench. The secret is that the point is off-set so that the hook presents a 'thicker' aspect when the strike is made. Even if pulled directly sideways through the fish's half-open mouth, the off-set point is likely to find a hold.

Spade-end and eyed hooks: these are loose hooks as opposed to those sold already attached to gut or nylon 'bottoms' or hook-lengths. You tie them on yourself with a whipping knot. There are many varieties of hook eyes, upturned, down-turned, straight, all of which terms are self-explanatory. Trout hooks are always eyed hooks since they invariably have to be tied to the end of the cast.

'Ayrbro': a proprietary brand of hook with a lightly loaded spring clip attachment that enables the angler to use live insects such as may-flies and grasshoppers without crushing them to death.

Sneck, Limerick: these words refer to special shapes of hook preferred by some game fishermen.

HORSE MACKEREL or scad: *Trachurus trachurus*, family *Carangidae*. In winter this fish is a bottom-feeder but in summer it comes to the surface and moves close inshore, sometimes in vast shoals. The scad is a dark green with overtones of blue. The belly is light with greenish tinge. It has two dorsal fins set close together, and, from the front of the first of these is a sharp horizontal spine that can give an unpleasant wound to the careless. The lateral line shows up clearly and there is a large dark blob on the gill-cover.

Horse mackerel fall readily to all sorts of bait, especially after dark. They can be caught from surface level to 10 feet down on fish cuttings of all sorts, worms, prawns, sand-eels. Light float tackle serves well and the fight given on this gear can be reckoned as lively. Poor eating, but good sport.

HOUGHTON CLUB: the most exclusive trout fishing club in the world. Membership is strictly limited. The club has about four miles of water above and below the town of Stockbridge on the Test. Entry to the club is said to be in the region of £1,000 with shares of the keepering and running expenses to go on top of this. £1,200 for the privilege of fishing the best chalk stream in the land would not be too high an estimate of what Houghton fishing costs. Voting on new members is extremely stringent. Headquarters of the club is the Grosvenor Hotel, Stockbridge.

HOUTING: *Coregonus oxyrhynchus*, family *Salmonidae*. Rarely comes into British water. Lives as much in the sea as in brackish water round the North European coast. Has salmonid characteristics and is distinguished by the superior attitude of its top jaw. Colouring, greenish.

HUCHEN: *Salmo hucho*, a large fish of the salmon family. The rivers of Czechoslovakia give splendid huchen fishing up to 40 kilograms. The fish looks something like large sea trout. It is sometimes called the Danubian salmon. It was once stocked in the Thames but failed to establish itself.

HYBRIDS: there is no doubt that certain members of the cyprinid family of British freshwater fish do interbreed—with results that puzzle the angler. Too often when he fancies he has caught a near-record roach it turns out to have a strain of

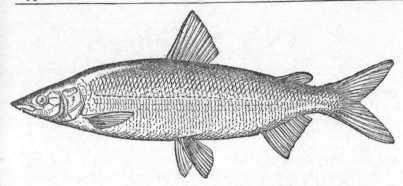

HOUTING. *This member of the salmon family is rarely caught in British waters.*

bream in it. Rudd and bream also produce crosses, and there is a suspicion that chub may join in this confusing exercise.

There are, alas, no absolute guides, though much can be told by experts by the examination of pharyngeal, or throat, teeth and scales. The layman angler should watch carefully in all cases of roach above the two-and-a-half pound mark, and, if a big contest is at stake, should submit the fish, pictures of the fish, or scales from the fish to the Curator of Fishes at the Natural History Museum, London. Usually this kindly department will help.

Where suspicion has been aroused, the ordinary angler should look closely for mixed external characteristics. For instance has your roach a breamy look? Or your bream the red tinge characteristic of a rudd, and is there something rudd-like about its dorsal fin? If in doubt apply to an expert. So little positive data has been collected on hybrids among coarse fish that the nearest natural history museum will probably be delighted to examine your evidence for you.

HYPOLIMNION: the lower layer consisting of the colder water in a lake. See THERMOCLINE.

I J K

INTERNATIONAL GAME-FISHING ASSOCIATION: body based in America standardising tackle, notably for big-game fishing. Also judges record claims.

JIM VINCENT SPOON: named after the famous angler and keeper from Hickling Broad. Among many other sporting talents, Vincent was a pike specialist. His method was sink-and-draw with a dead roach or rudd for bait, and sometimes the spoon. In both cases he believed in big bait for big fish. The Jim Vincent spoon that can today be bought at Hardy's is fully six inches in length. See SPOONS.

JOCK SCOTT: both the name for a salmon and sea trout fly and also (in the connection discussed here), a type of salmon fishing plug made by Hardy's and capable of adjustment as to depth and action through the water. One feature is that on hooking the rear triangle swings free of the plug on its own independent wire, leaving the fish free to fight. Obtainable also in pike, chub and perch sizes.

JOHN DORY: *Zeus faber*, family

JOHN DORY. *This rather comic and doleful looking creature is almost spherical. Rarely caught by anglers but known to inhabit the waters off the coast of west and south-west Britain.*

98

Zeidae. A queer-looking creature seldom caught by sea anglers. The body is deep-set and almost spherical, the tiny tail being attached by a narrow wrist. The front spines of the dorsal and anal fins are sharp and can give nasty wounds. Colouring on leaving the water is almost golden, but this quickly dulls. A big round black spot, gold surrounded, on each flank is said to be the mark made by St. Peter when he found the tribute money in a fish's mouth. The biggest of this species are usually taken off the West Country coast, the record of 8 lb. 8 oz. coming from Penzance. The John Dory has a rather defeated and melancholy appearance.

KEEP-NET: a net, usually made up of circular sections, but sometimes of rectangular section, used by coarse fishermen for preserving their catch in order to return it alive at the end of a day's fishing. Often, and particularly in hot weather, and almost certainly in match fishing, this has the opposite effect. Fish crowded together and deprived of oxygen suffer severe damage. On many rivers, anglers are asked not to keep too many fish in their keep-nets. However, it is very hard to see how match anglers can avoid doing so, since fish are needed for the weigh-in at the end of the contest. Keep-nets vary in length from a couple of feet to ten or twelve feet. There are many cases on record of pike attacking fish confined in a keep-net.

KELP: the long, flat crinkly brown weed that grows below low-water mark and is sometimes torn loose in rough weather and washed up. There are two varieties: the sort which holidaymakers take home to predict wet or dry weather, and a trident-shaped kind that grows on a long sinewy stem from the bottom.

KELT: the name given to a salmon which has spawned and is struggling back downstream to salt water. Kelts often look as thin as eels. To take fish in this state is illegal. Sometimes applied to sea trout in similar poor state of health.

KEEP-NET. *An essential item in the match angler's equipment.*

KIDNEY SPOON: a spoon, usually silver or copper, but sometimes a combination of both colours, that rotates freely about one end, the blade being kidney-shaped. Very effective for pike. See SPOONS.

KING CARP: a term used to describe all the partially scaled or scale-less variations of carp such as the so-called mirror carp and leather carp, as opposed to true wild, or fully scaled, carp.

KING RAGWORM: prime sea-fishing bait for billet, bass, wrasse, flat-fish, codling, whiting, pollack, and other species. Some species

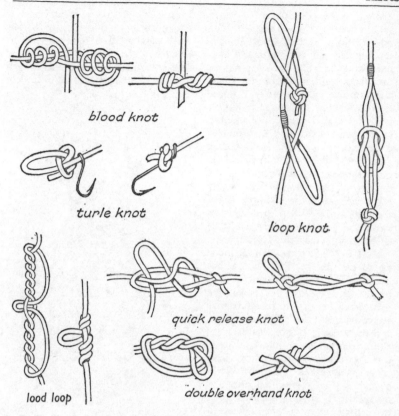

blood knot

turle knot

loop knot

quick release knot

lood loop

double overhand knot

KNOTS. *Showing the loose and tightened forms of those most useful to fishermen.*

grow to a foot or eighteen inches in length. Mostly they are green or greeny bronze and are found on muddy and gravelly shores, often under rocks near the low-water mark. Mostly they are cut up and used in pieces, but deep-water anglers sometimes put whole worm on for haddock, big cod and skate.

KNOTS: knots must be demonstrated by diagram rather than written about. They should be assiduously practised with thickish string. What I consider to be the most generally useful fishing knots, include:

Figure-of-eight for fastening reel line to loop in cast.

The Loop to be made in the end of cast or hook-link.

Blood-knot, the professional cast-maker's knot for joining lengths of silk-worm gut of varying tapers, and absolutely invaluable for joining any two lengths of nylon or gut.

Half blood used for tying reel line to swivel eye, or for tying fly to cast.

Turle-knot, the recognized way of attaching fly to cast.

 L

LAMPREY: family *Petromyzoni-dae*. There are two main species, the sea lamprey, *Petromyzon marinus*, which comes into the rivers to spawn, and *Lampetra fluviatilis*, the river lamprey, sometimes called forms of life that are found there.

LANCEWOOD: a light, springy Jamaican wood sometimes used in the tips of cheap rods, but of little permanent value since it takes a 'set' very easily.

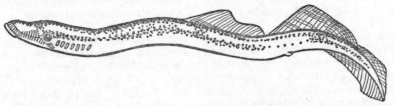

LAMPREY. *A parasitic eel-like creature which attaches itself to and feeds upon other fish.*

lampern. In appearance these are greenish eel-like fish but with a circular sucker-shaped mouth. In the case of the sea lamprey the latter is used to attach the parasite to the flanks of other fish off whom it lives until death of the host follows. There is some doubt as to whether the smaller river lamprey exists in this fashion, at least entirely. The river lamprey certainly grips with its mouth to rocks and parts of the river bed but it probably lives largely off the microscopic

LANDING-NET: a net with extended handle used for lifting from the water fish sufficiently large or lively to break the line or strain the rod top. For coarse fishing, where high banks are likely to be encountered, the main consideration is that the net has a long enough handle. One net of standard size and gape will do for everything except barbel and carp, and especially the latter. Special carp nets are now made. To be capable of enveloping really large carp they

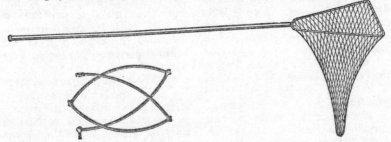

LANDING-NET. *A coarse angler's triangular-shaped net and handle, and a collapsible circular type of net ring.*

should be at least three feet in the gape and have a net-depth of four feet.

The main thing about a trout fisherman's net is that it should be unobtrusive, neat, and easily transportable. Ideally, it should be slung about the body but in a way that allows it to be quickly released with one hand and, if of the folding variety, flicked open. Folding nets should be tested for ease of opening at the start of the day. For rough-stream fishing and wading it is as well to combine net with wading staff. The staff can be fastened to the body with a cord in such a way that it can be released from the hand if necessary without being swept downstream. Bright, flashy, chromium-handled nets should be avoided for obvious reasons. A folding net strongly to be recommended is the 'Gye' made by Farlow's of London. In this model the wooden handle slides into the rigid wooden frame of the net itself when being carried. The whole net is slung round the angler on a lanyard. Nets are seldom used when salmon fishing. A gaff or tailer is a more certain way of landing a large fish which is needed for the pot.

LATERAL LINE: the line along the mid-point of the flank of a fish on which are grouped many of its sensory organs. Usually the line is marked by a series of dark spots or flecks on the scales. There is little doubt that the nerve centres on the lateral line are capable of detecting vibrations in the water, and that fish use these nerve endings both as a warning system and also as a means of detecting the whereabouts of prey. The pike undoubtedly 'homes' on its victims by means of this equipment. Other predatory fish probably do the same.

LAW, as applied to angling: I shall try my best to simplify what is, like all matters legal, a confusing and tortuous subject. In England and Wales the position as regards the angler and the law is broadly this.

(1) Except in extremely rare cases —the Thames below the Town Stone at Staines is the classic example—little fishing is free. The angler is always beholden to some one for his angling. Usually this will be the riparian owner through whose land the river flows. Or again it can be the tenant of that riparian owner, perhaps an angling club. From one or the other he must get permission to fish, and probably pay for the privilege. Moreover he is not entitled to fish another man's water from a place of vantage that is free to the public, like a bridge or a road bordering the stream. To do so is like leaning over a wall and picking another man's apples from his orchard.

(2) Having obtained the riparian owner's permission, the angler is still in the hands of the River Board—once again, the Thames is largely an exception to this rule: the biggest river in England, it is about the only one for which no fishing licence is needed. Elsewhere the angler will have to take out a River Board licence which will vary from a few shillings per season for coarse fish to several pounds for salmon and trout. This is perfectly fair and just, for the River Board, in whose hands is the safekeeping of the anger's sport, has its running costs to meet.

(3) The angler is always subject to the River Board's bye-laws concerning size of fish to be taken, numbers to be taken, methods of fishing, times of fishing, etc. If he breaks these he can be taken to account, and probably to court, by the

River Board's bailiffs who have quite wide powers. These powers are defined in the Salmon and Freshwater Fisheries Act, 1923.

If he catches a man in the act of illegal fishing, the bailiff can confiscate rod, line, reel, float, hook, and landing-net, but not creel, spare tackle, etc. He can take the gear actually used in catching and landing the fish, but nothing else.

In the case of a private fishery, if the private bailiff chooses to confiscate gear then he must do so on his employer's land. If the evil-doer can escape into a neighbouring landowner's field before the bailiff collars him, then he cannot be touched. In the case of a private fishery, seizure of the offender's gear precludes any further proceedings for damages or penalty—although of course the offender can be removed from the place if he is a trespasser. Seizure by a River Board bailiff, however, will be followed by proceedings for forfeiture of the gear, fines, etc. A private bailiff cannot seize any fish caught by the offender, but a River Board bailiff may do so. Take note that this applies only by day. By night the penalties are much more severe. Any person, let alone a bailiff, can arrest and take before a magistrate a malefactor found fishing illegally at night.

Finally, a word about riparian owners and their relationships with anglers. If you are a riparian owner —this can apply equally to the club to which you belong—holding only one bank, then you are entitled by law to fish to the middle line of the river and no further. In other words, long-casting under the opposite bank is trespassing. This, of course, is a technical point rather than one likely to play much practical part. The other point to be borne in mind if a club is dealing with a riparian owner about fishing rights is to get a written agreement, and have a lawyer vet it. Angling rights have been bought before now which have overlooked the fact that there is no right of access to the water concerned. What is more, for your own bailiffs to be properly and legally appointed they must, through the club, have a fiat from the original land-owner.

Those who have a desire to go more deeply into legal affairs are directed to *Pollution,* published by the Anglers' Co-operative Association; the Salmon and Freshwater Fisheries Act, 1923; the River Boards Act, 1948; Rivers, Prevention of Pollution Act, 1951—copies of all these Acts may be obtained from H.M. Stationery Office; also *Oke's Fishery Laws* (Butterworth & Co.); *The History and Law of Fisheries* (Stevens and Haines); *The Law of Waters* (Sweet and Maxwell).

LAYING-ON: a style of fishing which often accounts for big fish. Big fish usually feed on the bottom, and the term laying-on simply means placing your bait on the bottom when using float tackle. Obviously this method can be satisfactorily used only in swims of moderate current, unless a genuine leger weight is to be used in conjunction with a float: sensitivity is then largely lost. The advantage of laying-on is that the angler gets float indication of bites while fishing slap on the bottom. Roach, bream, chub, and even dace in winter are taken by this method, also other species. The float is usually seen at half-cock since some of the shot will be on the bottom with the bait.

LEADER: an American word for trace or cast.

LEADS: these take various forms but all have the same function—to get the bait to the fish, and, incidentally, to cock the float when one is used. Float-fishing weights take the form of small split-shot of various sizes. These are pinched on the cast, or even the hook-length, with flat-nosed pliers. A weight that is easier to use but more conspicuous to the fish is the half-moon lead which merely folds over the cast with finger pressure. Lead wire and small bored bullets stopped by split shot can also be used. Bored bullets have the advantage of concentrating the weight at one point, which is sometimes useful in heavy water. Lead wire instead of split-shot is helpful when hemp fishing to avoid the risk of the fish biting at split-shot, taking it for the bait.

Leger weights all work on the same principle. They are designed for holding the bait on the bottom in strong water. They usually consist of a lump of lead, either flat or round, and bored through the centre. The line runs through this, and the weight is stopped from sliding down to the hook during the cast by a shot, bigger than the diameter of the boring, and pinched on to the line. The most important thing about such a weight is that the line should run freely through it in order to prevent the fish feeling resistance when taking the bait and running with it. The hole through the weight should therefore allow ample clearance for the line. There is risk of the line jamming in a small hole, in which case the fish will start to lift the weight and feel the pull. The Arlesey Bomb type of weight is a great improvement on the standard article, having, besides a streamlined lead body that lessens the risk of becoming hung up on the bottom, a swivel eye through which the line passes. This allows maximum freedom from resistance

to a taking fish. The standard leger weights are either round bored bullets, suitable for rolling along the bed of a stream with the current, or else flat 'coffin' leads designed to hold the bottom.

Spiral leads are used mainly when livebaiting. Their advantage is that they have a wire spiral at top and bottom that allows them to be attached and detached from the tackle without disconnecting line from trace. When slightly bent they make a useful anti-kink device.

Anti-kink leads are used when spinning. Their job is to present a mass of weight that hangs below the axis of the swivels on the tackle. All swivels, save those on ball-bearings, transmit some twist from a spinning bait to the line. When an anti-kink weight of one of the several patterns available is fixed to the top eye of the top swivel, or to the line above the top swivel, this twist or kink is made negative. The rotary action of the lure is not powerful enough to spin the lead weight round and round, and the kink therefore never reaches the reel line.

LEAD WIRE: used sometimes in place of shot or slip-on weights. Useful for weighting self-cocking floats and for fishing with hemp. Fish sometimes mistake shot for hemp but cannot do the same with lead wire twisted round the cast.

LEGERING: sometimes written as 'ledgering', though I believe incorrectly so. It seems likely that the word is derived from the French *legere*, meaning 'light', for this style of fishing if properly carried out gives the lightest of resistance to a fish picking up and running with the bait. The principle of all legering is the same: a weight through which the line passes, and is free to run, takes the tackle to the bottom of the swim and holds it there stationary or else permits it to roll in a controlled way along the bottom with the current. Where, then, does the lightness of the tackle come in? Take a brief glance first at the make-up of a typical leger.

A spade-end or eyed hook is tied direct to the monofilament reel line. About eighteen inches from the hook —the distance will vary according to local conditions but should never be less—a split-shot is pinched on to the line. Above the shot, and threaded on to the line, is the leger weight. This may be (1), a round bullet suitable for rolling down a clear stream bed; (2), a flat 'coffin' lead for holding fast to the bottom; (3), an Arlesey Bomb, so named by Richard Walker who designed it for fishing Arlesey Lake, near Hitchin, for big perch. The first two are bored through their central axis to take the line. The Arlesey Bomb, a pear-shaped affair, has at its thin end a built-in swivel. It is through the eye of this that the line is passed. The swivel eye achieves its object

splendidly—it gives excellent clearance for the line; moreover, it presents a minimum surface to the line, so that a fish tugging at the hook feels no check from the weight. The bullet or coffin-type weights are not always so efficient in this respect.

The important thing to look for when buying leger weights is to see that the hole is large enough. Small boring often causes the line to stick instead of running out smoothly, particularly when affected by mud and debris from the stream bed. If the line sticks for an instant a taking fish will shift the lead weight and, feeling the check, drop the bait. Lightness therefore comes from line freedom.

Legering normally is done without a float, though compromise tackle can be made up in which a float is used for bite indication. With the float-leger, the float is often attached by the bottom ring only. When no float is used bites are indicated either by the movement of the rod tip, the feel of the line held over the

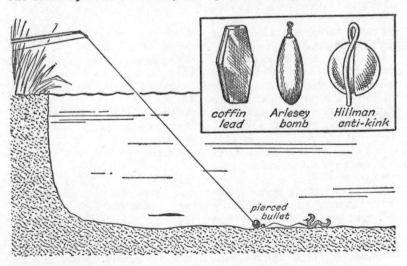

coffin lead   Arlesey bomb   Hillman anti-kink

pierced bullet

LEGERING. *The bait is held on the bed of a river or lake by a suitable weight Three other forms of lead, one of them detachable, are shown inset.*

finger tip, or by some form of bite-indicator. The most common of these is the well-known dough ball, or 'bobbin', squeezed on to the line and hanging down usually between reel and first rod-ring. When the bobbin jumps a fish is at the bait.

A further variation of leger weight, and one extremely useful when the bottom is covered with flannel weed, is the slow-sinking leger. The leger in this case is nearly weightless in water. The body is made of hard wood bored in the usual manner. Round the wood, lead wire is wrapped until the weight will just sink. The result is that it settles so gently on the bottom that it runs little risk of sinking into the weed.

Some anglers find legering dull fishing. This is, of course, a matter of personal taste. There can be no doubt, however, about its effectiveness for all sorts of fish: roach, chub, perch, tench, carp, barbel, bream, and, with deadbait, both pike and eels. Livebait on leger tackle, especially in rivers during flood conditions, and intense cold, can sometimes make a killing among pike if the angler can find where the fish are sheltering in the deeps.

Perhaps the ultimate in legering, although it doesn't quite qualify under this heading, is fishing where no weight is used and certainly no float. The weight of the bait alone is used to get distance during the cast. This is an effective technique when carp fishing, for these wily fish can then feel a check from neither float nor leger weight.

LEVEL-WIND: a device incorporated in reels and seen principally in multipliers. It carries the line backwards and forwards across the drum so that it will lie evenly as it is retrieved. A fixed-spool reel achieves the same object by virtue of the spool's in-and-out movement.

LICE, Fish: *Argulus foliaceus,* the fish louse, is often seen clinging to freshwater fish around the gill area. This small parasite lives on its host by blood-sucking. Towards the end of the spawning season fish are very prone to attack by it. *Argulus* probably accounts for much of the leaping, by fish of all species, seen in the early season.

LIMPET: *Patella vulgata,* a gastropod mollusc found firmly glued to rocks above and below tide marks. A fair bait for some sea fish.

LINE-DRIER: a device for doing precisely what the name implies. Usually in the form of a

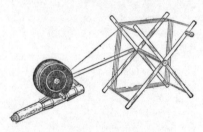

LINE-DRIER. *A rotatable framework for the drying of silk lines.*

metal frame round which the line may be wound. In most models the whole frame can be rotated by a handle to assist the drying process. Essential to the fly fisherman using silk line.

LINE-GUARD: device on a drum-type reel designed to prevent the line from falling off the drum and causing a 'bird's-nest' entanglement.

LING: *Molva vulgaris,* family *Gadidae,* is really a deep-water fish but is often caught in small sizes and large numbers from the South Coast. The fish has a barbule below its chin, is olive brownish and certainly reaches 50 lb. in deep waters. The record, from Penzance, is 45 lb.

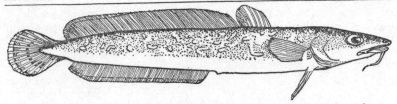

LING. *Deep-water specimens of this relative of the cod range from four to six feet in length. The barbule beneath its lower jaw is a notable feature.*

LIVEBAIT: almost any small fish will do for a livebait, though some are better than others. I would divide them as follows. Excellent: dace, gudgeon, perch, small pike, roach, rudd, minnow. Good: perch small carp, goldfish. Poor: bleak (no stamina), bream (wrong shape). Perhaps it is a mistake to suggest that livebait should be small or smallish fish, at least for pike. The Scottish record from Loch Lomond (47 lb. 11 oz.), was taken on a roach of over a pound. There is very definite support for the theory that if you want to catch really big pike use really big baits. On the other hand, the English record was nearly beaten in 1957 by Colonel Harold Atherton, of London, when fishing a four-ounce rudd.

Among the small baits used by anglers, dace and gudgeon are first-class. Dace because they are bright and lively; gudgeon because they are rare fish in still-waters and are thus a great attraction for pike. Goldfish, though expensive and rejected by many on humanitarian grounds, are excellent baits for the same reason. A word about perch: pike are perfectly capable of swallowing perch despite the spiny dorsal fins. They do so regularly in nature, and, to remove the dorsal fin, as some anglers persist in doing, not only causes unnecessary suffering but robs the fish of means of movement, weakens it, and renders it no more appetizing.

All predatory fish will take live-bait, and this, of course, includes trout. At the beginning of the season, especially, many other species will eat a live meal. Include among these chub, rudd, roach, bream, barbel, and carp. Minnows make the best bait for perch though other small fish, including small perch, do well. The rule about hooking livebaits is this: a small bait will quickly die if pricked by heavy triangles. Lip-hook it once with a large round-bend hook, or at most a small triangle. Baits of three ounces and upwards will usually stand attachment to the appropriate size of Jardine snap-tackle. Livebait should be carried to the water in a special can with a perforated inner liner. The sloshing of water through these perforations keeps the water aerated and the bait in good condition.

LOACH: family *Cobitidae*. There are two species, *Nemacheilus barbatula*, the stone loach, and *Cobitis taenia*, the spined loach. Both are found in clear, fast, pebbly streams and can easily be caught in the hand. Average length, three inches. Appearance, something like a gudgeon but longer and thinner. The tail of the stone loach (the more common of the two) is straight-ended and that of the spined loach convex (the gudgeon's, of course, is forked). Apart from all this, the loaches have a more mottled appearance and have six barbules round the lower jaw. In the case of the spined loach these are of even size: two of the barbules of the stone loach are exaggeratedly large. The spined loach is an inch shorter than the stone variety, and is more local in distribution. It is

LOACH. *The stone loach, shown here, is slightly larger than the spined loach.*

not present in Scotland, Ireland or Wales, and in England seems to keep to the East Midlands, Midlands and Wiltshire. The spines from which it takes its name are erectile, and are situated in grooves on each side of the head below and in front of the eyes. Both species can use atmospheric oxygen as an aid to breathing. Both make excellent bait for trout and perch.

LOBWORM: one of the larger earthworms, deadly for most freshwater fish and useful for a few sea fish when all else fails. Lobs are between three and six inches in length and should be fished on two- or three-hook tackle in cases where fish are likely to bite shyly. Lobs can be found lying out on flower beds or lawns after dark and particularly after a shower of rain. A torch, a silent approach, and a quick grab aimed at either side of their burrow is essential if they are not to escape. Best kept for a few days in moist moss, preferably spaghnum, before fishing.

LOGGERHEAD: slang name for chub.

LONG-TROTTING: an alternative name for the technique of swimming the bait a long way downstream. Sometimes also called long-

corking. Success of trotting depends on the tackle being paid out smoothly, preferably from a centrepin reel. Long-trotting is used extensively on such rivers as the Avon and Kennet, a fairly substantial float and heavy shotting is needed to take out the line. Trotting is especially effective for shy fish such as chub. There is at least one famous trotting swim on the Kennet where the bait can be sent down fifty yards below the angler. At this range both spotting the bite and striking to it becomes extremely tricky.

LUGWORM: a good all-round sea bait. Found on sandy and mud beaches between tide-marks, they can be spotted by the worm cast and the small indentation above their heads. The worm will lie in a U-shaped tunnel between these two points. Random digging will, of course, produce worms but the best

LONG-TROTTING. *The 'Slipstream' float is specially designed for this method of freshwater angling.*

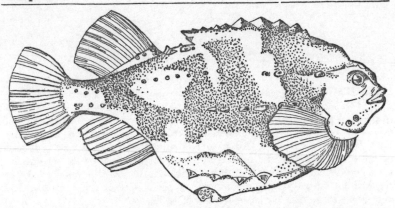

LUMPSUCKER. *An odd-looking sea fish which has a disc-like sucker on its underside by means of which it can cling to rocks and stones.*

lugs are found by expert diggers who attack individual burrows. Lugs should be kept in a wooden box in wet seaweed. After a day or so they will deteriorate and smell abominably. Fish will still take them in this condition, more avidly if anything, provided that they are firm enough to be kept on the hook.

LUMPSUCKER: an ugly yet gaudy brute, rarely fisl d for but sometimes caught off the Lancashire coast. Its colouring varies from yellow, in the female, to orange in the male. The upper half of the body has a rough lumpy appearance. The fish as a whole is oval-shaped, and its dorsal and anal fins are set well towards the tail, which is small. The name is taken from the orange-coloured sucker on the underside of the fish with which the creature is able to attach itself to anything and hold on with limpet-like force.

MACKEREL: *Scomber scomber,* family *Scombridae.* The mackerel is of the same family as the giant tunny and the bonito, mighty fighters both. Though a very small relation of these sporting fish, the mackerel shows much of their fighting quality. Hooked on suitably light tackle it will give a scrap that for sheer dash and spirit can rival that of a trout. It's a pity that many people's introduction to mackerel fishing is made when on holiday and while fishing with a heavy hand-line from a boat. In such circumstances it becomes merely a question of pulling the fish in.

Mackerel winter in huge shoals off the south of Ireland. When the spring comes they rise from deep water and migrate to the coastal areas where the shoals break up into smaller groups and the fish forage inshore at the surface. Mackerel during the summer months can be found almost anywhere round the coast of the British Isles. Mackerel need very little description with their elegant, tabby-cat markings that lose much of their sheen when the fish is taken from the water. The fish has two dorsals, the front one having 11–14 spines. Behind the second dorsal is a series of small finlets. Behind the anal fin is a similar line of finlets. The fish is voracious and predatory, eating fry of all species including its own. A good mackerel weighs a pound: the record stands at 4½ lb.

MACKEREL-FISHING: mackerel can be taken in a number of ways, light tackle always being used to give the fish the maximum chance to display its fighting qualities. Mackerel will take a gaudy fly. They can also be caught easily by three or four feathers fixed on dropper links and trailed behind a boat. When feather fishing, to deal with the drag of current and tide on the line, a fairly heavy rod is needed, and much of the sport is thus lost. However, if the number of lures is restricted, a stiff spinning-rod can be used.

The best fishing times for mackerel are the early morning and evening. Hot, calm weather is fine. The fish will take spinning baits including spoons, wagtails, devons, and fly-spoons. Line should be

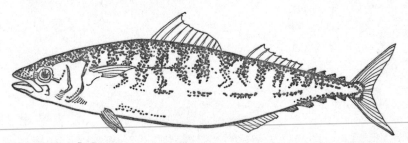

MACKEREL. *It has many of the fighting qualities of the tunny, to which it is related. The British record, caught at Looe in 1935, stands at 4½ lb.*

light, say 4–5 lb., and fixed-spool gear will serve best. Natural baits on spinning flights, including rag-worms and strips of fish skin, all work at times. Since mackerel operate at all depths between surface and bottom—though the top six feet will generally yield most fish—the spinner needs to vary his depth constantly if he is not connecting with the fish. Strike at once if a touch is felt when spinning.

MACKEREL FISHING. *A simple tri-angular-type spinner such as this makes an effective lure for mackerel.*

Float-fishing from rocks, pier and boat also takes a lot of mackerel. Baits include brit and sand-eels, worms and fish skin, particularly mackerel skin. Worms should be of the small variety: shrimps and prawns also will catch mackerel. Floats need to be as light as possible since the mackerel takes the bait with a sensitive touch. Lines must be greased to float, as sunken line is fatal to a quick strike.

Boat fishing produces fine hauls of mackerel during the summer months. The activity of sea birds often guides the angler as to the correct place and moment to make an attack from a boat. Gulls, cor-morants, gannets operating in a concentrated way in one spot suggest a shoal of mackerel. True, the birds may be at work on shoals of sand-eels or fry, but local knowledge will usually tell you whether the target is likely to be mackerel. Float fishing and spinning, and feather fishing as already described, may all be done from a boat, but drift-lining is probably as effective as any other

method when afloat. Any of the baits mentioned above will serve: weights should be kept as light as possible, consistent with the current.

MAGGOTS: sometimes called 'gentles', these are the larvae of the bluebottle, greenbottle and house-flies. Many anglers dye their mag-gots, but there is no positive proof that this makes them more attractive. Maggots are the classic roach bait but they will lure practically every freshwater fish including trout, and occasionally even pike. They are used in many styles, varying from one maggot on a No. 20 hook to a bunch of four or more on a No. 8. Inferior maggots, called 'squats' or 'feeders', are used as groundbait. The best maggots are said to be the liver-fed ones.

What matters most is that they are fat and lively. In hot weather they can be prevented from hurrying into the chrysalis stage by being kept in a cool place (they keep in a fridge for days). In cold weather some match anglers are even alleged to keep the next few maggots for the hook in the cheek in order to wake them up and make them lively. Generally speaking maggots are little use in chrysalis form, though good fish are sometimes taken when the maggots have just begun to pupate. The 'liver' maggot is the larva of the bluebottle. The greenbottle produces the 'pinkie'. 'Squats' come from the common house-fly. 'Specials' are the offspring of a larger-sized variety of house-fly.

MAGGOTS, Colouring of: maggots are often dyed in an attempt to make them more attractive to fish, notably roach. To dye mag-gots, put them in a sieve and run cold water on them. While they are wet, sprinkle dye powder over them, and let the colour spread, then wash again in water and leave to scour in breadcrumbs. This method works best for yellow maggots, using chrysoidine powder bought from the chemist. Deeper shades are not very effective since light does not penetrate far below water and dark red will soon appear black when submerged. For pink maggots use rhodamine powder, and make up a solution of one part powder to six parts water. Leave the maggots in this for at least three hours, then sieve them under the cold tap and rinse as before. Other dyes: auramine O—pale yellow; methylene, blue; methyl, violet; Bismarck, brown.

MALLOCH REEL: early version of the fixed-spool reel in which a conventional drum reel was turned so that its spool lay with its axis parallel to the rod. For recovering line the spool was turned back into its normal position. The snag with all such reels was that the line became kinked as each loop flew off the drum.

MANURING PONDS: it is the dream of every fishing club to improve its waters. Mostly this is attempted by restocking with better fish. However, this is a waste of time unless the water is, in the first place, sufficiently rich to support those fish, in addition to the existing population, and to help them grow. If the water is a poor one, then the fish will 'go back', that is to say, become stunted and possibly sterile. A fishing water is a direct parallel of a farmer's field. The field can only produce a given weight of crop consistent with fertility of the field. To make water produce more, it must be assisted with fertilizers, either chemical or organic. In the first place an analysis of the water is necessary, and here the local River Board may be able to help. If the water is basically too acid, it

may have to be treated with lime before any manuring can be done. As is explained in the section POND LIFE, the food chain on which fish ultimately depend begins with microscopic vegetable and animal organisms called plankton. It is the plankton that must therefore be stimulated if the whole water is to be improved. Manuring can be done directly with organic matter such as decaying vegetation (the equivalent of the gardener's compost), treated sewage liquid, or even by sowing a crop of red clover and tipping the turves into the water. The danger with the organic method, particularly during hot weather, is that the oxygen necessary to break down the organic matter may leave the water so depleted that the fish will suffer and possibly die. For improving trout stocks there is little to touch the putting of offal or minced horseflesh into the water, but this is so expensive that it is generally beyond the means of angling societies.

In the first place improvement, then, depends on the nature of the bed of the lake. The best bottom is a silty one with a rich mixture of organic matter derived from dead plants and animals. Peat-bedded lakes are poor ones. Here the bottom is composed of dead vegetation that has not rotted sufficiently, and the danger is that any fertilizer put into the water may be washed out before the slow breaking-down mechanism of the peat lake has had a chance to make use of it. The addition of lime can improve things here. Inorganic lake beds of sand, gravel, and clay can be improved by the addition of humus, stable manure, etc.

Phosphates have been found on balance to give the best results in improving fish crops. Superphosphate, basic slag, bonemeal are all other names for phosphates. Between 1 and 1½ cwt. of this per acre, applied once in May and again in July or August, has been found to give the best results. American experiments have produced a commercial mixed fertilizer consisting of nitrogen, phosphorus and potassium and known as '6.8.4. (N.P.K.).' The figure denote proportions of nitrogen, phosphoric acid and potash.

as the name suggests. Found on rough, acid streams rather than on placid chalk waters. In season more or less constantly. Artificials, both wet and dry, exist by the same name.

MARGIN FISHING: a recently developed technique for taking carp at night. Fishing should be done on the side of the lake to which the wind is blowing, and taking any

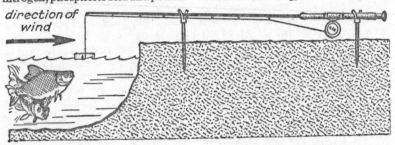

MARGIN FISHING. *The angler selects a lakeside swim into which the wind is blowing, and suspends from his rod a large piece of crust at surface level.*

This mixture is applied at the rate of 100 lb. per acre at intervals. The first dose produces such a rich crop of plankton that the bottom becomes invisible at 18 inches. When the water clears sufficiently for the bottom to be seen again, another treatment is applied: and so on throughout the summer. American experiments have shown that this costly treatment has raised productivity of certain lakes from about 100 lb. of fish per acre to 600 lb.

In Central European countries where fish are farmed commercially for the table, ponds are drained for long periods and sown with clover before being flooded again. The nearest the average fishing club can get to this is to put farmyard manure or even clover turves into the shallows.

MARCH BROWN: second largest member of the ephemerid family of flies. Brownish in colour

scraps of surface food, particularly particles of groundbait left by daytime anglers. The rod is set in rests so that the last three feet or so overhangs the water. A large piece of crust is put on the hook and lowered until it just floats on the water. In the dark hours, fish of all sorts, not only carp, patrol the banks looking for trifles. Large roach as well as carp have been taken by this method. The first run is usually spectacular when the hooked carp realizes how close he is to his opponent.

MARK: a known ground favourable for sea fishing. The usual way of locating this is to make a note of two pairs of prominent objects ashore. Imaginary lines drawn through each pair of objects will intersect at the desired mark. By memorizing these the angler can ensure that his boat will be anchored in the same position when he wishes to fish there again. An alternative method is to take compass bearings on each of two prominent landmarks ashore.

MARROW-SPOON: a long narrow spoon used for sampling the stomach contents of freshly caught trout. The spoon is pushed down the trout's gullet, twisted round and withdrawn. This action collects on the blade of the spoon some of the insects and molluscs most recently swallowed and, therefore, indicates what the trout in that stretch of the river are feeding on at the moment. If the angler is puzzled as to which of several flies the fish are taking, the marrow spoon can often give the answer. The stomach contents recovered in this way should be put in water, in a tin lid or saucer carried for the purpose. They will then separate and allow the angler to make his autopsy. See photograph facing page 145.

MATCH FISHING: this is a highly specialized form of fishing which dominates the angling scene in the Midlands and northern parts of England. It usually comprises two or more teams of fishermen competing against one another on a water, over a fixed period. The winning team being the one which accumulates the largest aggregate weight of fish at the end of the period. The competitors fish at fixed stations, or 'swims', which are decided previously by a draw: this is referred to as being 'pegged down'. Usually the competition lasts from four to five hours. Often it is a friendly match between clubs, but, on occasions, match angling is seen on a grand scale. Towards the end of the summer, the All-England Championship, the Birmingham Anglers' Annual Match, the Trent Angling Championship, and the Welsh Angling Championship draw between 1,000 and 5,000 competitors. These, as in the case of the Birmingham contest, are sometimes spread over 15 miles of river. At some of the big championships bookmakers can be seen laying odds against individual and team chances, and it has been known for a single angler to win £1,000 in bets and sweepstakes.

Match angling has recently assumed tremendous importance. It would not be a great exaggeration to say that it has become a minor industry. Certainly, bus companies thrive on the strength of it, for Midland anglers think nothing of travelling 100 miles to the 'venue' of even a friendly match. A match champion may spend up to £3 on maggots alone for a big occasion, and probably starts the season with a hundredweight sack of groundbait.

The angling match itself is no new idea. It has had its place in fishing for 50 years or more. Probably it owes its origin to industrial pollution. As the industrial development of the Midlands ruined more and more streams close to big centres, fishing became poorer and poorer in quality. Since big fish were out of the question, interest could be given to an outing by having a sweepstake on the total weight of small fish caught. Then, when even this sort of fishing was killed by pollution, it became necessary to seek fishing miles away from the city. Transport had to be organized. To make sure that there was a sufficiently large attendance to justify the transport some special attraction had to be attached to the day—a match.

The fact that big-scale match-fishing has never caught on in the South is due to two things: rivers in the south and west of England are as yet by no means as polluted as those in the north and Midlands; there is a distinct difference of temperament between the northern and southern angler. The latter likes to get away on his own, and fish on his own. Mass attendance at the waterside does not greatly appeal to him. Lately he has earned the strange epithet 'pleasure fisherman', for that is what the match angler calls him.

But to say that the match angler is primarily concerned with catching small fish is not to decry his skill, which is very considerable. His art consists of attracting the fish to his swim by clever groundbaiting, of holding them there against the blandishments of his up- and down-stream neighbours, of spotting and striking the most minutely indicated bites (for every half-ounce fish counts in the total weight). His fishing technique is a time-and-motion study. The crack match man wastes not a second nor makes a superfluous movement. His tackle is disposed around him with the order and regularity of a surgeon's instruments.

He casts with the delicacy of a fly fisherman, strikes at the bite, and swings his small captive back into his hand with one movement, removing it from the tiny hook (he uses sizes 22–16: nothing larger) and flips it into the keep-net. If he hooks a big fish like a 2-lb. tench when the roach are biting, he will do a quick calculation of how long it will take him to land the tench on his superfine tackle (he commonly fishes with tackle whose weakest link is a pound-and-a-half breaking strain), and whether in that time he could pile up a greater aggregate of 3-ounce roach. If the latter, then he will unhesitatingly break off, tie on a new bottom and continue fishing for roach.

By far the most famous of all big contests is the 'All-England', properly called the Annual Angling Championship of the National Federation of Anglers. Here are some extracts from the rules:

1. *The competition shall be a peg-down one. Pegs to be not less than 60 feet apart where practicable.*

2. *Competitors to have in use only one rod, one line, and one hook at one and the same time. No competitor will be allowed to have a second rod put together. Any bait may be used except blood-worm, live or dead fish, or spinning baits. All baits must be thrown in by hand—no other method allowed.*

3. *Competitors must play and land their own fish. All fish of the following species (of whatever size) are eligible for weighing-in: pike, barbel, grayling, tench, chub, perch, dace, roach, bream, rudd, gudgeon, ruffe, and bleak.*

4. *Competitors must provide themselves with keep-nets, as all competitors must (if practicable) keep alive all fish caught, which, after being weighed, must be taken to the water's edge and carefully returned to the water.*

Recommended reading: *Match-Fishing* by Frank Oates.

MAXILLARY: the upper jawbone of a fish.

MAY-FLY: largest member of the *Ephemeridae*. There are three species on British waters: *Ephemera danica, E. vulgata, E. lineata.* The last named is so rare that for angling purposes it can be ignored. *E. danica* has a yellowish body with brown markings on the dorsal surface of the last body segments. *E. vulgata* has dorsal markings but in the form of two dark triangular blotches. *Ephemera danica* is by far the most common and therefore important to the angler. The may-fly is quite the most spectacular of all our aquatic insects, having beautiful transparent wings set in the upright position of the ephemerids, six legs and three *setae* or tails. Nowadays the name is something of a misnomer, for, history having played about with the calendar, the fly is much more likely in most seasons to begin hatching in June. Actually, the hatch varies from river to river. On the Kennet and Lambourn in Berkshire, chalk streams both, the hatch begins in early June. On the Test and Itchen in Hampshire one is likely to see the fly in quantity by 15 or 20 May. The quantity and quality of the hatch depends largely on the weather, as does the quality and quantity of the hatch two to three years later, for this is the time it takes for the eggs laid in one year's hatch to go through their many nymphal changes and rise to the surface to hatch as flies again. Thus, if this year you suffer a vile east wind that evening after evening gets up and blows your female may-flies away from the water, few of them will reach the river to lay their eggs, and a subsequent generation two to three years hence will suffer.

The story of a may-fly's life-cycle briefly told is this: a fertilized female may-fly lays her 6,000-odd eggs on the water. As she does so she is known to the angler as a 'spinner'. Egg-laying done, she falls exhausted on the water and dies: she is now a 'spent spinner'. The eggs drift down to the bottom and fall into the silt. Soon they hatch into minute larvae. These larvae are capable of existing in moving or still water, since they create their own aeration by gill movement. During their two to three years on the river bed they increase in size, splitting their husk each time to emerge in bigger form. At last comes the day when the light or the temperature, or both, tells them it is time to hatch. The larvae (known to the angler as 'nymphs') swim to the surface. There they split their skins for the last time and out comes a fly. The skin ('husk' to the angler) floats away. But the may-fly, sitting on the water, has not yet finished its process of evolution. The angler now refers to it as a 'dun', since the perfect fly is still covered by one last transparent skin. It sits on the surface drying for a few seconds, then flutters to the bank. There it will rest in the shelter of a bush for perhaps twenty-four hours when the final metamorphosis will take place. The skin splits once more and out flies the perfect, shining, transparent and wonderfully beautiful fly —the 'spinner'. The males now commence a strange dance, usually in the shelter of bush or tree, up and down, up and down, until a female happens along. A pair mate, the male usually falling to die soon after on land but the female making her way to the water. There she flies upstream —a provision by nature for the ground the fly lost yesterday in hatching—dips to the surface time and again to lay her eggs, and then falls to die herself. As larvae the flies have lived for many months. Emerged, they have had but 24 hours of life and one purpose—to mate. Nature does not even provide them with a mouth. It is not necessary.

That's the whole story, except for the angler's part in it, and the trout's, and the swallow's, and the swift's, for all these find excitement in the may-fly. At all stages of its life as nymph, dun, spinner and spent, the mayfly is a rare delicacy to the trout. As dun and spinner it is hunted relentlessly by swallow, swift, and marten.

As far as the angler is concerned the great thing about the may-fly hatch is that it turns the head of every trout in the river. Fish so big that normally they eat only other fish, are tempted to come up for the mouthful that a may-fly provides. Four-, five- and six-pounders are caught on the chalk streams every year during the 'mayfly'. But this is not to say that the hatch is truly what it is sometimes called—'duffer's fortnight'. Often it is easy to catch the smaller fish, but with every trout in the river feeding the skilful angler naturally wants only to go for the big fellows, and these may still prove mightily elusive. The timing of the strike will probably be different from that you are used to when using smaller flies. The fish may elect to feed only on spent when spents and duns are coming down together, and a spent in the first stages of dying can look very much like a fresh fly. Or again, infuriatingly, the trout may not wish to feed at all, at least not at the start of the hatch when the angler is all impatience.

The may-fly is not confined to the chalk stream. You will find them in smaller quantities on many rivers from the Thames to the Barle on Exmoor. To see a really large hatch is truly a staggering sight. Motorists driving close to rivers during such a time have to put their windscreen-wipers on to clear the flies away. Sometimes, during a shower of rain, the female spinners dip to the surface of the road imagining that they are laying their eggs on the surface of their home river.

MEGRIM: this member of the flatfish family is seldom fished for though it is sometimes caught in deep water. Scientific name, *Lepidorhombus megastoma*, family *Pleuronectidae.*

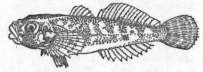

MILLER'S THUMB. *Known also as the bullhead, is useful as livebait.*

MILLER'S THUMB: *Cottus gobia,* family *Cottidae.* Another name for the small freshwater fish generally known as the BULLHEAD.

MINNOW: *Phoxinus phoxinus,* family *Cyprinidae.* Maximum length about three inches. Streamlined, powerful for its size, lives on shallows over a clean bottom in fast, well-aerated streams. Its markings are something like that of a tabby-cat. In the breeding season the males assume a reddish colouring round the mouth and gill area. A most effective bait for perch and trout. Good to eat if enough can be

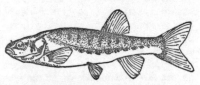

MINNOW. *Lives in the shallows and makes a good bait for perch.*

caught. Usually caught for bait in a trap: can be taken on a frament of redworm fixed to a No. 18 or 20 hook from which the barb has been removed.

MINNOW TRAP: these are sold in tackle shops and are made of plastic or celluloid. They consist of a transparent cylinder, the entrance to which is funnel-shaped. The opposite end of the cylinder is perforated to allow the current to flow through. The trap is baited with scraps of bread, fragments of worm, or gentles, and is lowered to the bottom. The minnows see the free feed, swim in through the funnel, which is placed at the downstream end, and are unable to get out again. Perfectly good minnow traps can be made from clear wine bottles that have a cone in the bottom. All that has to be done is to knock the 'marble' out of the cone. The best way is to fill the bottle with sand and bury two-thirds of it in the earth. Thus packed it will not shatter when the bottom of the glass cone, or 'kick-up', is hit smartly with a poker or cold chisel. Muslin should be tied over the wine bottle neck and string looped round it at each end so that it can be lowered to the stream bed on an even keel.

MODEL PERFECT: a proprietary brand of hook which has an off-set point and consequently gives great holding and hooking power.

MONA'S SCALE: Mona was the name under which a well-known contributor to the *Fishing Gazette* once wrote. His scale, first published in 1918, gives a reliable estimate of length-to-weight ratio where pike are concerned. It is based on the fact that a pike of 40 inches in length weighs 20 lb. Here is the scale:

MINNOW TRAP. *A collapsible form of trap for catching livebait is most effective in shallow, streamy runs.*

MONEL METAL: a nickel alloy now being used in the manufacture of reel and rod fittings. Its virtues are that it does not corrode and is extremely durable. The metal is now being adopted for making fine wire lines.

MONKFISH: *Squatina squatina,* family *Squatinidae.* This fish is in appearance a sort of cross between a shark and a skate. In Cornish waters and off the west coast of Ireland fish of 40 lb. plus are quite often caught. The monkfish feeds largely on a fish diet and is particularly partial to flatfish, patrolling the sandy bottom in search of prey. Tackle should be as for tope, the bait where possible being a live flatfish. The battle is usually a dour, drawn-out affair, the hooked fish heading for cover and then holding on for all it is worth. As when skate fishing, 'pumping' tactics are called for. The species seems to be crucially affected by weather. When cold sets in the monkfish leave inshore waters.

MONOFILAMENT: synthetic monofilament has revolutionized the business of buying and choosing fishing lines. To all intents and purposes monofilament has ousted silk from the tackle bag. It is cheap, can be obtained in any breaking strain the angler chooses from 1 lb. to 50 lb., takes camouflage dye readily, is easy to knot provided the correct knots are used, and floats well in the smaller breaking strains.

Length	Weight	Length	Weight
20 in.	2·5 lb.	38 in.	17·1 lb.
21 ,,	2·89 ,,	39 ,,	18·5 ,,
22 ,,	3·3 ,,	40 ,,	20·0 ,,
23 ,,	3·8 ,,	41 ,,	21·5 ,,
24 ,,	4·3 ,,	42 ,,	23·1 ,,
25 ,,	4·88 ,,	43 ,,	24·8 ,,
26 ,,	5·49 ,,	44 ,,	26·6 ,,
27 ,,	6·15 ,,	45 ,,	28·4 ,,
28 ,,	6·8 ,,	46 ,,	30·47 ,,
29 ,,	7·6 ,,	47 ,,	32·44 ,,
30 ,,	8·4 ,,	48 ,,	34·58 ,,
31 ,,	9·3 ,,	49 ,,	36·77 ,,
32 ,,	10·2 ,,	50 ,,	39·06 ,,
33 ,,	11·2 ,,	51 ,,	41·45 ,,
34 ,,	12·2 ,,	52 ,,	43·94 ,,
35 ,,	13·39 ,,	53 ,,	46·5 ,,
36 ,,	14·58 ,,	54 ,,	49·2 ,,
37 ,,	15·8 ,,	55 ,,	51·9 ,,

Perhaps its only drawback is its stretch, but this is becoming less and less.

Braided nylon and Terylene lines share the market with monofilament. These are more expensive but are preferable for spinning, particularly with a fixed-spool reel.

MUCILIN: a proprietary flotant for lines and flies.

have two barbules below the chin. They are perfectly splendid to eat, but it is the grey mullet family that intrigues the sea angler, for the mullet of this branch is as wily and hard to catch as a big roach. Indeed, many anglers never succeed in catching a grey mullet.

The three varieties are fairly easily identified apart. The thick-

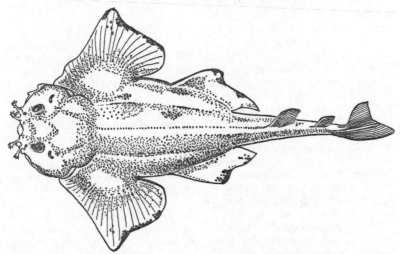

MONKFISH. *Sometimes called 'shark-ray' because of its resemblance to those species.*

MULLET: there are four mullet to be caught in British waters. Three come from the same family—the *Mugilidae*. These are the thick-lipped grey mullet, thin-lipped grey mullet, and golden (grey) mullet. The fourth kind, the red mullet, is a member of a different group, the *Mullidae*. The red variety can be dismissed straight away as it is really a warm-water and Mediterranean fish. Occasionally they are caught accidentally by rod-and-line anglers off the south and west coasts of Britain, when they are said to give a good account of themselves. They are pinkish, blunt-headed, and

lipped characteristic is immediately apparent. Moreover, this fish has its second dorsal and anal fin partially scaled. The grey mullet is torpedo-shaped, large-scaled, thick of body, and has a forked tail. The thick-lipped version has four very pronounced spiked rays to its front dorsal: this is the fish that the angler is most likely to meet. The British record, only partially substantiated, is 10 lb. 1 oz., and there is little doubt that the species grows larger than this.

The thin-lipped fish has the same blue-grey colouring and external characteristics, except for the fact that its fins lack scales. The golden (grey) mullet is again a thin-lipped fish. It is most easily identified by the golden spot on the gill-covers and by a smaller spot aft of the eyes. It, too, has no scaling on its fins. Mullet spawn in deep water but come into the shore in early summer where they stay well into the autumn. They have a habit of shoaling for a brief time in vast numbers close to the shore. However, they quickly move on. If the angler can get amongst them at this period, he is likely to make a killing.

Mullet are certainly shy, although they appear to be able to acclimatize themselves to noisy conditions, as in harbours. One great thing in the angler's favour is that they are extremely inquisitive in search of food. They can often be seen to suck in the most unlikely objects such as pebbles, and then as quickly eject them. They also like fresh or rather brackish water and are therefore to be caught in estuaries.

MULLET-FISHING: there are two principal methods: (1), float-fishing close to the surface; (2) surface fishing. The former is done off piers, rocks, or from a boat. Tackle needs to be something close to that used for roach and a 5–6 lb. line will be strong enough. The float should be kept as small as con-

ditions allow. A number of baits will take mullet thanks to the species' natural curiosity about possible foodstuffs. Among the best favoured are: breadpaste, worm, macaroni, and partly-boiled cabbage stalk. Where worms are used, tiny ragworms will be found most effective and a number should be threaded on a fine wire hook. Because of the fact that mullet suck in the bait cautiously, the float will rarely dart under and away. Instead it will tremble and shift up, down, or sideways, exactly as when roach fishing. Groundbait can be used in the form of cloud made from breadcrumbs and flavoured with pilchard oil. Floating bread-crust will also catch mullet during calm weather when the fish can be spotted. When ground-fishing, the technique is to use a light lead as in slack-water bass fishing. Float or surface fishing is usually better.

MUSKELLUNGE: *Esox masquinongy*, largest of the pike family and found only in N. America and Canada. It has no scales on the lower half of the gill-cover and cheek, and has a barred rather than spotted marking towards the rear half of the body. It grows to great size and has a formidable reputation as a fighter. The record, from Wisconsin, is 69 lb. 11 oz.

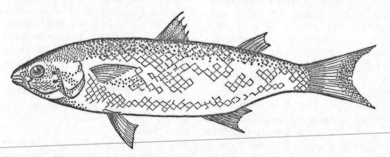

MULLET. *The thick-lipped grey mullet has a thick torpedo-shaped body. In summer, mullet often shoal in great numbers close inshore.*

NATURAL FLIES: in approximate order of importance to the fly fisherman come the following families of flies found on the water, and to which fish, both coarse and game, rise.

The Ephemeridae: these are primarily flies of the gentle lowland, and particularly chalk, rivers, also of many lakes. The most important is probably the may-fly, although it has only a short season, usually from mid-May to mid-June, according to the water on which it is hatching: the over-all weather also affects the time of hatch. The may-fly is a very large, gossamer fly which in common with all the ephemerids is up-winged, has an up-curved body ending in *setae*, tails, or whisks, and sits the water well on six legs. The may-fly has three tails, sharing this distinction with one other member of the family—the Blue-Winged Olive. The other ephemerids have two only. Fish feed avidly on the may-fly in all its forms—nymph, dun, spinner and spent spinner. Frequently they go into a slump period after the may-fly feast and will look at nothing else for quite a time. Certainly the may-fly period causes fish of a size that would not otherwise look at a fly to feed greedily at the surface. May-flies are often called Green-drakes, Grey-drakes, and Black-drakes. These refer to different stages of development and even to different species, and have local variations. The term 'spent gnat' refers to the female dead on the water after ovipositing, or egg-laying. Trout frequently select 'spents' in preference to anything else.

The Olive in its 50 or more different forms, hatches throughout the year on many rivers and lakes. Trout take it at most seasons though they will at times select other flies in preference, perhaps because it is such a universal item of diet. It is a medium-size fly varying from olive green to practically transparent, and occasionally dark green. It has two tails and goes through the normal ephemerid life-cycle: nymph (two years or so), dun, and spinner. The spinner of the Olive is known to anglers as the Red Spinner.

The Iron Blue is a small dark fly which the trout appear to like very much. It has two tails only and the spinner is called the Jenny Spinner.

Pale Watery ephemerids are colourless little flies that hatch fairly regularly throughout the season.

Blue-winged Olives share with the may-fly the honour of having three tails, have a smoky appearance, and generally seem to hatch towards evening. The spinner is called the Sherry Spinner.

The March Brown, a large dark brownish member of the group, favours mountain and moorland streams rather than the alkali waters of the south of England.

The Trichoptera: the word is derived from the Greek meaning 'hairy-winged'. Float fishermen refer to them often as caddis-flies since the larval stage is the well-known caddis, or cad-bait of the coarse angler. The nymphs of the species build themselves small protective cases of sticks and stones and other debris stuck together with a natural

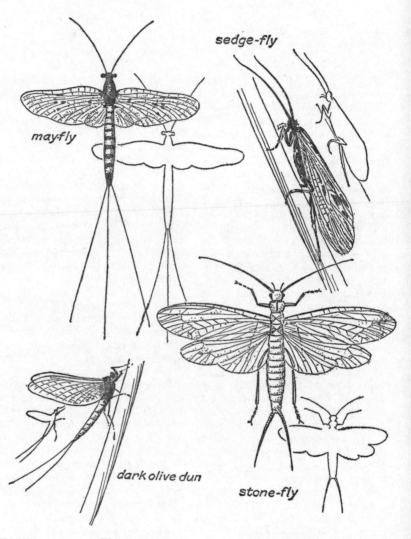

mayfly

sedge-fly

dark olive dun

stone-fly

NATURAL FLIES. *The outline sketches show actual sizes. Though shown as a winged insect here, the stone-fly is of far more interest to the trout angler in its larval form, when it is called a 'creeper'. The flies on this page represent the three main families of fishermen's flies—the Ephemeridae (may-fly and olive), the Perlidae (stone-fly), and the Trichoptera (caddis, or sedge-flies).*

secretion. Trout anglers call the species sedges. They are somewhat moth-like in appearance, having back-folded wings that slope like the roof of a house. The life of the adult fly is considerably longer than that of the Ephemerids, or Ephemeropterans (the name means 'one day on the wing'). Caddis-flies will survive days, even weeks, in a suitably moist atmosphere. They are found on almost every water and give splendid dusk fishing to the fly-angler. Many a trout that has sulked all day will make its fatal mistake in half-light to a juicy sedge. The best-known forms of sedge-fly are: the Grannom, the most killing patterns of which are the females with green eggs clustered at the tail; the Silverthorns, of which the larvae usually make their cases ot fine sand and which have long fine antennae; Halford's Welshman's Button, a large dark, almost purple sedge, known on the Test as the 'Caperer'; The Great Red Sedge, Large Cinnamon Sedge, Speckled Peter, and Silver Sedge are other well-known varieties, all rather similar in appearance: brownish.

The Perlidae: or stone-flies are important to the rough-stream fisher, and the stone-fly itself is the moorland trout-fisher's equivalent of the may-fly. Strangely enough the most effective way of fishing it during its May and June hatching time is in the larval form, or creeper. This large nymph can be found in the shallows under stones, especially in the early morning when it crawls out to hatch on land. The creeper can be swung out on light tackle as in upstream worming. Very few fly dressings have been attempted of this large insect, but recently some foreign plastic nymphs have appeared notably from Norway and Italy: their value has at the time

of going to press yet to be proved. There are about twelve common species of *Perlidae*. The wings of all are small and back-folded, being flattish rather than sloped when at rest. In many of the males the wings are virtually useless for flight. The principal representatives of the group are: the February Red, the Early Brown, Needle-fly, Yellow Sally, Willow-fly, Stone-fly.

The Diptera: these are the two-winged flies which anglers usually refer to as gnats or smuts. Reed smuts are often taken infuriatingly by trout when bigger and better species, easier meals to represent artificially, are ignored. The reed smut is like a tiny house-fly. Most of them are too small to imitate successfully with an artificial fly-dressing.

The Chironomids: these are the midges, many of which hatch from the familiar bloodworm. The trout feed keenly on them, particularly on lakes. Blagdon has special dressings known as the Olive Midge and Green Midge. A dark Greenwell artificial sometimes works. The midges have long legs and a rather hump-backed appearance.

Among other flies that must be mentioned are: Angler's Curse, a pale-winged, minute two-tailed fly that is hard to imitate and frequently upsets fishing because the trout persist in taking it. The Alder, a member of the *Sialidae*, a fly that crawls out of the water to hatch, and frequently kills on all waters. Cow-dung fly, the small brownish fly seen on the excretion from which it gets its name.

Recommended reading: *An Angler's Entomology* by J. R. Harris ("New Naturalist" series).

NATIONAL FEDERATION OF ANGLERS: or N.F.A., the largest affiliating body for angling clubs in Great Britain. It does excellent work in all branches of angling, campaigning for better understanding between anglers and industry, acting as official arbiter in many disputes, and lobbying on vital issues such as the threatened closure of many canals. Its member clubs also organize and take part in the most famous of all match-fishing events, known to most as the 'All-England'. It must be added that

in good light away from the water: even actions such as casting should be practised blindfold, or at least in darkness, previously, in the garden. It is surprising what a difference darkness can make to an angler's control of his tackle. If an all-night session is planned, take warm soup in a vacuum flask, a comfortable seat and blankets. Even a warm August night can turn chilly in the small hours.

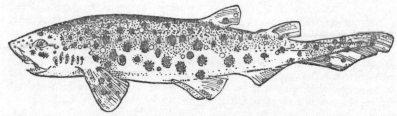

NURSEHOUND. *Also known as the Greater Spotted Dogfish or Bull-huss.*

the N.F.A. by no means represents all the anglers in Britain. There are still many other angling associations outside its orbit.

NIGHT-FISHING: some societies, and some River Boards, ban night fishing. In a few cases there is a sound reason. For instance, angling boats moored without lights on a busy river in summer could be a menace. Generally, however, there is no reason why anglers shouldn't fish throughout the night if they wish. For many species, in summer, night is the best time for sport. These species include: bream, carp, tench, eels, and sometimes roach.

If you go night-fishing the main thing is to see that all your staffwork is done well in advance. It isn't simply a question of packing a torch with your usual gear. Gear should be reduced to a minimum, hooks tied to hook-lengths and readily accessible, rods assembled

NORTHERN PIKE: American and Canadian name for our own pike, *Esox lucius.*

NOTTINGHAM STYLE: a method of casting by drawing additional loops of line from the reel, originally developed for giving extra distance to Trent fishermen, now the style adopted by the majority of coarse anglers. Treated fully under CASTING.

NURSEHOUND: *Scyliorhinus stellaris,* family *Scyliorhinidae.* A small shark growing to about five feet in length and found over rocky ground. It can be distinguished by its very rough texture and brownish skin covered with blotches. The nasal flap is double. Other names given to it by anglers are Greater Spotted Dogfish, Bounce and Bull-huss. The British record, from Poole, is 21 lb. A good fish is, however, an eight-pounder. Tope tackle should be used, the fish giving a good fight. Fresh fish baits will take these fish.

NYLON: a synthetic substance derived from coal, air and water, that has many of the properties of hair, silk and gut. Increasingly used by anglers in its many forms for casts and lines. Nylon monofil is made by the raw material being melted and forced through a small aperture into a current of cold air in which it solidifies as a filament. The filament is then stretched to about four times its original length. This process rearranges its molecular construction and gives it its strength.

NYMPH: the angler's term for the larval stages of aquatic flies. Though the perfectly formed fly has a remarkably short life—that of the may-fly is only a day or two—the larva lives for two to three years on the bottom. In this state is is highly mobile and feeds avidly on small vegetable, and sometimes animal, organisms. When it grows it splits its skin, or shuck, and emerges in bigger form, repeating this process many times during its life. Eventually it rises to the surface—in the

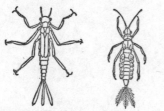

NYMPH. *The larva of the dragonfly (left) and may-fly (right)*

case of the may-fly family; or crawls out of the water, as with the alder— in order to hatch. Fish feed on the nymph at all stages, and when seen to be darting about on an established 'beat' sub-surface, or rolling over —'bulging'—just below the surface, they are almost certainly nymphing.

This is particularly true of chalk-stream trout.

NYMPH-FISHING: it was G. E. M. Skues (he took to fly-fishing late in life) who pioneered the theory of nymph-fishing. At first this was taken to be heresy since the diehard chalk-stream men of the Test and Itchen were wedded to the dry-fly, which, they believed, was the only artistic and gentlemanly way of taking trout. During the days when trout were uncatchable at the surface, Skues noticed that they were darting about taking nymphs. He therefore tied patterns of fly to imitate ephemerid nymphs. These had little hackle and slender bodies, and the merest suggestion of the wing-case which the nymph carries. It was no good fishing them downstream to the fish as in established sunken fly practice, for, in the clear chalk water, the angler was immediately visible and put the trout down. The nymph had to be fished upstream, and furthermore, to an individual fish that the angler had spotted. The technique at last found acceptance with the diehards, and is, in fact, every bit as skilful and satisfying as dry-fly work of which it is now a standard variation. Great nicety is needed to judge the 'future position' of the trout since it is frequently roving after nymphs on a small beat. Then, the take is by no means easy to spot, as difficult in fact as in upstream wet-fly fishing which nymphing greatly resembles. The angler may see the flash of the fish turning over, or the bulge it makes at the surface, or the disappearance of a few inches of gut. Good eyesight is essential for success with the nymph.

It might be described as upstream wet-fly fishing to a located fish.

O

OLD SCALE: the original method of numbering hooks by sizes, and that now mainly used by coarse anglers. In this scale the smallest hooks have the largest numbers. Thus the smallest hook that even a match-angler is likely to use is a No. 20. After reaching No. 1, at the ascending end of the scale, the numbering becomes 1/0 etc. up to 6/0. These large hooks are the ones generally used by sea fishermen. The New, or Pennell, Scale takes the reverse view, and is the system usually preferred by the trout fisherman. Here the largest sized hook is an 8, and the three smallest 0, 00, and 000 respectively.

OLIGOTROPHIC LAKES: lakes in which the lower layers are never depleted of oxygen during the warm weather. Their opposite, the eutrophic lakes, are always shallow, rich waters in which dead animal and vegetable matter falling to the bottom layers decays in warm weather and uses up oxygen. Oligotrophic lakes are not necessarily poor ones as far as life is concerned. They may be just that, of course, if there is not sufficient surface life to fall to the bottom in decay, in which case they are scientifically distinguished by the term 'edaphically oligotrophic'. Those lakes which are both rich and so deep that the fall of decaying organic matter never takes the oxygen from the depths are known as 'morphometrically oligotrophic'. This information, frankly, is not likely to help you catch more fish.

OPAH: a gloriously exotic creature mainly seen in south-western waters of the British Isles during very warm weather. It is otherwise known as the Kingfish, and also Sunfish, and grows to a weight of 50 lb. and a length of about four feet. It has an almost spherical body, blue at the dorsal surface, shading to red, to green, and eventually to pale yellow on the belly. It is covered with silver spots and has long anal and pectoral fins shaped something like those of fantail goldfish. It is also caught by professional long-line fishermen off the East Coast and in the Shetlands.

ORFE: *Leuciscus idus*, family *Cyprinidae*, sometimes called ide. Found in Continental waters and in its natural state coloured something

OTTER. *Serves fishery to some extent by eating a great many eels.*

like the carp. Breeding has produced a fancy fish-pond variety called the 'golden' orfe. They feed readily at the surface on fly life.

OTOLITHS: or earstones, a vital part of the auditory equipment of a fish. Otoliths also help a fish to maintain its balance in water.

OTTER: *Lutra vulgaris,* a large aquatic mammal, the dog sometimes weighing a stone-and-a-half and more. The otter lives in holes in the bank, or sometimes on the sea-shore in caves. The hole is called a 'holt'. The animals raise one litter a year and live largely by taking fish. They do, however, eat mice, voles, crayfish and frogs and destroy an enormous quantity of eels. When in playful mood they may kill hundreds of fish which they have no intention of eating: this is likely to happen when the parents are instructing cubs in hunting. The call is a whistle. Otters have a great sense of fun, making slides down the bank and diving off ledges rather like sea-lions. Keepers will often destroy them. In a salmon river they probably pay for their wickedness by keeping down the eels. Trout fishermen, particularly where a stocked lake is concerned, cannot afford to ignore them.

OTTER, Tackle Releasing: The angler's otter is a piece of equipment used for releasing tackle caught up on the bottom. It is invaluable, especially in fast-running streams. It consists merely of broom handle or similar wood about eighteen inches in length. An old piece of line, about 30 inches long, is tied to each end so that line and stick form a triangle. Now, at about one-third from one end of the line, tie in a chicken ring, or split ring. When caught up, the

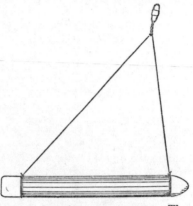

OTTER, TACKLE RELEASING. *The Hardy 'Giffard Smith' pattern of this useful device.*

angler slips the chicken ring over the reel line, lets the otter slide down into the water, and pays out line from his reel until the stick is well downstream of the obstruction. He then begins to wind in. The pull on the bait is now coming, because of the force of the stream on the otter, from beyond the bait. This will frequently shift it. As the released spoon comes back to the angler it catches in the ring and brings the tackle releaser back to the bank. I have often made otters at the riverside from a bit of branch and a spare length of nylon.

 P

PALMER: a type of artificial fly with a bushy body wound the whole length of the hook shank to make it look something like a 'woolly-bear' caterpillar.

PARR: the name given to young of salmon in the early stages of their river life. They then look remarkably like young brown trout. Apart from the parr markings, like finger tip marks, along the flanks, the parr's maxillary, or upper, jawbone reaches only to the centre of the eye. That of the brown trout extends beyond the eye.

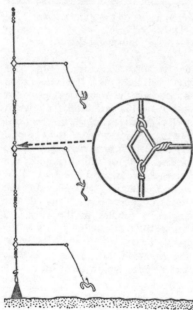

PATERNOSTER. *Three-boom sea paternoster showing, inset, the manner in which the booms are attached. A spiral fitting at the bottom enables the lead to be detached.*

PASTE: the name given to bread bait made from crumb of loaf and water. Paste can be made direct from flour and water. Some anglers like to mix in colouring or flavour, a favourite additive being custard powder. Paste bait when made up should be kept in a damp cloth and kept out of the sun. It differs from 'flake' in that it is tightly compressed dough: flake is loose crumb. Used mainly for roach, bream, carp and tench. Paste will take chub, particularly when flavoured with cheese, also dace in flood conditions.

PATENT-BAIT: a local name for the artificial sand-eel that is made of rubber.

PATERNOSTER: as far as freshwater is concerned, a complicated and untidy, but nonetheless effective gear used generally for fishing livebait in a fixed position. It probably takes it name from the medieval monks who were great fishermen. Because of its many appendages it may have been thought to have borne some resemblance to a monk's beads. Its essentials are always the same, though details vary. At the bottom is a heavy weight for keeping the tackle in one spot. Above this at intervals are fixed two or more wire or plastic booms. From these booms hang the hook lengths. For livebaiting the latter will be of fine wire.

The booms are free to turn round the central line of the paternoster so that a small bait can swim in circles in this limited orbit. When paternostering for perch the booms are often dispensed with: a hook link is then run direct from the central line.

Fishing from the weir apron at Hambleden, on the Thames.

Horning Ferry, a popular spot on the Norfolk Broads.

The tackle is ideal for fishing small holes in weed beds. When cast out some distance the gear tends to slope from bottom to rod top, which is a disadvantage. This can be avoided by fixing a large float at the exact depth of the water.

For sea anglers the paternoster is an invaluable piece of equipment for all sorts of ground-fishing for anything from bass to conger. All kinds of baits, but usually worms or pieces of fish, are used on it.

PELVIC FINS: the paired fins on the belly of a fish; known also as ventral fins.

PERCH: *Perca fluviatilis,* family *Percidae.* British record: 5 lb. 15 oz. 6 drams, from the Suffolk Stour. Perch cannot be confused with any other fish save possibly their poor relation, the ruffe. The perch has a humped back, and has a double dorsal fin, the front section of which is vigorously spined. In addition it has a spike on the rear of each gill-

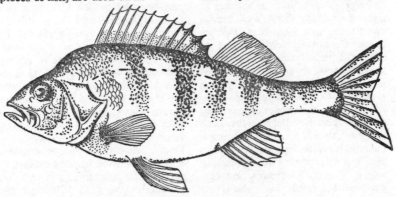

PERCH. *Readily identifiable by the pronounced striped pattern on its body and by its double dorsal fin, the perch is a freshwater predator. The front dorsal fin has sharp spines as do the gill covers.*

PEAL: West Country name for sea trout.

PECTORAL FINS: the breast fins of a fish, situated just behind the gill-covers and at about the level of the lateral line. These fins are used principally in turning.

PEG-DOWN: a match-fishing term that refers to a contest in which swims are previously marked out and drawn for. Each swim is usually at least ten yards long.

PELAGIC: a term used to describe forms of water life that live in the surface and upper layers. Those forms that frequent the bottom and near-bottom are called 'demersal' forms.

cover, and is marked with five to six black bars running from ridge of back to a little over halfway down the flank. The top of the back is dark green to black, the belly is white to yellow and the fins and tail a rich red. There are, however, considerable colour variations in fish from different waters. Even the stripes are absent in some specimens The perch is a fierce predator, preying on its own kind as well as on other fish of all species up to a quarter of a pound. The mouth, though apparently small, on opening expands like a Gladstone bag and can accommodate quite formidable loads. Perch swim in shoals, the smaller the fish, the larger the shoal. When the fish top the three-pound mark you do begin to find solitaries, but even at this weight two or three similarly sized fish will often be found swimming and hunting together. The stripes on the flank give the clue to the perch's method of attack. Like the pike it is a creature of ambush and is equipped with natural camouflage for the purpose. It can make only short bursts at any speed and seems to like to attack its target from behind. It appears to try to cripple the victim's tail before swallowing him head-first. But its tastes are not entirely confined to small fish: it will eat insects, larvae, shrimps, small frogs, eggs and almost any of the animiculae found on the river bed. On the whole, lakes seem to produce the larger specimens, possibly because the fish there do not have to waste energy fighting a current. Nevertheless, four-pounders and upwards do come out of running water. The chalk streams, notably, produce fine perch. But most rivers up and down the land have perch capable of filling a glass case. As a fighter the average perch is nothing spectacular. It pulls and jags at the line. The chief danger to the fisherman lies in the soft membrane of the mouth. A hook hold in this all too easily pulls out. A lot can be learnt by watching perch feeding in an aquarium. The fish take up the bait —say a worm—and suck it in then blow it out several times before swallowing it, a fact which accounts for the continual bobbing of the angler's float. Perch are 'on' all the year round. In winter rivers they move into the deeps, as do all species. Lake fish can be found after October in the deepest water the lake holds, being caught sometimes at a depth of thirty feet or more. Perch are extremely good to eat (I put them next to trout), being white, sweet and firm-fleshed. They can safely be grilled or fried with their scales left on. The latter are extremely hard to dislodge and won't come off in the cooking process.

PERCH-FISHING: perch can be caught in three ways: on bait, on livebait, and by spinning. I exclude the use of wet-fly (sea trout patterns), which will on occasion work, as being too out-of-the-way for most. Let's take bait first. There is only one worthwhile bait for perch and that is worm—brandling, lob or redworm. If a lob, it should be mounted on two- or three-hook Stewart or Pennell tackle to ensure connecting with your fish. Gentles will sometimes catch perch, as will the freshly extracted gills of another perch. Tackle can be any Avon rod with fixed-spool or centre-pin reel. Legering, trotting or sink-and-draw, in the latter the worm is cast out and worked back in jerks against or across the current, will all on occasions take fish. Whatever the bait, the angler must remember that his quarry will be found in a shoal. These shoals keep on the move. It seldom pays to stay in one place for perch angling, particularly after the first few fish have been caught.

It is said that a pricked fish fleeing from the hook will often panic the rest of the shoal and take them with it. From my own observation I believe there is a lot in this theory. Remember, if float fishing, to let the perch finish bobbing about before you strike. Walton said of perch: 'I will give you but this advise, that you give the perch time enough when he bites, for there was scarce any angler that has given him too much.' Walton was not very often right when it came to fishing technique but here he is certainly at the heart of the matter: on the other hand, the strike must be gauged to a nicety or else the perch will gorge the bait and you will hook him in the top of the gut. Strike when the float goes right under and away.

Small livebait usually take the best perch. A minnow, gudgeon, small fry of any species, including perch, all do well but of the lot I favour a nice fat minnow. These small livebaits can and should be fished on the lightest tackle possible. A quill float or a cork and quill will support a minnow, and, on this gear, the bait can be floated down to where the perch are shoaling. If the livebait is being fished in a fixed position, say in a gap between weeds, I like the float-paternoster. This is simply light paternoster gear surmounted by a float set at the exact depth of the water. The gear is thus vertical between float and weight, a great advantage if fishing at any distance from the bank, where a normal floatless paternoster would slope at a sharp angle to the bottom. When river fishing in winter this gear can be used by roaming from eddy to eddy: long stops should not be made in one place.

Perch are difficult fish to groundbait for. Almost the only way of enticing them is to groundbait for other fish—small ones. Stirring up the bottom for gudgeon often brings round the perch. Feeding the water with match-fisher's cloud bait will sometimes have the same effect.

Perch take almost any small, bright spinning lure. Tiny plugs, Devon minnows, wagtails, small dead fish such as bleak mounted on a spinning flight, and spoons all kill on occasions. The rod for perch spinning should be a light seven-footer of fibre glass or split-cane and the reel a fixed-spool armed with line not above a five-pounds

breaking strain. This gives the fish the best chance to show its paces. The spin should be fast and bright and be continued until the moment that the lure leaves the water. In summer, keep watch for perch attacking fry in the shallows and spin a small lure amongst them. Small Vibro spoons, Colorados, tear-drop or fly spoons, Mepps spoons, and kidney bar spoons remain my own favourites for taking perch. When handling perch the angler should be careful of the spines on dorsal fin and gill-covers as these can give unpleasant wounds.

PERLIDAE: a family of aquatic flies commonly called stone-flies. They are flies of rough streams and climb from the water to hatch. The *Perlidae* fold their wings back along the body so that they overlap the tail. The largest, the stone-fly itself, is called the 'may-fly' of the rough moorland streams. Over an inch long, it is deadliest when fished in larval form, when it is known as a 'creeper'. The needle-fly is the smallest of the tribe. Others include the willow-fly and February red.

PERLON: a proprietary brand of synthetic monofilament line.

pH: a scientific term that describes the acidity or alkalinity of a given water. pH7 is a norm. Below pH7 the water is an acid one, and an alkaline one if above that figure.

PHANTOM: a type of spinning lure made in close imitation of a fish but with spinning vanes at the head; trebles (usually three) are attached by wire flights. Practically indistinguishable in movement from a Devon and having no additional advantages.

PHARYNGEAL TEETH: these are throat teeth found in the *Cyprinidae*, the family of fishes which includes most of the coarse angler's quarry. The teeth are used to crush food against the bony palate and look something like an incomplete set of dentures. To the angler-scientist the teeth are invaluable in identifying doubtful species, though obviously the fish must be killed before examination can take place

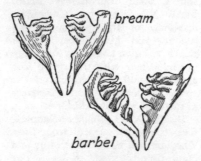

bream

barbel

PHARYNGEAL TEETH. *The throat-teeth of two species of freshwater fish*

Pharyngeals of individual cyprinids are of a varying formation. For instance, those of the carp, which are like human molars in shape, are set in three rows. Reading sideways across the mouth you see on each side of the 'jaw' a single tooth, another single tooth, and three teeth. Tench teeth are longer and narrower. Tench have five in one side and four in the other. Roach have five teeth one side and six the other. Chub teeth are in four rows —two, five, four and two: they are long and hooked.

PICK-UP: the part of a fixed-spool reel that engages with and pays back line on to the spool during recovery. Sometimes called the 'flier'. Practically all pick-ups these days are of the 'full bail' type in which the pick-up is made in one continuous loop of steel. The point over which the line passes needs to be specially hardened. Nylon soon cuts into insufficiently tempered metal.

PIKE: *Esox lucius*, family *Esocidae*. Record: Irish, 53 lb. from Lough Conn by John Garvin; Scottish, 47 lb. 11 oz. from Loch Lomond by Tom Morgan; English, 37½ lb. from Hants Avon by C. Warwick. The pike is the only fish of its kind in British freshwater though it has two close relatives in transatlantic waters—the muskellunge and the pickerel. In America and Canada our pike is known as the Northern Pike: the 'musky' is a bigger and fiercer fish, and the pickerel smaller.

In shape *Esox lucius* is built for sudden acceleration rather than sustained effort. All its motive power is grouped round the tail, and the dorsal and anal fins are therefore set well back. Its colouring is designed for camouflage—dark to olive green with primrose spots that blend easily with surrounding weed growth. The head of the pike is flat topped and the jaw pointed and armed formidably with teeth. Those of the lower jaw are seizing teeth like a series of dog's canines. The upper jaw is completely roofed with hundreds of 'ratchet' teeth sloping from front to rear. Once prey has been grabbed, these prevent it escaping. As long as the pike keeps a firm hold on its meal the latter can go only in one direction—down. For swallowing fish at least half the size of itself the jaw of the pike can expand enormously, so that when it is wide open one seems to be looking down a vast tunnel.

Pike thrive in both still and running water and there is every reason to think that they are of benefit to both—except in the case of stocked trout streams. There they definitely take trout in preference to anything else, and, since the trout are invariably living in competition with coarse fish, the presence of pike is undesirable to say the least. The trout angler's point of view can be better understood when the price of farm-raised fish is considered. In coarse fish waters pike, in reasonable numbers, are a useful property. Any water will support only a given weight of fish, just as a field will produce a crop only of a certain size and richness. The total weight will be distributed among the inhabitants of a water. Thus a lake poor in natural food and salts will, if unstocked with predatory fish, grow only a population of dwarf rudd or roach. Introduce some healthy pike and the total number

of pike. Slapton Ley in South Devon is a classic example. There specimen rudd abound: so do specimen pike. There is ample room for the growth and development of both species. The motto then for the fisherman is: don't ruthlessly slaughter every pike you catch. They are worth eating only when between 3 and 6 lb. Unless you want to put it in a glass case, slip the fish back.

The pike is a fish that always has captured the angler's imagination. Most tales of huge pike are unfounded, and few waters are sufficiently rich to hold pike of over

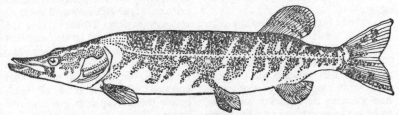

PIKE. *The fiercest predator in British lakes and rivers. It is able to swallow fish half its own size. This is a young fish of under 2 lb.*

of dwarf rudd or roach starts to fall. The total 'crop' of the lake is still the same. Some of it will have gone into making the pike fat; the rest will be split up among the remaining coarse fish. The net result will be large roach and rudd, though fewer of them. The pike will regulate their numbers according to food available, and will breed and survive in large numbers only where food is plentiful.

Large pike like eating small pike. If too many hatch out and reach the fingerling stage in a water that is poor in natural resources, the pike fry will quickly become a natural resource and will be gobbled up in large numbers. In a rich water—for coarse fishing at least—no one need ever worry about the presence

25 lb. The appetite of the pike is one of the things that gives rise to innumerable legends. There is little doubt that when really on the feed a pike can eat at least half its own weight in a day. Stories of big pike swallowing duckling, moorhens, and even full-sized mallard are authentic. So are stories of ten-pound pike being found choked to death with six-pounders stuck down their throats. That pike feed in a cycle that starts slowly and builds up to a crescendo seems also beyond doubt. There are days when the pike 'go mad' and everything and anything is gobbled up as soon as shown to them. These are the days on which livebait floats are attacked as soon as they are cast out. On other days, pike can be seen lying dormant amid

shoals of roach, with neither side taking the slightest notice of the other.

To attack, the pike likes to lie deep and watch his prey pass over his head, making a sudden upward swoop. The eyes of the fish are sighted for this purpose, being on top of the head. The pike also has binocular vision, which is much more use to it as a predator than the side-operating monocular eyes of fish such as roach and chub. The latter needs to be able to see all round at the side to save themselves from being surprised. The pike is interested primarily in aggression.

There is little doubt that the pike is highly sensitive to the vibrations set up by fish travelling nearby. He likes easy meat, and so the sick or wounded fish making an unusual beat as it passes along appeals to him because he knows it is going to be easier to catch than a fit member of the community. The pike therefore probably is able to sort out the unfamiliar vibration: this accounts for the success of spoons and plugs, all of which make a beat quite unlike any normal fish. I don't believe the pike's main benefit to fishing is that he takes the sick fish. They would die anyway. He is valuable because he takes any fish and thus ensures that the food supply will better suffice.

Experiments at Windermere have shown that pike do select their prey. Stomach contents of pike netted over a long period include more perch and trout than other species. Once swallowed a meal lasts a pike a remarkably short time. Its digestive juices are phenomenal. Stories of hooks being eaten away by stomach acids can safely be believed.

As with carp, there are numerous legends about the age to which pike grow. Twenty years is probably a maximum. Rate of growth depends on richness of water. In eight years in comparatively infertile Windermere a pike grows to an average of 28 inches; the same period in a fertile water such as Lough Conn would probably produce a fish of 40 inches (roughly a 20-pounder).

In spawning, pike are prolific. A female probably sheds at least 40,000 eggs. Few hatch out, of course. From an estimated 2 million 1,500 survivors were counted in one experiment.

Anglers are usually filled with admiration for the pike, admiration not unmixed with awe and even an element of fear. I believe that the latter can be traced to the fact that because of its binocular vision the pike is the only freshwater fish to look you full in the face. This coupled with the rows of teeth below the staring eyes can give one quite a shock.

PIKE-FISHING: when feeding naturally, pike do undoubtedly eat small crustaceans, worms, larvae, etc. However, the economy of predation is such that unless the trifle appears right under the pike's nose it is not worth the looking for: energy expended in hunting would scarcely be replaced by the reward. Except by accident, pike are rarely taken on worms or other normal bottom-fishing baits. The pike's natural food is fish and the bait to take him must, therefore, be a fish or a representation of one.

Live fish, or livebait, are the usual answer of the unadventurous fishermen, but recently there has been considerable development in a new form of pike fishing with deadbait. Great success with big pike has been obtained by using a herring on leger tackle. The theory is that pike can detect, probably through smell, the

oils given off by the dead herring.
One angler who has done a great
deal of work on deadbait experiments swears that in a canal the fish
will come from five hundred yards
distance, attracted by the herring
oils. Certainly the shark—which,
of course, is no relative of the
pike—is attracted by the 'rubby-
dubby' bag of chopped herring
which the big-game angler trails
over the side of his boat. If herring
oil does attract pike, then the
obvious inference is that you should
groundbait with crushed or chopped
herring.

Livebait is usually fished on float
gear and is attached to two-treble
Jardine snap-tackle which gives a
maximum chance of hooking in the
jaw with an almost immediate strike.
It should be kept in mind that the
pike looks upwards for his meals and
that the colder it is the deeper the
fish will tend to lie. The usual gear
is a big float (called a 'bung'), then
a swivel; attached to the swivel a
two- to three-foot trace of Alasticum
wire, another swivel, and attached
to this the snap-tackle. About two
feet from the snap-tackle on the
trace should be a lead to keep the
livebait working sufficiently deep: a
Jardine spiral lead does as well as
anything. As a refinement, a small
pilot float may be fixed to the line—
provided the rod is long enough—
above the bung—to keep the line
afloat. Incidentally, line for livebaiting needs to be well-greased, as
nothing is more fatal to the strike
than yards of sunken line. It takes
a good clean blow to put the hooks
home into a pike's bony jaw.

The only possible rod for this
work is a proper livebaiting rod.
Few good ones are specifically
designed. Thus you find anglers
using either barge-poles that give
the fish no chance (because a barge-
pole demands a correspondingly
thick line); or, fishing with a wand
that allows the fish a sporting chance
but is much over-strained by the
effort of throwing heavy tackle.
There are no light spinning rods
capable of casting a four- to six-
ounce fish, and bait as big as this
and far bigger will be needed on
occasions. The test curve of a
powerful rod like the Mark IV
carp rod allows for a casting weight
of only one-and-a-half ounces. One
answer is to throw the bait out by
hand, but this is a messy and unsure
procedure. If boat fishing, the bait
can be allowed to drift away with
wind or stream, but most pike
fishers are bank anglers.

Either a fixed-spool or free-running centre-pin drum reel serves
excellently at the butt end of the rod.

Livebait themselves have been
discussed elsewhere. I would select
my livebait in the following order of
preference: dace, rudd, roach, perch,
gudgeon. There is continual argu-
ment as to the size that a livebait
should be. I believe that if you seek
specimen pike then you should
persevere with really big baits. It's
quite true that big pike do eat small
fish, but it's obviously to their
advantage to get their meals in one
lump. You may lose a lot of smaller
fish by using baits of half-a-pound
and upwards, but sooner or later
you will click with a monster. The
Scottish record was taken on a roach
of over a pound. Though it is not
quite the same thing, a friend of
mine took a 42-pounder in the River
Boyle, Ireland, when trailing a one-
and-a-half-pound dead rudd. For
all-round pike anglers who just seek
good sport, I would advise baits of
not less than four ounces. All these
baits should be used on snap-tackle
with one treble through the ridge
of the back in front of the dorsal

fin and the other laid inside the gill-cover. Alternatively, with small baits, a single treble may be used as a lip-hook. If you object to these practices, as you are fully entitled to, livebaiting is not for you and you must turn to deadbait or spinning.

Two other methods of fishing livebait must be mentioned. In river flood conditions, when deep holes contain concentrations of hungry pike, success can often be had with livebait on leger tackle. For fishing between beds or in pin-pointed holes where exact presentation of the bait is necessary, paternoster gear, either with float or without, does well. A pike paternoster should have its hooks mounted on wire or plastic booms, clear of the central trace and free to revolve round it. For paternostering, smaller baits will generally be used: gudgeon do well in these circumstances, and pike have a definite liking for them.

We come now to spinning. All that has been said about the feeding habits of the pike show that it likes its prey to be crippled or at least incapable of full movement. Thus the spinning bait that imitates this ideal prey stands most chance of being snapped up. The spinner who can make his lure move along in fits and starts, rising and falling, hesitating and darting by turns, is likely to take pike: the man who simply winds in at an even rate is not going to be successful very often, and the angler who recovers his bait at full speed may catch a perch or two but it is doubtful whether he will touch many pike.

The ideal rod for pike spinning is of split-cane or fibre-glass and between seven and nine feet in length. At the heavy end of the scale a salmon spinning rod can be used with lines of up to twelve pounds. Most pike can be taken, however, on eight-pound lines. With spinning the big bait rules again applies. Big fish will be caught on spinning lures that either are large, as in the case of the six-inch Jim Vincent Broads Spoon, or on baits that give the impression of bulk by the way in which they spin. Among these I include the Horton Evans 'Vibro' spoons in their larger sizes, and also the old-fashioned kidney bar spoon. There are some extremely efficient miniature spoons of foreign make available, notably the Mepps, made in various sizes—all small.

Plug baits do excellently for the very reason that their action imitates the wounded fish of the pike's dreams. They have the added advantage that, since they do not revolve, no swivels are necessary on the trace. Among plugs some of the rubber French baits, such as the 'Plucky', work very well.

I myself, though, am more and more in favour of the old-fangled methods of using deadbaits on spinning tackle. Good, bright, freshly killed roach or rudd, or even bleak, make baits that obviously approach as closely as possible in texture, appearance and smell to the real thing. Even baits preserved in formalin have some of the qualities (smell excepted) of the genuine article. Luckily, there are numerous tackles that can give these baits the throb and thrust of life again.

Deadbaits can be spun, wobbled or fished sink-and-draw. Spinning flights can be bought to reproduce all three of these actions. Scarab tackle, for example, is a plastic sheath with spinning vanes at the nose into which deadbait is slipped. With wobbler gear, a central pliable stiffener is stuck down through the bait and the whole given a bend that

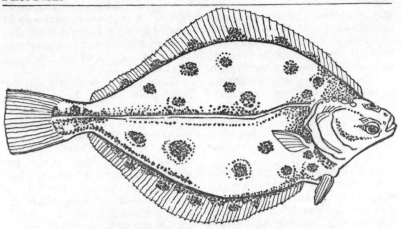

PLAICE. *It can be readily distinguished from other flatfish by the pattern of orange or reddish spots on its upper surface.*

the stiffener retains. The bend makes the bait wobble and dart when retrieved. Sink-and-draw tackle usually mounts the dead fish head downwards on the line: a weight is put inside it and treble hooks are wired to its flanks. The whole apparatus is allowed to dart and dash to the bottom, being retrieved in swoops towards the bank. Yet another variation puts the deadbait facing up the line with the weight two to three feet above it. This is a variation of sink-and-draw and wobbling which is properly called trolling. With all these the rule again is to make the bait limp home.

When spinning, the strike will come almost automatically as the angler feels the fish take hold. With livebait the angler should wait until the bung goes under and away, wind in any slack line, then strike at once.

To land a pike a gaff is permissible especially if the point is slipped in through the soft membrane in the bow of the lower jaw. This does the fish no harm if it is desired to return the pike to the water.

As to who takes the most pike, the spinner or the live-baiter, the matter has never been decided. My money is on a skilful spinner, however, for he has so many more tricks at his disposal.

PILOT FLOAT: small, round, bored float used for keeping the line afloat when livebaiting for pike. It may be left free to roam on the line or can be pegged to the line when the length of rod allows.

PLAICE: *Pleuronectes platessa,* family *Pleuronectidae.* The plaice can be distinguished from all other flatfish by its red spots. Just occasionally these are missing, and controversy begins. For the record, then, other identifying features are: eyes: on the right of the lateral line, small lumps of bone behind the eyes, teeth larger on the blind side of the fish. A three-and-a-half-pound fish is a specimen, though there are probably eight-pounders to be caught somewhere. The plaice hunts for molluscs and worms over muddy or sandy ground. All the usual baits will catch plaice, and to these squid, razor fish, and sprats must be added. The fish are usually caught on light paternoster gear either from shore or boat. One hook only is sufficient, since plaice rarely feed anywhere save on the bottom.

PLANKTON: a term to describe many different forms of minute surface and sub-surface life. Tiny crustaceans, molluscs, etc. Valuable food for fish of all sorts, including even such giants as the basking shark.

PLAYING A FISH: the principle is always the same. Maintain maximum strain on the fish as long as it is safe to do so. When you must, then let the fish run, but always against the maximum safe pressure you can exert. This pressure, no matter with what type of reel you are using (except big-game and heavy sea fishing) should come from the fingers rather than from any mechanical device. Slipping clutches, drags and the like are made to be set at a useful medium. In freshwater at least, when the fine limit of breaking point is neared, only finger pressure can be relied on, and sensitive finger pressure at that.

The other vital thing to be remembered is that a rod is exerting maximum strain when butt and line are at right-angles, even if the rod top is so bent as to be at right-angles to the butt also. To achieve this position, or any fraction of it, the rod must be kept up when playing the fish. Remember, too, that the springy nature of the rod top acts as a buffer to shock, and this resilience can work only if the rod is kept well up. An angle of seventy degrees from the horizontal is a fair working average.

When playing a powerful fish that must be turned before he reaches cover, side-strain plays an important part. A fish can often be turned by bringing the rod point down and putting on pressure momentarily in a more or less horizontal plane. But even so, the line and butt must still be at right-angles to get maximum results.

When the fish is played out, the landing-net should be well submerged before an attempt is made at landing the catch. Then the fish, preferably beaten and on its side, should be gently drawn over the sunken net and lifted. Never jab with the net or try to scoop the fish out. Even at this stage watch for a sudden last-minute rush which can break the line.

PLEASURE ANGLERS: a term, largely of abuse, used by match anglers to describe those who would rather fish on their own. A strange term when one considers that all angling is, presumably, done for pleasure.

PLUG: a type of lure, generally for pike, which dives and darts through the water rather than rotates like the conventional spinning bait. Plugs are divided into two main classes—sinkers and floaters. Practically all have a plate fixed to the nose so that the action of winding in causes them to dive.

With sinkers the plate is designed to give them more of a wobbling action. The floater can be splashed along on the surface, or made to dive at any depth according to how fast is the retrieve. In addition, there are 'poppers' that are worked on the surface until required to dive almost vertically. Sharp work with the reel causes them to disappear towards the bottom with a *plop*. Plugs come in all colours, and all seem to work well in different conditions. You can buy them single bodied or double-jointed according to taste and experience.

When fishing a plug no swivels are required since the bait imparts

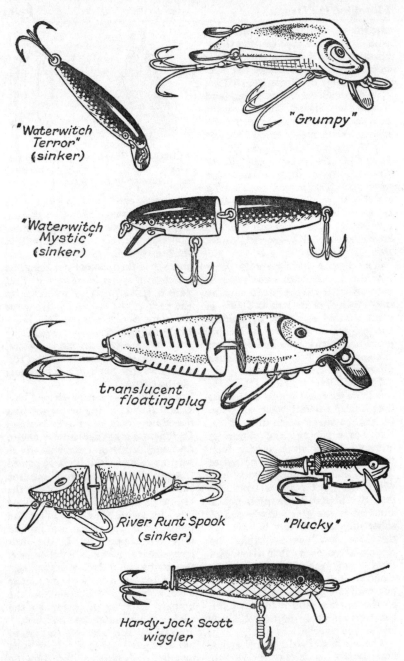

"Waterwitch
Terror"
(sinker)

"Grumpy"

"Waterwitch
Mystic"
(sinker)

translucent
floating plug

River Runt Spook
(sinker)

"Plucky"

Hardy-Jock Scott
wiggler

PLUG. *A few examples of the numerous forms of plugs available to the angler.*

no kink to the line. The Americans, who still make by far the most effective plug baits, produce them in infinite variety. Perhaps the most famous plugs of all are the Heddon Bait Company's 'River Runt' and 'River Runt Spook'. The Americans believe in fancy baits and fancier names. Witness—Meadow Mouse, Go Deeper Crab, Weedless Widow Jr., Old Zaragossa, and Crazy Crawler. Many of these are bass plugs and all come from the Heddon stable. At this moment the latest is a sonic plug which actually makes a noise—claimed to be attractive to fish—as it passes through the water.

The French have recently come into the market with some remarkably effective rubber plugs such as the 'Plucky'. This bait is about as good an impersonation of a small fish as you could imagine. British plugs are catching up and have the virtue of being far cheaper than those of foreign competitors.

PLUMBING THE DEPTH: this is an essential operation for the float angler in freshwater, and also for the sea angler when drift-lining. For coarse fishing, lead plummets are sold which have a wire loop through which the line is passed at the top, and a section of cork, into which the hook point is stuck, let into the bottom. The plummet is attached to the gear and allowed to shoot quickly to the bottom. If the float now lies flat, then the setting is too deep: if it disappears from sight, the float is set too shallow. If it stays at the surface, but with a slight slant, the bait is on the bottom. And if the float sits bolt upright, then the bait will fish just off the river or lake bed.

The sea-angler drift-lining from a boat needs to know the depth accurately. To find this he will

PLUMMET. *Two forms of this very useful gadget which is attached to the hook for determining the depth of a swim.*

probably used a hand-line with heavy weight attached. He casts out up-tide so that the weight finds bottom under his boat, then pulls in the line, measuring it with full arms' spans. He then counts out the same number of spans from his reel line, adds a fathom or two according to the pace of the current to allow for the slant of his line, and makes a mark on his reel line, preferably with waterproof sticking plaster. When this mark comes off the reel he knows that his bait is fishing just off the bottom.

PLUMMET: a cone-shaped lead weight having a ring at the top and a section of cork let into the bottom. Its function is to enable the angler to find the depth of the swim. It is used as follows: the hook is passed through the ring and stuck into the cork. Tackle with float set at the estimated depth is then dropped into the swim. The weight of the plummet is such that no normal float can support it. If the float immediately disappears, therefore, the setting is too shallow and adjustment must be made. Some plummets have a recess for tallow at the bottom in order to bring to the surface a sample of the river bed.

POINT: the last two feet or so of a tapered fly-cast. Since this invariably becomes shortened by the tying on and cutting off of different flies, the fly-angler always carries spare points which he ties on when necessary with a blood-knot.

POLARIZED LENSES: specially treated tinted lenses of immense value to the game fisherman specially since the use of them eliminates surface glare from the water. He is thus able to see the bottom. Trout and salmon can often be spotted when with the naked eye or plain dark glasses they would remain hidden. Polarized lenses have the effect of neutralizing surface glare. They also greatly relieve the eyes when float fishing. They can be bought as complete glasses, 'shields' or 'clip-ons'. Care must be taken if worn over other glasses to get them at the correct angle, or much of the effect will be lost.

POLLAN: another little-known member of the salmon group found in Ireland, where it is netted in great quantities for food. Loughs Neagh, Erne, and the Shannon Loughs all hold pollan. The fish is silver, has an adipose fin and seldom grows to more than twelve inches. Latin name: *Coregonus pollan.*

POLLACK: *Gadus pollachius,* family *Gadidae.* The pollack comes from the same family as the cod, hake, and haddock. The record, from Newquay, stands at 23¼ lb. A tenpounder can be reckoned as a most useful fish. The fish is olive green with a silver-white belly. The lower jaw sticks out well beyond the upper, and there is no barbule. Pollack are often found near rocks for the shelter of which they dive with great power when hooked. At night they rise closer to the surface, and are readily attracted by lights. They are poor eating.

POLLACK-FISHING: the best pollack fishing in Britain is to be found in the west. The rocky coastline seems to give the species everything they desire. Hooked on the right tackle the fish show considerably fight. Luckily they will take a wide range of baits including the usual fish, crab and worm baits, but also valve-rubber, rubber sandeels and strips of 'Porosand'. The recognized methods of catching pollack are drift-lining from a boat with strongish boat tackle; trolling with spinner or feathers. Pollack vastly prefer a moving bait so that even from a moored boat the bait should be constantly lifted by means of the rod and given a sink-and-draw motion. For the latter tactics a 6-lb. line fished from a two-pound test-curve rod will do well. Pollack

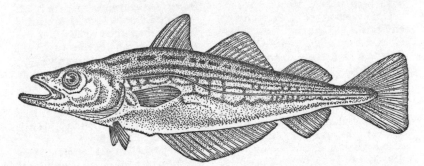

POLLACK. *A member of the cod family that is found in considerable numbers off the south-west coasts of Britain.*

can be taken by spinning from the rocks, though this is a difficult and specialised art. Rubber sand-eels prove deadly bait for this work: they are most effective armed with strips of fish skin. In the evening, float fishing with the bait set fairly shallow pays dividends. Pollack tend to rise towards the surface as night sets in. Bites vary from a quick vicious slash to a sly tug that strips the bait from the hook. The only possible answer is a sharp, decisive strike.

POLLUTION: with water extraction, the great evil of fishing today. Pollution can be caused by any industrial effluent or sewage outfall that is not treated adequately before being passed into the river. Pollution can kill outright by poisoning—as with cyanide: or it can deplete the river of oxygen to a point at which life can no longer exist: or it can cloud the water with suspended matter and sicken fish life, as with gravel and coal washings. There are many other ways in which pollution can attack our waters. Unfortunately there are not as many ways of fighting it. River Boards are vested with certain powers but owing to the diversity of interests represented on any River Board—fishing having a very small representation—these powers have been proved insufficient.

One method of redress exists, and this is at Common Law. There is an ancient right under Common Law that says that a riparian owner is entitled to the flow of water through his land as pure as it left his upstream neighbour. Many notable battles have been fought and won over this point, and this is entirely due to an organization called the Anglers' Co-operative Association. Individual subscription to the A.C.A. is one guinea per year; there are also club and association

memberships. The A.C.A. can act only on behalf of its members, however. The association provides expert legal and analytical aid to any of its members whose waters have been attacked. The cases successfully fought number many hundreds. Every fisherman would be well advised to subscribe if only as an insurance policy.

The most spectacular case ever fought by the A.C.A. was on behalf of a small working-men's angling club, the Pride of Derby A.A. with waters on the Derwent below Derby. When the River Derwent became an overheated sewer, the A.C.A. succeeded in a classic legal battle in getting injunctions against Derby Corporation, British Electricity Authority, and British Celanese. Renovations and alterations made necessary to plant-treating effluents are estimated to have cost over £2 million. One other thing should be added: pollution does not only attack fish; it attacks every living thing bordering rivers, including livestock and farmland.

POMERANIAN BREAM: the lower fins of this species are red, although in the main it resembles the silver bream, 'bream flat', or 'tinplate'. It is probably a cross between the silver or white bream (*Blicca bjoernka*) and a roach or rudd.

POPE: *Acerina cernua*, alternative name for the ruffe, a small fish of the family *Percidae*, having a drab, brownish appearance and only slight resemblance to the perch, mainly through its spined dorsal fins. Found in comparatively few rivers including the Thames. Will take worm or gentle avidly. Never deliberately fished for.

POND-LIFE: the whole elaborate structure of life in water, of which fish are the pinnacle, can best be studied in a still-water, preferably a small one. Everything in water is part of a food and life chain. This finally enables the fish themselve to live.

At the bottom end of the scale are the millions of small animals classified as zooplankton. Though most of these can be seen clearly with the naked eye they can only be studied accurately with a magnifying glass or, better still, microscope. Most of them are filter feeders, that is to say they pass water through some part of their system, extracting in the process the nourishment they need. Some so-called water-fleas, such as *Chydorus*, have paddle-shaped legs that help them to scuttled along and collect food. The movement of the legs draws water into the shell. Another variety, *cypris*, looks rather like a tiny bean and has small legs that enable it to move along the bottom; it, too, is a filter-feeder although it can consume comparatively large solids by pulling them into its shell. *Diaptomus and cyclops*

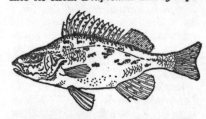

POPE. *Alternative name for the ruffe, a small member of the perch family. Its front dorsal fin has the characteristically sharp spines.*

look similar with their elongated, carrot-shaped bodies and long feelers. The female cyclops carries two egg bags at the rear of her body. Both these animals can deal with quite big food particles.

Next come the freshwater molluscs, of which there are a surprising number. The biggest is the freshwater, or swan, mussel which has a

special process for spreading its kind. The young mussels develop inside the parent shell and then launch themselves into open water by means of opening and closing movements of their shells. At this time they trail a long sticky filament that becomes entangled with weeds. There the baby mussel waits for a passing fish, hooks itself on and grows into the scales of the fish, the host producing a cyst to cover it. After some three months of feeding on the fish the mussel drops off to live its own life.

There are two kinds of freshwater cockles: the pea-shell variety which are very small and have a pinkish shell, and the orb-shell cockle with a brownish and much larger shell.

There are also two main kinds of water-snail, the species that look very like a garden snail (these are the pond-snails) and the trumpet snails with the curled, horn-like shell. The main varieties are: giant pond-snail (large, twisted pointed shell); dwarf pond-snail (tiny miniature of the former); wandering snail, a mollusc that falls in size somewhere between these two; trumpet snail (a very small, horn-shelled mollusc); the ramshorn (very large, horn-shelled snail).

Also among the freshwater molluscs are the limpets, a very small replica of the sea variety; and the freshwater winkle, perhaps the biggest of all the freshwater shelled species. All the snails come to the surface to breathe. The winkle however, has gills, while the limpet gets its oxygen direct from the water. But whereas the molluscs are mainly vegetarian many of the pond insects are fiercely predatory. The jungle world in which they live can hardly be imagined without a shudder.

Take for instance the nymphs of the various dragon-flies. These are equipped with a rapidly extending mask that can shoot out and seize its prey in order to pull it to the mouth for other jaws to tear up. The best-known dragon-flies are: (1), *Coenagrion-puella*, the slender blue-bodied creature popularly known as the damsel-fly. (2) *Aeshna cyanea*, a far larger slender-bodied dragon-fly. (3) *Agrion splendens*, like the damsel-fly but slightly larger and having coloured wings. (4), *Libellula depressa*, the largest dragon-fly of all with a thick stubby body.

The larvae of the great diving beetle (*Dytiscus*) have especially horrible habits. These large insects seize their victims with long front legs, puncture them with a needle-like projection, inject them with digestive fluid that turns their flesh to liquid form, and then feed by sucking the nourishment back into their own bodies. The water scorpion (*Nepa cinerea*) behaves in much the same way, and can often be seen poised for action hanging from the surface film. All the water beetles and bugs, of which latter the scorpion is one, breathe directly from the air. When seen in the sub-surface position, the scorpion is taking in oxygen through a schnorkel-like tube fixed to its rear end.

The other main insect carnivores are: the whirligig beetle, a small oval creature that can be seen swimming round and round at the surface; the water-boatman, which swims upside down, propelling itself by means of its long legs; the water-spider, which not only traps its prey, as does the great diving beetle, but kills it with a poison injection before pumping it full of liquefying saliva, and then sucking its liquid flesh back as food. The water-spider, which looks very like a medium-sized land version, is remarkable in that it carries below the surface a coating of air bubbles attached to its body. Once down below it shakes the bubbles off into a web that it has previously spun. As more and more air accumulates in this web, the latter balloons upwards towards the surface. Eventually the spider has a comfortable diving bell of its own construction filled with air in which it can live and lay its eggs below the surface.

Among the insects that these and other creatures prey on must be included the larvae of most of the fishermen's flies: the caddis family the stone-flies, the may-fly group and the mosquito and midge groups. These are practically entirely vegetarian.

This picture by no means exhausts the list of a typical pond's inhabitants. There are the amphibia: the common frogs, toads (common and natterjack), smooth and crested newts, the fish themselves, birds, water-shrews, and voles. Also the pond-skaters and freshwater shrimps (a very important item of fish food, for which some running water is essential). The woodlice-like pond-skaters crawl about on water plants. There are also the flatworms and leeches.

Recommended reading: *Life in Lakes and Rivers* by T. T. Macan and E. B. Worthington (Collins' "New Naturalist" series.)

POROSAND: a proprietary form of plastic bait which is bought in strips and can be cut up to resemble ragworms, sand-eels, etc., for trailing and spinning: very effective.

POUTING: or pout whiting, *Gadus luscus*, family *Gadidae*. A marine fish similar to the whiting proper, except that it has a barbule beneath the chin and tends to look shorter and more squat. In habit it differs also in that the whiting

Safely in the net — a 7-lb. pike taken at Wallingford-on-Thames.

Examining the stomach contents of a freshly caught trout.

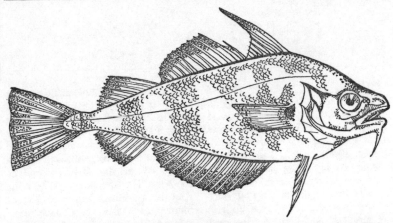

POUTING. *This member of the cod family is known also as the pout whiting.*

prefers a sandy bottom while the pouting likes rocky ground. Pout can be taken on light paternoster gear and will eat almost anything offered, including worms, mussels, and fish baits. Another distinguishing feature is the four broad bronze bands on the flank.

POWAN: *Coregonus clupeoides* is the Scottish version of the Irish pollan. Silver in colour with a roughly dace-like appearance and an adipose fin. Swarms in Lochs Esk and Lomond. The fish are netted rather than caught with rod and line.

PRESERVING BAITS: bleak, gudgeon, small roach, or rudd, minnows and fishmonger's sprats all make good spinning baits for use with sink-and-draw tackle or on spinning flights. To preserve them, put the fish when fresh into a solution comprising one tablespoonful of formalin to one pint of water. Leave them in it for two days. Wash the baits in cold water then place them in a shallow dish filled with a syrup made from one part of sugar to four of water. Bottle in syrup in airtight jars.

PRIEST: a weighted club for killing fish quickly. The name comes from an old fishing joke. A killed fish was said to have been 'visited by the priest'.

PUMP, To: an expression meaning to raise a fish that has 'sounded' or sunk to the bottom. The trick is to wind the rod top down towards the fish and then raise it with steady pressure, thus regaining a little line at a time.

PURE RIVERS SOCIETY: an active anti-pollution body.

 Q

QUILL: birds' primary feather quills are used both in fly-tying, where the quill in strips is wound round the hook shank to form a body (notable examples: Orange Quill, Ginger Quill, etc.), and also in making coarse fishing floats. Minute floats can be made from song-bird feathers but these are suitable only for livebait catching. Crow quill is the smallest for general all-round use. while really heavy floats are made from swan, goose, and porcupine quills. Any large feather should be picked up and saved. To make a float, strip off the fibres, cut almost through at the feather tip end but leave a strip of quill attached. Slip a wire or nylon loop over this quill strip and bend the quill back against the body of the float. Whip the loose quill to the body to hold the ring in position. The addition of paint and a float cap made from valve-rubber completes the job For added buoyancy a balsa or cork body can be mounted round the quill and glued to it.

 R

RAY, STINGRAY: See SKATES AND RAYS.

RAZOR-FISH: sometimes called spout fish, scientific name *Ensis*

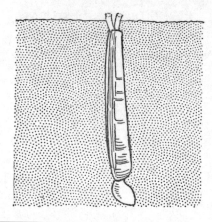

RAZOR FISH. *A useful bait which may be found on the beach at low tide.*

siliqua. The species has a long shell like an old-fashioned cut-throat razor in shape and grows to about eight inches in length. Razor-fish make valuable bait when removed from the shell. They can be spotted in the sand at low tide by the keyhole-shaped depression they leave. Razor-fish can burrow quickly, so light footwork is essential if you wish to catch them. A two-barbed spear made from two straightened and re-tempered sea hooks fixed to a wooden handle is the ideal weapon. This is plunged quickly down the burrow and withdrawn once the barbs have taken hold.

REDD: gravel shallows on which salmon and trout spawn.

REELS, Freshwater: here are brief notes on the main types.

Drum or Nottingham reel: This can be as plain as you like.

Allcock Aerialite

Orlando III Supreme

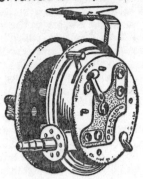

SEA REELS

Featherflo

Milbro Favourite

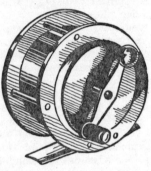

FRESHWATER REELS

Hardy's "Perfect"

"Gildex 2"

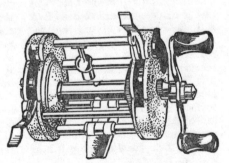

FLY-REEL

MULTIPLYING REEL

REELS. *Some examples of drum-type reels for anglers.*

Some of the old wooden 'starback' reels, so called because of the star-shaped brass frame on which they are mounted, still give excellent service. About the only refinement they have is a check that can be put on or off.

Centre-pin: this is a drum reel but with a difference. It is extremely free-running being mounted at its central axis on a carefully machined steel pivot. Often the reel has bronze bearings. Moreover, for lightness it will be made of alloy and cut away as much as strength permits. This is the kind of reel needed for long-trotting and swimming the stream. There are many excellent patterns. It usually has a line-guide.

Fixed-spool: in the first place this reel was designed for throwing light spinning baits long distances. Its main features are: a drum or spool mounted at right-angles to the axis of the rod; a slipping clutch; a pick-up arm, and stepped-up helical gearing to speed recovery of line. Some patterns have anti-backwind devices and audible checks to indicate when fish are taking line.

Multiplier: this is essentially a geared drum reel of an exceptionally free-running variety. It should be used on a short bait-casting rod when it is fished on top of the butt. The cast is made with an overhead flick and the reel is braked by the angler's thumb being pressed on the revolving drum or spool. For recovery the multiplier has a travelling line guide that distributes line evenly across its drum's rather wide surface. Another feature of most multipliers is an adjustable drag by which tension can be put on a running fish. Ideal for plug fishing and beach casting.

Fly-reel: a fly-reel does not need to be at all complicated. It must take up to thirty yards of fly line

and backing. Above all it needs a sweet-sounding check. When buying a fly-reel you should first try it on the rod, as balance of the outfit is all-important. Some American fly-reels have a self-retrieving device. As the angler strips off line to cast he winds up a spring. Press a trigger and the drum winds back its own line. Useful, possibly, with a big fish running towards you.

Drum, multiplier and fixed-spool reels are all made in larger sizes for sea fishing.

REELS, Sea: in general sea reels are simply larger versions of their freshwater counterparts. Line capacity is a vital factor as is adequate braking power to stop or tire a runaway fish. The main types of reel used by the sea angler are:

Centre-pin or Nottingham reel: the drum should never be under 3½ in. in diameter and, where big fish are expected, 4–4½ in. may be advisable.

Fixed-spool reel: the advantages of this weapon remain the same as they are in freshwater fishing, namely that a light lure can be cast long distances provided it is attached to a light line. Though big salt water versions of some fixed-spools are made to take lines up to 30-lb. breaking strain, much of the advantage in casting is lost when lines of this size are used. Moreover, it is not the easiest reel on which to play a really big, strong fish. Fixed-spools are useful when float fishing in salt water.

Multiplying reel: ideal for casting from the beach. Many sea anglers favour free-running multipliers in which the rotation of the spool during casting is checked and controlled by the angler's thumb. More complicated multipliers employ magnetic brakes, centrifugal governors, and so on, which guard against an over-run during casting. However, sea reels being exposed to salt and sand as well as water should, perhaps, be kept as simple as possible. Sea fishing reels should be of non-corrosive metals. As a precaution against rust they should always be washed in fresh water after use and kept well oiled. Two hundred to 250 yards is a useful line capacity for any sea reel.

Big-game reels: these are in a class of their own. Large drum reels can be used to play fish of 100 lb. or slightly more provided they are fitted with a powerful brake. However the damage done to the angler's hands and fingers by madly gyrating reel handles can be considerable. Most big-game reels are really out-size multipliers embodying a clutch which is tightened against a running fish by a star wheel or capstan bar: the clutches are specially designed to lose the great heat generated by the friction set up when a big 'un

runs. The gear ratio of such reels is 2½ to 1, or thereabouts. They have a single handle and the reel is locked or screwed to the rod butt. Lugs on top of the reel, which is fished above the rod, connect with the straps from the angler's harness. The reel thus takes the double strain of fish pulling down and angler bending his weight back. A big-game reel may hold 500 yards of line and weigh as much as 8 lb.

REFRACTION: this is a question of vital importance to the angler who wishes at all times to keep out of sight of his fish. Discussing the trout's WINDOW in another section I said that the trout, or any other fish, saw through the surface at a fixed angle only. This angle is just over 48 degrees to the vertical and applies at whatever depth the fish may be lying. The fish can only see out through the surface as though through an inverted cone the sides of which form an

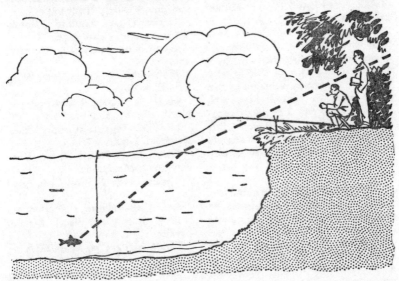

REFRACTION. *Owing to the bending, or refraction, of light rays the bystander would be within the fish's range of vision, whereas the angler would not.*

angle of approximately 97 degrees. This might make it seem that the angler is invisible unless he is standing almost on top of the fish. Unfortunately this is far from so. Light rays, on entering the heavier medium, water, from the lighter medium, air, are bent or refracted. This means that the line of the fish's vision which passes to the surface at an angle of 48 degrees to the vertical is suddenly bent downward at the surface to an angle of about 12 degrees to the surface. The motto is that to be unseen you must keep mighty low down on the bank.

RISE: the term given by fly-fishermen to a hatch of fly, or, more correctly, to trout reacting to a hatch of fly. The best moment, perhaps, of a trout angler's day is the evening rise which usually takes place as twilight falls. A rise: the disturbance made by an individual fish taking food from the surface.

RIVER BOARDS: the powers of these important bodies are defined in the River Boards Act, 1948. Broadly speaking, the Boards have total authority over everything the angler does. He must obey their bye-laws as to methods of fishing, size of fish to be taken, numbers of fish to be taken or kept in keep-nets, close seasons, etc. The Boards impose licence fees and their bailiffs can start proceedings against anglers who fail to obtain licences before fishing, or indeed break any other bye-law.

One Board usually administers one river, but in some of the smaller counties a group of rivers fed by one catchment area will come under the jurisdiction of one authority as, for instance, the Cornwall River Board. As far as the fisherman is concerned, the most important member of the Board is the Fisheries Officer. If he is alive to his job he can improve

fishing conditions by encouraging insect life, seeing that there are adequate spawning grounds, restocking, and watching the pollution problem.

Here are some River Boards and their addresses. (See also Appendix.)

Avon & Dorset: Rostherne, 3 St. Stephens Road, Bournemouth.

Bristol Avon: 18 Bennett Street, Bath.

Cheshire: County Hall, Chester.

Cornwall: St. John's, Western Road, Launceston.

Cumberland: River Board House, London Road, Carlisle.

Dee & Clwyd: 45 Nicholas Street, Chester.

Devon: The Castle, Exeter.

East Suffolk & Norfolk: 'The Cedars', Albemarle Road, Norwich.

East Sussex: 1 Upper Lake, Battle, Sussex.

Essex: Rivers House, Springfield Road, Chelmsford, Essex.

Glamorgan: 'Tremains House', Coychurch Road, Bridgend.

Great Ouse: Elmhurst, Brookands Avenue, Cambridge.

Gwynedd: Highfield, Caernarvon.

Hampshire: The Castle, Winchester.

Hull & East Yorkshire: 37 North Bar Within, Beverley.

Isle of Wight: County Hall, Newport, Isle of Wight.

Kent: River Board House, London Road, Maidstone.

Lancashire: 48 West Cliff, Preston.

Lee Conservancy: Brettenham House, Lancaster Place, Strand, London, W.C.2.

Lincolnshire: 50 Wide Bargate, Boston.

Mersey: Liverpool Road, Great Sankey, Warrington.

Nene: North Street, Oundle, Peterborough.

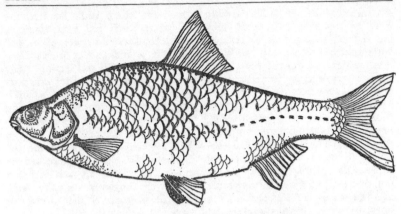

ROACH. *Widely distributed throughout the lakes and waterways of England and Wales, the handsome roach is the most popular quarry of the freshwater angler. Its reddish fins are less strong in colour than those of the rudd.*

Northumberland and Tyneside: 'Dunira', Osborne Road, Newcastle-upon-Tyne, 2.

Severn: Portland House, Church Street, Great Malvern, Worcestershire.

Somerset: 12 King Square, Bridgwater.

South West Wales: Penyfai House, Penyfai Lane, Llanelly.

Thames Conservancy: 2/3 Norfolk Street, Strand, London, W.C.2.

Trent: 206 Derby Road, Nottingham.

Usk: 'The Croft', Goldcroft Common, Caerleon, Newport, Mon.

Wear & Tees: 'Greencroft East', 158 Coniscliffe Road, Darlington.

Welland: 11 Market Place, Spalding, Lincs.

West Sussex: County Hall, Chichester.

Wye: 20 East Street, Hereford.

Yorkshire Ouse: 21 Park Square South, Leeds, 1.

ROACH: *Rutilus rutilus,* family *Cyprinidae.* British record: 3 lb. 14 oz. from Hampton Reservoir by Bill Penney. Roach are as universal as perch. From the chalk stream to the gravel pit, from the Fenland drains to the Thames they will be found in quantity, though not always in quality. A good roach weighs a pound; a roach to be pleased with, a pound-and-a-half; a roach to put in a glass case, two pounds; and the roach of a lifetime anything from two-and-a-half pounds upwards. Small roach are astonishingly easy to catch but big ones are frustratingly difficult.

In appearance the roach is a silver fish with large scales that have a bluish tinge on the flanks. The fins are reddish. Along the lateral line they have between 40 and 46 scales; in a transverse count from root of dorsal to lateral line there are between 7 and 9 scales. The dorsal fin has three simple rays (no bifurcations) and 9–11 branched rays; the anal fin, three simple and 9–12 branched. The underlip of the roach is overlapped slightly by the upper lip (the fish is a bottom feeder).

Unfortunately it is possible to confuse a roach with a number of other fish. Small chub are often mistaken for large roach. Rudd have a similarity that is only partially offset by colouring differences (they are redder, particularly as to eye, with golden sheen), and the facts that the dorsal fin of the rudd is set further back, and the underlip overlaps the upper slightly. Then, alas, we come to the hybrids, for the roach interbreeds freely with bleak, bream and rudd. Sometimes a mixture of characteristics can be detected by the trained observer. To try to describe possible means of detection of crossbred roach is impossible in a few words. I think perhaps the safest advice to give any angler who fancies he has caught a two-pound roach is: if there is a competition or award at stake, submit two or three scales of the fish to an expert, or to an angling paper for a decision.

Roach are vegetarian by nature rather than carnivorous (I include larvae, etc. among a vegetable diet to distinguish it from a predatory menu). Early in the season they will, without doubt, take small fry. They breed prolifically in all waters, holding on grimly against pollution. However, they grow best in clear rich water, and nowhere better than the Hampshire Avon and Dorset Stoue. In fighting qualities the roach varies immensely. The Avon fish will give you a battle all the way to the net while a gravel pit fish of similar weight may come in with scarcely a struggle. Roach are shoal fish, the shoals containing fish of mixed sizes. The angler finds roach a testing quarry in that they show immense caution in approaching the bait and great stealth in taking it.

ROACH-FISHING: this is the basic fishing of Britain's two million or more coarse anglers, so that every possible style and every imaginable kind of tackle is used in pursuit of roach. Unfortunately, the universality of the roach has given rise to the term 'roach rod'. In fact, the so-called roach rod sold by some tackle makers is a poor effort, and no sort of rod at all. As has been pointed out in the rod section, every rod is ideally designed for one purpose. The rod that would be ideal for catching roach in a Fenland drain would make a poor showing on, say, the Kennet. The Thames rod certainly wouldn't do for the Witham. So, plainly, there can be no such thing as a roach rod that will work anywhere equally well, regardless of size of fish or state of water.

The thing to do, therefore, is to consider varying styles of roach and roach fishing and the rods that individually suit them.

The roach, first of all, is the match angler's stand-by. The competition fisher catches a great number of small roach, often in clear, over-fished water. It follows that he must fish far off, with fine tackle, and light floats. The match rod and the Sheffield style has been developed over the years to cope with these problems. The match rod is all tip-action. Roach do not fight strenuously, at least below a pound, and few pounders come to the Sheffield man: a tip-action rod can therefore deal with his quarry. The rod is used with a vertical flick something like that of the fly-caster. The line is very fine monofilament, perhaps of only a pound-and-a-half breaking strain. Floats are tiny quills and hooks are minute affairs sized 14–20, Redditch scale. The reel will usually be a centre-pin but increasingly often a fixed-spool. The bait is usually a single gentle, and the groundbait is cloud or feeder maggots put into the swim a little and often. The bite given in such roach fishing is a mere flicker and the strike has to be quick and sharp to put the hook home. Sometimes the float merely moves sideways, or lifts a fraction.

The Hampshire Avon man is at the other extreme. His roach are big and powerful just as his river is big and powerful. The only thing he has in common with the Sheffield man is the clarity of the water. He, too, will have to seek his fish far off, and the probability is that he will do so by long-trotting. Using this technique he will sometimes swim his gear down thirty or even fifty yards to the fish. To pull out this length of four- or five-pound monofilament from the reel will demand a heavy float and correspondingly heavy shotting, also a freely running centre-pin reel. The float will usually be a cork and quill capable of supporting quite a large bored bullet or else 14–16 medium shot. This heavy weighting is also necessary to keep the bait down where the fish are. On the hook the Avon man will use a much more generous bait than the Sheffield angler. Breadcubes of up to half-an-inch in length, bunches of three or four maggots, or large pieces of flake will be needed to entice the one- and two-pounders that are the quarry.

Similarly the rod will have to be suited to the river. To lift forty yards of line in a long-range strike as the float flashes under far downstream requires a rod with action throughout its length. The most famous of Hampshire chalk streams has given a generic title to all powerful yet sensitive rods. They are called Avon rods, and are usually of three pieces, made of the best splitcane and are capable of striking a hook home into quick-biting roach or fighting it out with a big barbel. They would prove too heavy and whippy for the matchman, but, outside his specialist orbit, they are the finest all-round coarse rods made. It needs only to be added that groundbait must match the stream, too. Avon groundbait should be rich, puddingy stuff that can hold the bottom like an anchor and only gradually break up to drift down between the weed channels to the waiting fish.

Variations of both the Sheffield and Avon styles are endless and will be found up and down the country on rivers of all sizes, pace and clarity. Often there is a compromise between some of the best features of each. Perhaps most anglers refer to their technique as the Nottingham style, but since this term really only refers to a method of casting, a method that is rapidly losing its importance as the fixed-spool reel and first-class centre-pin gain more and more ground, I don't propose to dwell on it: the Nottingham style of casting is described in the CASTING section.

Some of the biggest roach ever taken—including the record fish— have been caught regering, and this is the method used by most stillwater experts. Breadpaste or flake is the bait most likely to succeed, and, in deep water lakes such as reservoirs, success is most likely to come when the angler disdains comfort and decides to fish with the wind in his face. The action of the wind on deep still-waters is fully described under THERMOCLINE. All the principles of legering apply to roach, only more so. The roach is a very shy fish and every care must be taken to see that the line can pass freely through its attachment to the leger weight.

Roach can be taken on a number of baits, the most successful of which are maggots, bread cube, flake or paste, wheat, barley, rice, hempseed, caddis. They will also take both dry- and wet-fly, especially early in the season. Occasional roach are landed on small livebait, by accident.

ROACH-POLE: this type of rod has now largely been abandoned, though it was once much seen on the Thames and the Lea. It is usually between 17 and 20 feet in length, and of five sections made of whole cane with a whalebone or split-cane tip. The butt is often weighted with mahogany and lead so that the angler can maintain balance when fishing. The line, which is as long as the rod plus the top joint, is fixed to the tip with a special knot consisting of two twists, a half hitch and a bow. For resting the roach-pole the angler uses two supports, one U-shaped and the other O-shaped. The latter, of course, is designed to hold the butt of the rod.

The great virtue of the roach-pole is that it enables the angler to fish exactly over his float and to drop in most precisely. Extremely big fish can be played successfully by the skilful angler. The art consists in preventing the fish from 'pointing' you, that is to say escaping to a position at which it can exert a straight pull on the rod tip. The expert is able to stay above his fish and keep the most telling strain on it. When landing a fish the roach-pole angler frequently dismounts the bottom two joints of his rod so that the quarry can be swung easily to net. Some match anglers who habitually fish waters where only very small roach are encountered, use a French variation of the roach-pole (French anglers are great fixed-line men). A 'French Cane' is of 13–19 feet in length and has the line fixed to the tip by six inches of three sixteenths cata pult elastic which in turn is whipped to the rod top.

RODS, Freshwater: there are two vital considerations in choosing a rod. The first is that it must be suitable for the job of work you have in mind. The second, that you like the look of it and the feel of it, for you will be in its company, all being well, for a number of years. The question of fitness for purpose is all-important. For example, there is no such thing as an all-round rod. There are combination rods, it is true. These enable you to change tops, bottoms and middle joints around until you have produced permutations and combinations suitable for several types of fishing. But even the makers of these rods don't claim that they are the answer. One rod, one task, remains a basic rule.

What task have you in mind? The build and action of the rod will differ in each case. Let's look first at the rod which demands minimum action throughout its length—the match rod.

The match fisherman is not primarily concerned with big fish. In fact, his aim in life is to extract from the water in quick succession a multitude of small fish. If he hooks into something of two pounds or more it's likely to be a bream, and bream give little fight. He can therefore afford to have a long (for getting out far from the bank), light (because he will be handling it continuously for perhaps five hours), stiff (because big fish are not expected), weapon with all its action in the tip. The match rod may be 12 or 13 feet in length with bottom and middle joints of hollow Spanish reed, and tip of split cane or fibre-glass. Because he will be using super-light lines that stick to a rod when wet, the match man will take care to see that his weapon is equipped with high bridge or stand-off rings.

The same rod faced with a four-pound tench or barbel would be quite inadequate, however. The nearest thing to an all-round float fishing rod that can be found is one of the many three-piece Avon types having at least two split-cane joints. These are sensitive enough to strike a quick-biting roach yet have a powerful action if a big fish has to be subdued.

Spinning rods are of two main kinds. The so-called light spinner, between six and eight feet in length, is designed for flipping a small spinning bait thirty or more yards. Built of split-cane or fibre-glass, this rod, if skilfully used, will stand up to any fish swimming in British waters.

The second spinner is the short bait-casting rod. Perhaps only five feet in length and made in one piece, this has a detachable handle or butt with a special winch fitting. The latter is offset to take a multiplier, the correct reel for this type of fishing. Moreover, the reel is seated on top of the rod, for the cast is made with an overhead flick, the thumb being used to brake the rotating spool of the multiplier.

Heavier spinning rods are made, of course, particularly for salmon fishing. An example of first-class workmanship is the Milward 'Spinversa' that has a reverse taper under the butt, fining down towards the butt cap. Richard Walker's 'Mark IV' comes into the same class. Though Walker's rod was designed primarily for carp, it makes a first-class salmon or heavy pike spinning rod.

Livebaiting again requires its own weapon. The problem here is that of dealing with large weights. When bait and lead are reckoned with, anything up to half-a-pound may have to be cast. Obviously, considerable backbone is necessary in such a rod. But a stiff, stubby rod means poor sport, and will need an ultra-heavy line.

Fly rods are something quite apart. Here action is needed all the way since the drive given to a fly-line comes right from the wrist. Split-cane is the accepted material for the best fly-rods. Greenheart, these days, tends to be unseasoned and unreliable, though the wood when sound gives a beautiful action. Fibre-glass is coming up fast as a material for use in fly-rods. Lengths vary from six-and-a-half feet for small brook trout to eleven feet for sea trout. Dry-fly rods are far stiffer in the action than those for use with the wet-fly. The reason is that a dry-fly has to be driven through the air to a closely defined target. Moreover the fly is picked up off the water after the cast with the line floating. Wet-fly casting can afford to be slightly less precise. The real difference, though, comes in the recovery. The wet-fly fisherman has yards of line out downstream and underwater. To get his line into the air again he has to pull against a considerable weight of water and the current. A stiffer actioned rod would ultimately suffer under the strain.

A word now about rod-making materials.

Greenheart: is a close-grained timber giving a splendid action for all types of rod. As has been said, it lacks maturity these days. Even in its heyday it was inclined to be unpredictable. It appeared to suffer from a sort of vegetable equivalent of metal fatigue. After years of faithful service a tip would break in mid-cast without the slightest warning. Just the same, if you are offered an old greenheart in good condition it should be snapped up quickly—at the right price, of course.

Whole-cane: whole bamboo, stiff, tough, unrelenting. Suitable for butt joints of tip-action rods.

Lancewood: timber used in the top joint of some cheap rods. Serviceable up to a point.

Spanish reed: hollow, light, ideal for match rod lower joints. Split-cane can be, and often is, spliced in at the tip.

Split-cane: the classic material from which all first-class rods are made. Usually hexagonal, the rod is made from six separate pieces of carefully machined split-cane glued together. Immense strength is combined with extreme lightness.

Fibre-glass: a newish material coming along nicely. Fabric wrapped round a moulding rod is impregnated with synthetic resin. The result is a hollow, strong, light, and durable rod section that is impossible to break during normal, or even abnormal, usage. Because of the growing shortage of skilled craftsmen, split-cane will eventually die out for all but the most expensive rods. Fibre-glass rods are also made solid.

The best rods are, of course, scientifically designed. Here we must touch upon the question of 'test-curves'. The test-curve of a rod determines how much weight it can safely cast and what strength of line it can take without risk of a powerful fish fracturing the rod. To determine this it is necessary to find out exactly the amount of strain that can be imposed upon the rod to make the tip, and consequently line, stand at right-angles to the butt. The test is made against a spring balance. For every pound of weight needed to achieve this, the rod will safely cast one ounce: likewise reckon that the rod will fish securely with line of a breaking strain calculated at 5 lb.

for every pound of test weight. A rod with a one-and-a-half pound test-curve will thus take a 7½-lb. line and throw a weight of one-and-a-half ounces. There is usually a tolerance of about 30 per cent. either side of this figure.

RODS, Sea: the tendency in the past has been for sea anglers to make do with any old rod, the stouter and less flexible the better. This in itself has given sea fishing the reputation, at least among river fishermen, of having little sporting quality. Lately, great developments have taken place in both sea fishing and tackle with the result that sea fish are now seen for the first time in their true sporting perspective. A mackerel, for instance, hooked on a light spinning- or fly-rod, can give a battle which would show up many trout in poor light. However, light rods are not always possible for sea angling, if only because of the size of weights that have to be used to cope with heavy tides and currents. Generally speaking, though, the modern sea angler fishes as lightly as he possibly can and consequently enjoys magnificent sport: for a sea fish, weight for weight, is always much stronger than a freshwater fish.

The basic rods required for all-round sea fishing are: (1), a boat rod for handling heavy leads; (2), a spinning rod; (3), a surf rod (it is possible for this and the boat rod to be interchangeable); (4) a fly-rod; (5), a big-game rod. Many anglers will settle for two rods, however, in which case a beach-cum-boat rod, and a spinner are probably the best bets.

The spinner should be about eight feet in length. This will take bass and pollack and can also be used for trailing for these fish and even for legering in shallow water. It can be

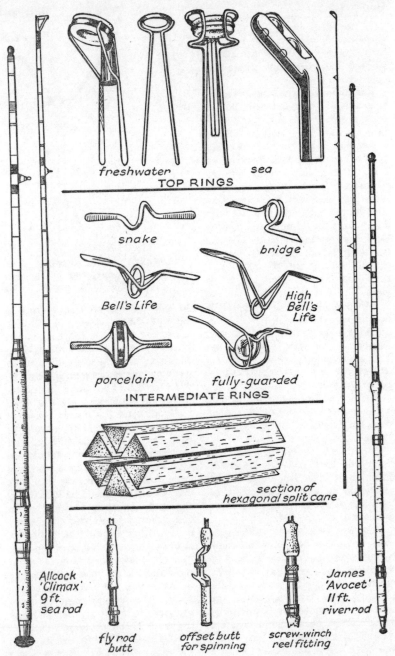

freshwater   sea

TOP RINGS

snake

bridge

Bell's Life

High Bell's Life

porcelain   fully-guarded

INTERMEDIATE RINGS

section of hexagonal split cane

Allcock 'Climax' 9 ft. sea rod

James 'Avocet' 11 ft. river rod

fly rod butt   offset butt for spinning   screw-winch reel fitting

RODS. *A sea and a freshwater rod together with some alternative forms of rod-ring and butt fittings, and a sectional view of split-cane rod construction.*

used for drift-lining for mackerel and black bream and also for bass. Drift-lining for pollack demands a stouter rod, probably a ten-foot spinner.

For surf-casting and beach fishing an eight-foot boat rod will do the trick provided it is not too stiff: it has to have sufficient action to throw the heavy tackle smoothly. Special tackle has been evolved for surf fishing, and much of the research in this direction stems from America. The standard American urf-casting apparatus is a rod with a one-piece tip fitting into a hickory butt about 30 inches long. The rod tip itself is six to seven feet in length and made of split-cane, beryllium copper, steel, or fibre-glass. The reel to use with this rig is a free-spool multiplier capable of holding 250 yards of 9-thread line. Such rods are usually made to cast weights of between 4 and 6 oz. The multiplying reel is fished on top of the reel seating instead of below the rod.

For thread-line spinning in salt water a seven to eight-foot rod of steel, split-cane, or fibre-glass with a 20–24-oz. test curve is ideal.

For trolling, or trailing a bait, the eight-foot boat rod can be used, although it may be found to be unnecessarily stiff. A seven-footer with a 2–3½ lb. test-curve would fit the case nicely.

Big-game rods are of fibre-glass, steel, or hickory and split-cane combined, with the hickory built into the side of the rod that is convex when it is curved towards a fish. Hickory gives elasticity while the split-cane provides the power. Big-game rods are usually about five feet in length, are made in one piece, and have a butt designed to sit in a leather socket worn by the angler. The reel seat has a locking device

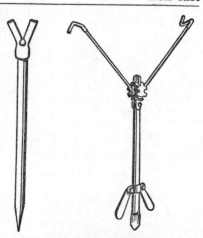

ROD-RESTS. *Two examples from among the many forms of rod-rests available to the angler.*

to hold the reel securely, since it is through straps connected between chest and reel that the angler puts his weight into the rod when fighting the fish. Often the line-guides are of a pulley type rather than agate rings.

ROD-RESTS: these important pieces of equipment are too often badly designed. They are of most use when legering. They should be adaptable to any bank surface. The perfectly designed rest should be capable of standing on a concrete embankment or digging into soft clay. Equally it should be sufficiently strong in the shaft to stand up to being rammed into hard clay. Apart from all this it should be adjustable as to height by use of extension legs. Perhaps most important of all it should allow free passage to the line below the rod. Certain brands on the market incorporate most of these features. It is a pity that so many anglers still rely on forked sticks.

ROLL-CAST: a fly cast in which the line is picked off the water without being thrown behind. This is done by a rolling movement of the rod tip. The circular path of the tip obliges the line to follow so that very little, if any, passes behind the angler. Invaluable where there are obstructions to the rear of the angler.

ROTENONE: powdered derris sometimes used when, before re-stocking a lake, existing fish popula-tion has to be poisoned. Permission to do this has almost invariably to be obtained from the River Board concerned. The water quickly clears itself, after which new fish can be introduced. A probable use for this poison is where a coarse fish lake is to be restocked with trout.

RUDD: *Scardinius erythrophthal-mus*, family *Cyprinidae*. Takes its name from the Anglo-Saxon word meaning redness. Redness is the keynote to the rudd's appearance. It seems to be infused with red where the roach is plain silver. Colouring, as has been said, is seldom a sure guide to identifica-tion, however. Since rudd are often mistaken for roach, and vice versa, the following simple differences should be stressed: the roach is a bottom feeder, therefore its top lip overlaps

its lower; the rudd feeds mainly on or near the surface, so the reverse is true of its lips. Also, the dorsal fin of the roach is almost directly above the ventral fins. That of the rudd is set much further back. As to scale counts, the roach has from 40 to 46 along the lateral line and the rudd 39–43: from root of dorsal to lateral line the roach has 7–9, and the rudd 7–8. Counting the rays in the fins of both fish is, perhaps, more helpful. The rudd has, dorsal: 8–10 branched rays, and the roach, 3 simple and 9–11 branched. The rudd, anal: 10–13 branched, and the roach, 3 simple and 9–12 branched.

Apart from its red tinge the rudd has a greenish back and in some cases a golden sheen to the flanks. The species fight hard when hooked and go to a good weight. A glass-case rudd is a three-pounder: the British record, by the Rev. E. C. Alston at Thetford, is 4 lb. 8 oz.

In rivers, rudd usually keep to certain spots and are not spread about the stream. Rudd are not known in Scotland but abound in Ireland. The Norfolk Broads hold fine rudd as do many Midland and

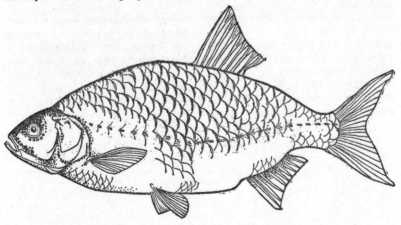

RUDD. *Sometimes confused with the roach. The dorsal fin is, however, set farther back. Also the lower lip overlaps the upper. Rudd abound in Ireland.*

Sussex lakes, also, of course, the classic rudd water, Slapton Ley in South Devon.

The spots favoured by rudd are often overhung by trees, since they feed on insects that drop to the surface, and close to lily beds from the underside of whose leaves they suck minute aquatic organisms.

RUDD-FISHING: most of these handsome fish are taken on or near the surface, though a bottom-fished worm will sometimes connect. Tackle used for roach will suit admirably for rudd. The first requirement is to locate their feeding stations. In a lake they can be seen cruising near the surface attacking floating insects, their back fins breaking water. They can be attracted by groundbait moored near the surface. The classic bait is half a stale loaf moored to a stone. Marshall Hardy, the well-known expert, advises dry bread moored in a hair-net. The fish can be taken on breadcrust, gentles, worms or wasp grubs. The main point to remember is that the bait must sink slowly to keep it in the vulnerable sub-surface layer as long as possible. If float tackle is used—and a very light float is essential—the shotting should be as far from the hook as possible. Indeed, it may pay to make the float self-cocking with the addition of a little lead wire, leaving one tiny dust shot about a foot from the hook. A single maggot fished in this way can prove deadly, especially when dropped near the moored groundbait. Another method is to use a half-filled bubble-float on fixed-spool tackle. You can cast this gear a long way, and once in the water it is almost invisible and offers little resistance to a taking fish. Single maggot or a fragment of crust can be put on the hook about two to three feet from the bubble. Whatever float is used, the bait should rarely be set more than three feet from it, for, by the time it has sunk to that depth, it will be out of range of the fish.

Rudd are also fine targets for the fly-rod. A single maggot on a small hook can be used at the end of a dry-fly cast; or ordinary dry-fly, in which case a small bright pattern, such as a Wickham's Fancy or a Black Gnat, will do well. Rudd, like carp, are primarily fish of summer. Once September has gone, the sport, particularly in lakes, slows down. On the Continent, rudd are being caught at the beginning of the season on small spinners and fly-spoons. There is little doubt that they would fall for similar treatment here.

RUFFE: *Acerina cernua,* family *Percidae.* A poor relation of the perch, alternatively called 'pope'. Brownish in appearance, has no side stripes. Chief resemblance to the perch is in its spiny fins, especially the dorsal. Found in comparatively few rivers, notably the Thames. Seldom deliberately fished for. Will take worm or gentle avidly.

 S

SALMON: there are many species of salmon, but *Salmo salar*, the Atlantic salmon, is the only salmon that runs up British rivers to spawn. The British rod-caught record is 64 lb. by Miss G. W. Ballantyne from the Tay in Scotland. Bigger specimens undoubtedly visit our rivers. In appearance the salmon can be mistaken only for the sea trout, and this only in its smaller sizes, say between five and fourteen

shallows are called, the egg hatches out and becomes an 'alevin'. This minute fish has attached to it a yolk sac containing nourishment for the first few weeks of its existence. In the first year the fingerling salmon is known as a 'parr'. Then it looks very much like a small brown trout except for the finger-like marks along its flanks and the fact that the upper jawbone (maxillary) of the salmon does not protrude, as does

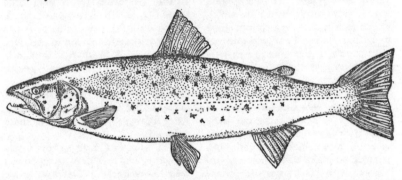

SALMON. *The salmon enters pure fast-running rivers from the sea and journeys upstream to spawn on the gravel-bedded shallows of the headwaters.*

pounds. Even so, a simple scale-count reveals the difference. Between lateral line and dorsal fin the salmon has, in a slanting line, 10–12 scales and the sea trout about 16. Both fish have the same overall silver sheen with blue-black spots and, of course, the adipose fin of the whole salmon family set just in front of the tail on the ridge of the back.

The salmon's life story is the reverse of the eel's. It starts its days as an egg laid in the gravel shallows at the head-waters of its native river. On the 'redds', as these

the trout's, beyond a line drawn vertically through the centre of the eye. It is illegal to take such parr and they must be put back if hooked by accident.

The next stage comes when the salmon is preparing to go down to the sea. It then begins to take on a silver appearance, looks not unlike a herring in shape, and is called a 'smolt'. The eel goes to the sea to breed, but to the salmon the ocean is home. Rivers are simply places in which to be born, to mate, and often to die. In the rich feeding grounds of the sea, the salmon grows at an astonishing rate. A fish that has gone down as a smolt of half a pound may return a year or so later as a five- or six-pound fish. In two years the salmon will have reached double figures. If it returns to the river in its first year, the fisherman refers to it as a 'grilse'.

Undoubtedly many homing salmon return to the same river they left at least twelve months previously as smolts. Experiments with ringed and tagged fish have established this beyond doubt. Recent experiments in America have gone a long way towards solving the mystery of how they do this. There now seems little doubt that the salmon has a very subtle sense of smell, which in a fish is very closely allied to that of taste. Tank experiments have shown that salmon are capable of recognizing and reacting to minute shades of difference in water taste. Fish homing along a river in Washington were netted above a fork. Half of them then had their nostrils plugged and the fish were taken a mile below the fork and released to make their choice again. Those with free nostrils chose exactly the same fork as before. The salmon that had been plugged milled about uncertain which to choose and eventually selected apparently at random. The inference is that the taste-smell of every river differs, and that, even off the coast, the salmon can detect his home river smell and make for it. He swims up the coast until he finds the river he seeks.

Once in the river the salmon no longer feeds. His body, firm and full with sea feeding, carries all the nourishment it needs for the upstream trip to the spawning beds. His flesh is now full of oils and has that red colour that delights all lovers of good food. Now the fish is possessed by one urge—to push on to the headwaters and spawn. In most rivers there are two big runs of fish—the spring and autumn runs. In between, of course, smaller parties of fish continuously make the journey. The upstream trip is carried out by fits and starts. When the salmon has made some distance he rests in one of the recognized deep holes, and this is where the angler looks for him. Sometimes when there is a shortage of rain— for almost all salmon rivers are subject to spate, having hill or moorland origins—a number of salmon become trapped in a pool. If this continues for a long time some of the fish may be seen to be taking on a red tinge: this is a sure sign that they have been in the river a long time. A 'fresh-run' salmon is bright silver, and, if it has come in from the sea only during the past two or three days, will often carry small dark sea lice on its head and flanks. After a few days in fresh water these drop off.

The salmon's urge to travel upstream is best seen demonstrated at a weir or waterfall. The fish make leap after leap to clear the obstruction until they finally surmount it. Those that fail and fall back into the pool take their place at the tail of the queue waiting to jump. Recent hydro-electric schemes have sometimes blocked salmon rivers completely. In such cases the electricity authorities have made salmon passes or 'ladders' which give the fish a graduated series of leaps in an artificial channel, by which means they can circumvent the power installation. Perhaps the best known is that at Pitlochry.

If it is true that a salmon does not feed in freshwater—and repeated post-mortems have failed to reveal stomach contents from a river-caught fish—why does he take the angler's lure? Often he grabs it at the tenth or the twentieth offer, as if he had been provoked into seizing fly or spinner. The question has never been answered satisfactorily but my own theory is that he acts from a conditioned reflex. For months, maybe years, he has been darting at small bright food-objects in the sea. Suddenly his metabolism has violently readjusted itself. For a reason he cannot comprehend he has ceased to need food. But this does not mean that he has entirely lost the urge to hunt or chase food. A small bright fishlike object, be it fly or spinner, waved about in front of him may easily be sufficient to trigger off the impulse to pursue and catch. Once he has caught it, the salmon perhaps realizes that he does not need the food in his mouth, and ejects it with gill pressure. But supposing the object has a hook in it. Then it may not be so easy to get rid of it. I stress that this is only a personal theory, but one that may account for the strange inconsistency of non-feeding fish taking imitation food.

At last, cock and hen salmon reach the headwaters where they are to spawn. By now the cock certainly will be pretty red, the red colour showing on his flanks. It will also have developed a hooked lower jaw for fighting other males. The fish lie side by side on the gravel spawning grounds, the hen scooping out a hollow with her tail and belly in which to lay her eggs, the male afterwards shedding his milt over the spot. The hen fish finally buries the fertilized eggs with a sweep of her tail. And so the whole life-cycle starts again. Many of the spawned fish will be so exhausted that they will fail to get back to the

sea. Some make the journey two or three times during their lives. Those that survive spawning struggle down the river, thin, emaciated creatures that look more like eels than salmon. They are then called by the angler 'kelts'. Those caught must be returned to the water.

Salmon will breed in any pure, fast-running water. Though Scotland is thought of as the land of salmon, equally fine fish run up the Severn, Hampshire Avon and Welsh rivers. A little over 100 years ago there were salmon spawning in the Thames. Even today the occasional fish is taken off Southend as it feels its way along the coast to the first friendly river. The barrier of filth between Hammersmith Bridge and the Estuary has, however, shut off the salmon from England's 'first river' for all time.

SALMON-FISHING: it is often said that the problem in trout fishing is to hook the fish. After hooking it, playing and landing it are fairly easy, whereas with salmon fishing exactly the opposite is true. Hooking a salmon is relatively easy but the real trouble begins when the angler starts to play it. Both these pictures are largely false, of course. However, it is a fact that compared with a chalk-stream trout on the dry-fly, moving and hooking a salmon—once you know where he is lying—is a fairly simple business. But when the tremendous strength of the salmon comes into play, the angler needs every bit of rod-craft he can muster. Many salmon anglers will naturally contest this view of the proceedings, but I believe it to be a reasonably fair one.

However, to fish consistently well for salmon, without benefit of advice from ghillie, demands one hundred per cent. skill and knowledge. No question then of simply being led to such-and-such a pool and directed by a hotel ghillie to flog it. The man who succeeds throughout the season, fishing single-handed, must know every mood of the river, its reaction to spate, flood and drought. He must know every lie and hole in it, when to fish with bait or lure and at what depth. Under such conditions the consistent hooking of salmon becomes comparable to any of the skills of the dry- or wet-fly man. It is the casual salmon angler—and this includes most who live in the South and Midlands—who must rely on local knowledge and more or less 'chuck-and-chance-it' tactics.

Many salmon are taken these days on the spinning tackle of the visiting angler. This is highly understandable since many of the casuals are coarse fishermen who already have excellent fixed-spool gear and pike spinning rods. Little need be said here except that spinning is an effective and sometimes the only way to catch salmon; it is by no means the most artistic or satisfying though. As to baits: spoons and plugs will catch salmon, but small Devons (1–2-in.) are more effective in most conditions—plain silver, gold, or blue and silver all working well. For strong water, reflex Devons give the necessary added weight. When spinning, the cast is usually best made across and slightly upstream, the current being allowed to sweep the bait down towards the fish before the retrieve is begun.

The cast should be fished right out as salmon, like pike, sometimes take at the last minute right under the bank. Natural dead-baits such as sprats, both dyed and natural, eel-tails, prawns, and worms all kill fish in the right conditions. The natural baits can be mounted on any of the well-known spinning flights such as Archer or Aerial to give spin or wobble. Eel tail works very well at the opening of the season: three inches of tail, either preserved or fresh, and mounted on a flight like the Geen Corkscrew does very nicely. In estuarial waters, the tail of a sand-eel is very deadly. Minnows and loach in some parts (the North particularly) make fine early-season baits.

Prawns are most effective from May until August and kill well in low-water conditions. The prawn is mounted head downwards on the spinning flight, in other words, with tail towards the vanes of the tackle. The cast is made downstream, the bait being fished sink-and-draw. The angler must keep himself out of sight. Worms should not be despised in flood conditions or when the river is clearing. A bunch of juicy lobs is fixed on the hook so that almost all their length is free to wriggle. This bait, juggled slowly in a sink-and-draw manner in a deep hole, or even left to rest on the bottom, will catch fish when the river is highly coloured.

Fly-fishing for salmon is done with a rod of between ten and fourteen feet. Nowadays the average is likely to be about twelve feet, although not so long ago monstrous weapons of up to seventeen feet in length were often seen. A tapered line is used of much the same construction as, but of course of greater weight than, the trout fly-line. A heavy level cast is used and the fly, which is tied to the end of this, is more properly called a lure since it resembles no insect known in nature. The cast is usually three yards long and will vary in thickness according to the size of fly used and nature of the river. The size known as 3/5 will serve for the very large patterns while 6/5 is stout enough for smaller stuff. A cast with a salmon rod is usually made double-handed, the right hand being at the top of the cork butt, and the left at the butt cap.

In principle, salmon fishing with a fly much resembles wet-fly fishing for trout on a grand scale. The throw is made downstream and across and the fly is allowed to work down past the suspected salmon lie with the current, recovery being made in enticing jerks and jiggles until the fly is lifted and cast again. Unlike a trout, a salmon can often be irritated—or apparently irritated —into taking the lure. Many fish will hook themselves on the take. With a fish that grabs the lure well below the surface it is as well to tighten and strike automatically. More time should, however, be allowed a fish that swallows the fly at the surface.

In playing a salmon the same rules governing the tiring of any powerful fish come into force. Pressure must be kept on at every moment. If the fish decides to run for it the angler must slow him down with every ounce of safe pressure he can put on. At times he may have to risk pressure highly dangerous to the success of the operation, as when a fish, hooked in a small pool, decides to make a break for broken water downstream where the fisherman cannot easily follow. Then it may become a question of risk all in an attempt to stop the rush. When a salmon sulks it must be roused to keep it on the move. If possible its head must be pulled across the current by steady pressure from the correct angle. This will throw the fish off balance and expose its flank to the thrust of the stream, which force will probably set it off again. On light tackle—particularly light spinning gear—the fish may have to be tired by being walked along the bank in a downstream direction in order to flood its gills from behind. This will be possible only where banks are open—a rare occurrence.

There is one further important technique in salmon fishing and that is the method pioneered by the late Arthur Wood and is called 'greased-line' fishing. Wood worked out his theories on the Aberdeenshire Dee. He discovered that in certain conditions, notably low water when the salmon wouldn't look at a fly fished well sunken, they would take a lure on or nearly on the surface. He also found that a salmon that had taken in this way tended not to eject the artificial lure once it had felt the deception. Instead, the salmon appeared to turn the bait in its mouth as if examining its find. To strike immediately, Wood found, frequently pulled the lure out of the salmon's mouth. If, however, a lot of slack line was allowed to drift downstream of the fish, the pull of the current on this line frequently set the hook. Wood found that the most effective flies in these low-water states were very sparsely tied dressings, indeed some of his lure had practically no trimmings to hide the hook shank. It seemed, moreover, that the salmon found such a fly drifting down broadside on to the stream more enticing than one that came down tail first. Out of all this came the greased-line theory which works as follows.

First, these special flies are used. Second, the reel line is greased nearly to the cast; the last yard or so is not greased, nor is the cast; the fly is not oiled. The angler throws across and slightly upstream, and with plenty of slack. The fly begins to float down broadside on. Directly drag begins to exert itself on the line, tugging the lure across stream in an unnatural fashion, the fisherman 'mends his cast'. That is to say, he lifts any loop of the line lying on the water with a downstream 'belly' on it and converts it into an upstream curve. He does this as many times as necessary until the cast is fished out.

SAND SMELT: sometimes called the atherine. This small greyish fish has a silver stripe along one side, two dorsals, and very large eyes. Six inches is a good size; they are found inshore during the summer, particularly on the South Coast. Excellent baits for mackerel and bass and other species. Family, *Atherinidae.*

SCHOOL BASS: small bass up to about three pounds which swim in dense shoals, pillaging one part of the shore then quickly moving on. An angler who locates such a shoal of 'schoolies' can often make a killing. The bigger fish are usually solitaries or at least move about in smaller groups.

SEA-BED, Nature Of: this factor greatly affects the sea angler. He can usually get a fair idea of conditions to be expected on new fishing grounds by studying Admiralty charts of the area. Plumbing with a lead weight which has a grease or tallow filled hollow in its base will always bring up for the angler a fair sample of the ground beneath him.

On hard sea beds the angler may find: down to 5 fathoms, wrasse; 5-15 fathoms, blue shark; 10-15 fathoms, conger, pollack, pouting; 10-20 fathoms, bream; 15-20 fathoms, coalfish, cod, ling; 15-30 fathoms, mako, and porbeagle shark; 20-70 fathoms, halibut.

On soft beds: 5-10 fathoms, dabs; 5-15 fathoms, soles, plaice; 10-15 fathoms, brill, turbot; 10-20, tope; 10-30, rays, skate; 15-30, whiting;

5-40, gurnard; 10-40, haddock; 15-40, cod.

Herring and mackerel move constantly and must be found before they can be fished for. Their presence can be detected by riffles on the surface. Dogfish are ubiquitous.

SEA FISHING: the following section gives an outline of the main techniques used in sea fishing.

Drift-lining: this means fishing just off the bottom either from a drifting or anchored boat, without using a float. Wrasse, pollack, mackerel, black bream, bass, cod are among the species to be caught by this method. The type of tackle to be used depends on quarry, depth the quarry will be found at, and strength of current or tide. This latter is most important because a strong tide will obviously slant the line away from the boat at a greater angle than a slack one. The spiral weight needed to hold the bait down may vary from a few ounces to half-a-pound or more: the rod will be selected in proportion to the stresses involved.

If often pays to plumb the depth first with a heavily weighted line, measuring off the line taken out and then marking a similar depth off on the reel line, adding one or more fathoms to allow for slant, and then marking the spot with sticking plaster. When fishing, provided the line is paid out until the sticking plaster leaves the reel, the bait will then be just off the bottom. When drift-lining, the bait should be wiggled about by hand to give it life by retrieving and releasing a yard or two of line occasionally.

If the fish are not found at one depth, then line should be wound up from the bottom, the revolutions of the reel being counted, until the quarry is contacted. Fishing thus from a drifting boat is only really

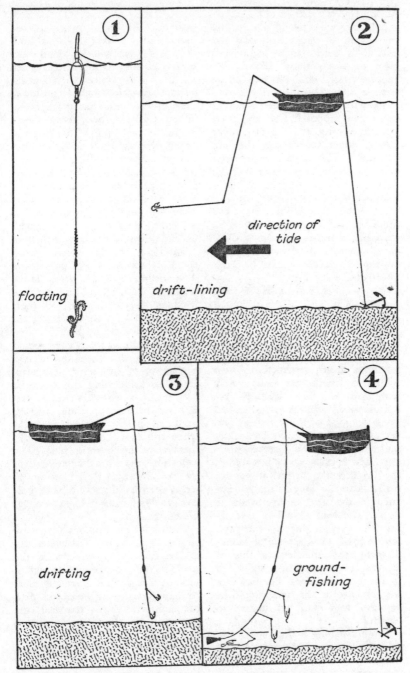

SEA FISHING. *Four examples of the techniques used by sea-anglers.*

satisfactory when no definite fishing mark can be established, and the bottom is known to be sandy and clear of obstructions. Worm, fish strips, or lasts, sand-eels may all be used as baits when drift-lining.

Feather-fishing: this is not, as sometimes supposed, anything to do with fly-fishing. It is, in fact, more closely allied to trailing, the lure being a feather instead of a metal one. Some anglers decry feather fishing, perhaps because it is a relatively easy way of catching fish (it is certainly an effective one), but more probably because it is a favourite stand-by of the professional fisherman. However, with appropriate tackle it can be both effective and sporting.

The technique is to fish from a drifting boat with tackle, weighted at the end, to which are attached, paternoster fashion on short snoods, a number of rudimentary feather lures. These lures, which may be anything from an inch to two inches in length, are really vastly simplified wet-flies, tied to resemble small fish. A long-shanked hook wrapped with silver tinsel and with four or five long cock's hackles tied in at the head will serve admirably. The hackles can be any colour, the brighter the better: it doesn't really matter as long as the appearance of the lure in the water is lively. The lead should be streamlined for easy sinking and recovery. Above the lead is a trace of monofilament and attached to this at intervals of anything from six inches to a foot are the lures. The link that ties the latter to the trace should be between four and six inches in length.

Feather-fishing is done mostly in daylight and in clear water. It will catch many species, including coalfish, cod, pollack, whiting, and

gurnard. But many other species, including tope, have taken this form of bait. These will be found close to the bottom, while mackerel can be taken a fathom or so below the surface. Rods will vary according to weights used and quarry expected. When feather fishing there always exists the possibility of hooking two or more fish simultaneously. Twenty-pound line, with 15-lb. dropper links for the lure, may not prove excessive. However, for mackerel, the appropriate breaking strains are more likely to be 8 lb. and 5 lb. Results are improved by working the feathers with up and down movements of the rod.

Mackerel nearly always hook themselves as the weight goes down. The weight must be heavy to be effective, for the bubbles created as it sinks attract mackerel in great numbers. With a heavy weight the hook rarely comes up bare.

Float-fishing: many anglers tend to think of this technique as the perogative of the river fisherman. In fact, float-fishing can often be very profitable in salt water, especially inside harbour walls, and in sheltered positions close to rocks when fishing either from the rocks themselves or from a boat. The following species are regularly caught by float-fishing: bass (on worm, strips of fish skin or livebait), pollack, coalfish, mackerel, grey mullet, bream, garfish.

Most of the conditions governing choice of tackle for freshwater use of the float, apply equally in the sea. The rod must be long enough to pick up line for the strike: it must be light enough to make its continual use comfortable and practical: the line must be greased to prevent it sinking so that a prompt strike is always possible: floats and weights should be as light as possible, consistent with weather conditions and fish sought: for deep-water fishing, sliding floats become necessary: rod rings should be of the stand-off type to facilitate casting.

Two rigs are really necessary, if heavy and light baits are to be fished. The first for small bass, mackerel, herring, etc., might be a ten-foot sea trout rod, or something similar, with a centre-pin reel holding 100 yards of line. Where long casting is necessary, a fixed-spool reel is a better proposition. Line need not be more than 6–8 lb. breaking strain, bearing in mind the test-curve of the rod. Traces, as in river fishing, should be of slightly smaller breaking strain than the line itself. Weights with this outfit can be large split-shot or lead wire. Floats may vary from a big fat cork-and-quill to an ordinary bottle cork painted and slit lengthways to hold the line. Sliding floats are of exactly the same pattern as that described in the entry on FLOATS, rubber stops on the line being used to set them at the correct depth.

When after bigger quarry with large baits or even live fish, gear will have to be appropriately scaled up. Big sea floats can be bought, or alternatively large pike bungs will serve. A rod with a test-curve of from two to two-and-a-half pounds will probably be necessary to handle the combined weights of bait, float and spiral lead (the best method of weighting such tackle). Very often the tackle can be allowed to drift away from the boat to the desired spot: then a centre-pin reel (15-lb. line) will do. Under adverse current conditions a large fixed-spool reel will be found better in action. For big pollack the trace needs to be heavy, since these powerful fish frequently make for the rocks.

Fly-fishing: this is nothing to do with feather fishing described earlier in this section. Saltwater fly-fishing is very closely allied to still-water wet-fly fishing as practised inland for trout and salmon. The difference is that there are no aquatic flies at sea. The lures used by the sea fly-fisher, therefore, are downright honest imitations of swimming worms, shrimps, fry and the like. Among the species to be caught by this method, number pollack, coalfish, sea trout, mackerel, bass and herrings. A sea trout or salmon rod will do the job, though the line should be Cuttyhunk dressed with tar, since salt water quickly ruins silk and Terylene fly lines. Flax line of about 25-lb. b.s. will work a sea trout rod quite well: a salmon rod will need line of nearly double that weight. Six feet of level nylon is all that is needed for a cast, since precise and delicate throwing is never necessary.

Lures for sea fly-fishing can be anything from a strip of bass or sole skin to a well-tied streamer fly. The main thing about sea flies is that they should have life and movement in the water, and that they should be bright. Bodies will usually be wound with silver tinsel, and 'wings' are made of large gaudy cock hackles or hair. The large and gaudier salmon and sea trout flies will also catch sea fish. A single fly, or a leash of three as in lake fishing, can be used to taste.

Now for some of the species that take a fly readily. Sea trout will be found offshore, particularly near river mouths, waiting their chance to ascend. Look for them in sheltered spots in sandy channels, and also where rocks and weeds give protection and feeding. The same principles that govern feeding and resting stations in freshwater largely apply in the sea. Pollack and coalfish can be taken on the fly, usually when the light is poor, at dawn or dusk. Bass can often be spotted feeding: if so get upwind of the shoal and cast across their noses. Mackerel can be seen offshore or in harbour mouths: cast among them and retrieve the fly in jerks.

In general, fly-fishing is not likely to be effective over muddy ground. Sandy beaches and river mouths give the best results. Sea fly-fishing corresponds closely to wet-fly fishing in a river, in that the fly is allowed to drift down-current until it hangs below the angler, and is then retrieved in jerks. The guiding principle to be remembered is that the lure must be given life either by movement with the hand on the line, or by action of the rod tip. Striking presents the habitual difficulties of wet-fly fishing and only practice can tell you when to hit the fish.

Bottom-fishing: this is fishing that is usually done from shore or pier. The gear used is likely always to be some variations of paternoster or leger. Almost all species feed on the bottom at one time or another, including bass, mullet, flounder, dab, plaice, turbot, cod, codling, conger, whiting, skate, tope. At slack water fish tend to feed at mid-water levels; during a strong tide they feed on the bottom.

For fishing in sheltered places such as harbours or on gently shelving beaches where surf and swell are never violent, lightish tackle can be used consisting of 12–15-lb. line with a 1–1½-oz. sinker. No wire boom gear or other ironmongery is necessary. The weight is attached to the end of the trace and the hook links, or snoods, are fixed at intervals above this. About 16 inches between hooks is all that is necessary, and two hooks (perhaps size 2/0) are quite sufficient. The main

object of the two hooks is that they give you a chance to try two different baits.

The rod to cast this gear can be a stout sea spinner, or beach rod with a test-curve of about 2 lb. Many anglers, particularly when beach fishing, prefer to rest the rod. It is not, repeat not, necessary to fix a bell to the end of your rod and then sit back and smoke your pipe. The 'bell-men', often seen on piers, are basically lazy anglers. It is the wait-until-the-bell-rings attitude that has earned sea-fishing the reputation of being clumsy and unskilled. As in rivers, a taking fish will give sufficient indication at the rod top of its intention to steal the bait, and the alert angler will strike accordingly.

On the subject of bite characteristics, the following may prove helpful. Big bass usually (usually is a word that applies to all these assessments) tug at the line in one vicious pull: school bass give repeated taps, and a slackening of the line until the run begins is often advisable; flounders give a series of tugs punctuated by brief periods of inactivity, so slacken off until the line straightens, meaning the fish has finally swallowed the bait; small pollack take gently and should be struck immediately, at least on paternoster gear.

The other main bottom fishing tackle is the leger, and again this is closely related to the river angler's tackle, although naturally heavier. Flat coffin leads are sometimes used, also the round, studded leads, and, nowadays, Arlesey Bombs. For gentle water a weight of 1–1½ oz. will suffice. A stop shot can be used on the trace below the weight exactly as when freshwater fishing. Two hooks can be fished. Heavy weed inshore usually renders legering impracticable. On a good, firm, sandy bottom a rolling leger will often take bass. In this case the gear used is something of a cross between paternoster and leger, the weight (preferably an Arlesey Bomb) being tied to the bottom of the trace with the hooks above it. The gear is allowed to wash in with the making tide, the bass often taking the bait as it comes right round into the shallowest water.

When legering, crabs are liable to be a thorough nuisance, but there in no sure remedy for this. A crab bite is felt as a grating sensation on the line rather than as a tug. The only thing to be said for crabs is that where they abound there usually fish abound also.

Surf or open beach fishing is a wilder and tougher variation of the legering and paternostering themes. Here the quarry is mainly bass, though other fish including skate, tope, and flatfish may fall to the surf-caster. The most favourable beaches for surf fishing are the gently shelving sandy strands found on the South Coast and in some parts of Cornwall. Here when the water is choppy the surf comes creaming up the sand, turning over and disclosing many of the creatures that have taken shelter in it with the receding tide. Bass often follow the breakers in until their backs are almost out of the water. There are no definite rules about the business but it's fair to say that the bass will probably be patrolling just beyond the third wave so excessively long casting is rarely necessary. As to what state of the tide gives best results it is safest to say that only local knowledge can provide the answer. In many places the first half of the flood tide gives the best results though there are estuaries where the ebb provides the best fishing.

The main problem from a tackle point of view with this type of fishing is how to hold the bottom. Even mild surf packs a powerful punch and one- and two-ounce leads will soon be rolled back to the feet of the angler. Leads of 4–8 oz. are commonly used, and under rough conditions bigger weights still may be necessary. The round, studded variety have good holding power: so have some of the leads made with flukes like miniature anchors. A useful type is the cone-shaped lead equipped with stout but soft wire prongs. These hold the sand under ordinary conditions. If they become embedded, a strong pull bends the wire and pulls them free.

The rod to cast such gear must not only be sufficiently strong but also must have sufficient action throughout its length to make the cast possible. Special surf-casting rods are made for use with both the free-running centre-pin type of drum reel and also the multiplier. The average line used is about 27-lb. breaking strain, and the reel should hold about 200 yards of line and backing. With the centre-pin reel the cast is made in a controlled side-swing, the reel being braked by finger pressure to control the flight of the bait and to stop over-run. The multiplier is fished on top of the rod as when river fishing, and the reel is braked by thumb pressure.

The surf-caster operates winter and summer, and frequently at night when the best fishing is often to be found, particularly at popular seaside resorts where daytime crowds make fishing impossible. At night, warm clothing is essential and waders are a 'must'.

Since the surf-caster's rod is usually held high to keep the line clear of the incoming wave tops, a strap-on leather rod-butt socket is extremely useful in taking strain off the angler. Few forms of fishing are more exciting, especially when a big bass is hooked at night. Landing a fish in surf is tricky and is largely a question of timing its beaching in shallow water with incoming waves. A big fish left high and dry to thrash about on the sand by a receding wave quite easily flips off the hook and is away in the next wave that catches it. Fish should be beached as high as possible. The tendency, provided the fish is still water-borne, will be for it to fight its way towards the angler in its efforts to escape. Once it is fairly beached the surf angler should waste no time in getting his catch as far up the beach as he can.

Some notes on surf conditions: heavy surf rarely produces good fishing. The aftermath of a two- or three-day blow is quite different, however. Fish, kept from feeding by rough weather, will now be inshore foraging for everything turned up by the rough weather. Flatfish tend to give best sport in calm weather. Cod and codling usually stand quite a long way out except in half-light which may be the time to try for them.

Bottom-fishing from a boat: the tackle used is either paternoster or leger, the governing factor in both cases being the weight needed to hold the tackle down in the tide. This may be anything up to one pound. Paternosters will usually be of the three-boom type, the top two booms having short leaders and the bottom a long one. The technique is to take the boat out to an established mark and then lower the tackle over the side until the weight rests on the bottom. The rod need have no casting action and its main requirement is that it should be able to stand the strain of lifting weights of a pound or more vertically off the

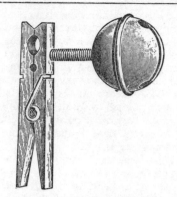

SEA FISHING. *The sea-angler's bite indicator is often a bell that is clipped on near the top of his rod.*

sea bed, through perhaps ten fathoms of water. Ground fishers may catch anything from conger to dabs, depending on the bottom and the locality. Line needs to be somewhere in the region of 15-lb. breaking strain for most fish. Congers, however, necessitate very heavy lines.

Pier-fishing: paternoster gear, either of wire or monofilament, is the most effective rig for pier fishing. The rod needs to have some casting action and will therefore tend to be more flexible than the boat rod. Weights will vary between 2-oz. and 6-oz. with 4-oz. a fair average. Line needs to be strong, perhaps 27-lb. Cuttyhunk, to make possible the lifting of played-out fish to pier level. It is true that few remarkable catches are made from crowded piers on summer holiday outings, but the serious pier angler, by picking his moments, can do very well. Piers, after all, shelter a host of small marine animals on which fish feed. Pollack, wrasse and flatfish are among the pier fisher's quarries. In winter, codling and even cod, also whiting (at night) fall to the pier fisherman. Excellent bass fishing is to be had from some South Coast rivers in winter.

Spinning: tackle roughly parallel to river gear for pike and salmon spinning will do nicely for saltwater work. Rods with test curves of between 2 lb. and 3 lb. will do anything asked of them in sea spinning. Lines will vary according to reel and quarry. For centre-pin reels and multipliers 15–20 lb. braided nylon will be excellent: fixed-spool reels demand something lighter if they are to work properly. Five to 8 lb. will probably be sufficiently heavy, in which case the use of all but the largest fixed-spools is limited to spinning for such fish as mackerel and sea trout. There is nothing to be said about casting when sea spinning that has not already been said under the freshwater section on casting: all the same principles apply. Lures used for sea spinning include most of those in the freshwater man's repertoire—spoons of all shapes and sizes, small plugs, Devons, wagtails, and specialist sea lures such as rubber sand-eels, also of course, natural baits both freshly killed and preserved. Among the latter you may number: fry, small fish, and sand-eels mounted on wobbler tackle or a spinning flight (exactly as in pike fishing); pieces of fish and strips of skin, notably from mackerel and pilchard; prawns and shrimps mounted on special prawn tackle and made to spin by celluloid vanes fixed on the trace; worms of various species, but notably rag and king rag, fished in a sink-and-draw method.

Artificial baits closely resemble those used by the river and lake man and are described in the section on spinning: only those that have marked characteristics of their own will therefore be dealt with here. First in importance is the baited spoon, a combination of artificial and natural bait that has been found very deadly for flounders. The spoon in this case should be of the freely-fluttering blade type and the hooks (a long-shanked one with a small hook mounted close to the point at which the main hook clears the tail of the spoon) should stand clear of the trailing end of the spoon. Flounders and flatfish seem to follow the spoon, especially if from time to time it touches the sandy bottom, are attracted by the bright spin and fall for the succulent natural lure they find attached to it. Worm on the spoon kills flatfish splendidly. Mackerel skin is an alternative attraction at the tail of the spoon and is very deadly for bass.

Rubber sand-eels are excellent pollack lures. The best ones spin freely when drawn slowly through the water—pollack do not like a fast-moving bait—and are pliant. Red and black kill well: the lure should be at least six inches long. A small strip of mackerel should be attached to the hook. Bass will also take this bait, though seem to prefer it white or green. The term sand-eel is a misnomer since these rubber baits in no way resemble the flashing silver of the true article. The rubber eel probably looks far more like a spinning worm, or even a baby conger.

Porosand: this comparatively new proprietary bait is a killer for bass and pollack at certain times of the year. It can be bought in strips and is then cut up as required. Porosand is a translucent (generally) crinkly plastic. When a strip of it is placed on a long-shanked hook and drawn through the water it probably resembles a juicy ragworm.

Nearly all that has been said about freshwater spinning tactics applies to the sea spinner. Keep down, keep a background of rocks behind you if possible; if one lure does not work, then try another; where there are special features to the beach or estuary, try to spot them at low tide. Look for channels, shelter given by rocks, try to work out where fish will seek food; remember that sea fish generally cruise at one level when foraging. They are quite likely to ignore a bait spun too far above or below them: vary your depth if you are not getting results; avoid splashing about with oars and banging bottom boards of the boat when feeding fish are sighted. Generally speaking, sea fish are not as shy as the freshwater kind, but they are still capable of being put off.

Trolling, or trailing: the strains imposed on a rod in this method of fishing are considerable. A six-foot fibre-glass rod is excellent. The rod needs to be stiffish to stand up to the pull of a heavy weight and lure towed behind a moving boat, for that is the essence of the business. The reel should be of the large drum type and must have a check or drag sufficient to prevent mere movement of the bait through the water from rotating the reel. When a fish takes, however, the first sign will usually be the scream of the running reel—and a very exciting sound that can be. An eight-foot rod with a test-curve of between 2½ lb. and 3 lb. will be just right for the job. On the reel should be at least 150 yards of 27-lb. (9-thread) line. Where possible line size should be cut down, for, the thicker the line the greater the drag, and the more weight, consequently, must be used to keep the lure at the right fishing depth. A longish Alasticum wire trace is necessary since the flax line itself can be spotted so easily. Generally

speaking, the heaviest lead likely to be used is an 8-oz. one: weights must be of the anti-kink type.

Lures include all the natural and artificial ones already mentioned in the spinning section. The technique is to lower the lure over the side, trail it for a few seconds to make sure that it is spinning properly, and then strip line off the reel until the predetermined length is in the water. If the bait is to be trailed at a depth requiring fifty yards of line, then fifty yards should be marked off at the appropriate point with a piece of adhesive tape. When this is seen leaving the reel the bait is trolling at the desired level and distance. The check or drag is then put on the reel and the rod either held or rested. If the latter, it should be put out at right-angles to the fore-and-aft line of the boat, being propped against a peg mounted in the gunwhale. In this way two rods, one at each side, can be used without fear of baits becoming entangled. It is, by the way, essential to trail the same amount of line on both rods, otherwise the lines are likely to foul each other on the turns. Occasionally it may be thought worthwhile to fish a third rod directly over the stern. When a big fish is hooked the two idle lines should immediately be recovered.

When trolling: the bait should be fished near the surface for bass, deeper for pollack during daylight but shallow at dawn and dusk; for flatfish the baited spoon should be trailed near a sandy bottom; whenever possible troll across the tide.

Recommended reading: *Salt-Water Angling* by Michael Kennedy, and *Sea Angling* by Derek Fletcher.

SEA FISHING BAITS: the novice tends to think only in terms of lugworm and possibly rag when it comes to catching sea fish. The truth is that the shore is littered with morsels acceptable to sea fish, since it is near the shore that many of them do their foraging. Here are some of the possible natural baits for the boat and beach angler.

Butterfish: this small, spotted eel-like creature, sometimes called stone-eel, is found on stony beaches. It can be discovered by turning over rocks and seaweeds. In length it seldom exceeds six inches, though it does grow to a foot long. It has a small, compact head, an anal fin that extends along about one-third of the body and a dorsal that stretches from tail to head. Along the base of this dorsal are blackish spots, each surrounded by a narrow gold ring. The colour of the eel itself is anything from olive to purplish. The name comes from its extreme slipperiness. Useful as a spinning or trolling bait for pollack, and sometimes bass.

Clam: a mollusc which buries itself deeply on muddy, or mud and sand, shores. The biggest of the clams, the gaper, may grow to six inches in length. It breathes through a long extension which reaches through the sand to the surface: the breathing tube may be a foot long. Look for the round tunnel going down into the sand and dig. On a large hook the gaper, or any other smaller clam, makes a good bait for ray, skate, haddock and cod particularly.

Cockle: detected in the sand quite easily by the discoloured surface and two small holes made by its breathing and feeding siphons. Easily raked or dug out, and quite easily opened. Because of the small size of the cockle's 'works', two or three shelled cockles are used on small hooks. They prove attractive to flatfish, whiting, and wrasse especially.

Crabs: apart from marine worms, these are the most important source of bait for the sea fisher. They come in various shapes, sizes and conditions. The edible, or fishmonger's, crab is rarely used as bait, if only because it lives in water too deep for the average bait-seeker to gather it. The shore crabs are the species that most interest the angler, and of these the deadliest is probably the peeler, pill, or shedder crab.

To understand the relative merits of different kinds of shore crab the angler must know something of the processes by which these crustaceans grow. A crab reaches a certain stage of development, then sheds or moults its shell and emerges a soft and helpless thing on which any creature can prey. In this stage it hides itself away to wait for its new skin to harden. The shed crab rapidly becomes encased in a progressively hardening shell so that it moves rapidly from 'soft crab' (just moulted) to 'leather-back', 'crackly back' and finally the genuine fully-fledged and well-armoured article.

The bait-seeker soon learns to identify the various stages. A crab found gripped by a larger crab is almost certain to be a peeler or soft crab, and a female. A crab that upon being discovered puts on a militant display of snapping and waving its claws is equally almost certain to be a hard crab, although leather-backs sometimes try to bluff out their comparatively defenceless state in this way. A crab that tries to hide itself and keep its legs well tucked in is likely to be a peeler. Soft crabs are wrinkled of back since their skin is only just out of the old shell; they can't walk properly either. Press the skin of a leather-back and its texture will probably give it away. If in doubt as to whether a crab is a peeler or hard crab, break off one of its legs. A hard-back's legs will snap off entirely. That of a peeler will leave the flesh of the leg intact—in its new skin in fact—and only the outside shell will break. If this sounds brutal, reflect that crabs frequently shed legs voluntarily to escape capture.

Where, when, and how to look for peelers and soft crabs? May and June are the best times, but you can find them right through until October.

Search rocks and rock-pools on sandy or muddy shores, particularly those well covered by weed. Low water at spring tides is the best moment, since a greater area of beach is uncovered. Notched and knotted wrack are the weeds that shelter most crabs. Use a prodding rod to rake the bottoms of pools and to turn over boulders, search crevices, etc., Try the sand and shell deposit along the base of rocks, raking it over gently. Carry a wet sack to put your catch in. If in doubt how to pick up a large specimen without getting nipped, press the crab down into the sand by finger pressure in the middle of its shell. When ready, grip across the back of the shell or carapace with finger and thumb behind its claws. Wet seaweed placed in the sack will keep crabs fresh for a short while, but if they are to be kept alive for any length of time they must be suspended in a perforated box in deep water so that the current can swish through the borings. The same boxes, well lined with weed, will assist in keeping the crabs lively in the boat or on the beach if fishing is to be done only some hours after the bait collection. In a sheltered cool place indoors, provided sea water is used to freshen up the weed from time to time, these boxes will keep the crabs alive and healthy for several days.

When baiting with peelers, break off claws and legs, strip off the shell: either put them on the hook whole, or else cut up in sections. Soft crabs need simply be cut up after removal of appendages, since there is no shell to remove. Hard-backs may be used in emergency though it will be difficult to find a hook hold: wool or rubber bands will probably have to be used to make them secure to the hook.

Edible crabs are usually found only at low water during spring tides. In peeler form they make excellent bait for almost anything.

Hermit crabs are found usually in discarded whelk shells; they make useful bait, and can be taken by baiting a drop-net with fish cuttings. Tapping the shell with a stone will probably help in persuading the crab to leave home.

Fish: either alive as fry, or dead as whole fish, or cut into strips, will take many sea species. For example, mackerel may be trolled whole for shark and tunny, and a whole dead mackerel will take tope. Half a mackerel is good for conger, while strips of skin (called 'lasts') about an inch wide and running from back to belly on one side of the fish make excellent ground-fishing and float-fishing baits. Mackerel strips will take mackerel, bass, also brill, cod, turbot, whiting and skate. They are only moderately successful baits for flatfish.

Herring can be used in the same ways as mackerel. In strip form it kills whiting splendidly. Pilchard have roughly the same range as herring. Sprats have many uses from spinning to drift-lining for pollack, cod, and conger, as well as for other species.

Pouting is good for shark and conger and will take tope. Pieces of this fish will also catch pouting itself quite well. Smelts are useful for spinning and also leger.

Sprats are good all-round bait for spinning or trolling, for bottom and drift-line fishing. Pieces of sprat will take many fish including bass and flounders. Whiting used whole is a first-class tope bait. Pieces of this fish will take a number of species including conger, bass, whiting, pouting.

Small flatfish of only a few inches long can be used as live bait when hooked through the upper jaw for bass: dead they will take congers and bass on the bottom.

Herring-bone: is a kind of marine worm not unlike a ragworm in appearance and of the genus *glycera*. The worm will usually be found in the areas where lug is plentiful, though it does not burrow nearly so deeply as lug, six inches being the depth at which to seek it. Generally it is pinkish in colour and has a row of feet along its flanks. It also has a deep line of purply hue along the centre of one surface. Its head and tail is pointed. Unlike the rag it has no nippers. When picked up it thrashes about in the hand, coiling and untwisting. The worms can burrow and swim freely and, probably because of their ability to move, are well liked by many sea fish. Among these must be numbered pollack, flounders, plaice, bass, pouting, wrasse, sea trout, gurnard, grey mullet, smelts and mackerel. The herring-bone is ideal for float fishing. Unfortunately these worms are difficult to keep alive for any length of time. They will, however, catch fish when dead.

Limpets: on the whole a poor bait, probably because few fish are capable of dislodging them and removing the meat from the shell. In fact, it takes a shrewd and sudden blow with a blunt instrument to dislodge a limpet from a rock. The flesh inside the shell of this gastropod mollusc can be improved greatly in bait value if it is dipped in pilchard oil.

Lugworms: probably the main stand-by of the sea fisher. Their presence is easily detected by the cast they throw out on the sand. The castings are formed by the sand which the lugworm has passed through its digestive system, removing nutriment en route, and then ejected. The worm itself may be anything up to a foot long and occupies a U-shaped burrow. One end of the burrow is marked by a small cup-shaped depression in the sand: beneath this lies the head of the worm. The other end beneath the castings is occupied by the tail. Lugs are plentiful on muddy or sandy beaches that are not violently beaten by surf or tide.

In digging for lugs the casual bait-seeker usually begins a random excavation over a large area. This will produce lug all right but much of the effort is wasted. The experienced hand seeks out individual worms and goes to work on them. He spots the cast and the hole above the head of the worm, tests the hole to see that it has not filled in: if it has the worm has probably moved on. Then, between cast and hole he makes two digs with the spade. A third dig from the other side of the excavation will probably produce the worm. The lugworm thus uncovered will have a long thick body section of dark red or almost black colouring and a tail, far narrower than the body, packed with watery sand. Lugs can be kept alive in well-ventilated seaweed-filled boxes for twenty-four hours.

Lugworms are valuable bait for flatfish. They also will take many other species such as bass, codling and whiting, wrasse, and gurnard.

Mussels: one of the best all-round sea fishing baits, though fairly difficult to keep on the hook. They can be taken off rocks, piers, breakwaters or almost any point regularly submerged by the tide, though the biggest ones come from below the low-tide mark. They attach themselves to their holding point by a fibrous device called a byssus. Once gathered they can be kept alive indefinitely if hung in the water in a sack, and for many days if placed in a sack filled with weed and kept moist with sea water. Mussels are not easy to open and a stoutish though flexible double-edged knife is necessary. They will take codling (one of the most effective baits for this fish), whiting, pouting, dabs, haddock, gurnard, plaice, wrasse and other species. To bait with them use a hook with a fairly prominent barb, pass the point through the tongue of the mussel, back through the joint of the two leaves of the mussel, twist the bait and put the hook through the joint once more.

Prawns: the most useful kind to the sea angler is the common prawn, *Leander serratus*. This crustacean, of the same family group as the lobster and crayfish, grows to four inches or so and is found in tidal pools among the kelp and notched wrack. There is also a smaller variety, an almost transparent prawn which sometimes swarms in rock pools during summer. Prawns of both types can be caught in a drop-net baited with fragments of fish, or, more effectively, in a stout prawn-net pushed through the pools so as to disturb the weed and push the prawns out of hiding. This bait is not an easy one to keep alive, though short-range results can be obtained by immersing the catch in a perforated box in the manner recommended for crabs. When first caught, prawns should be put in a canvas bag wetted and filled with moist weed. Prawns attract many species. They make good spinning baits for bass. As deadbait they can be fished either raw or boiled for flounders on the bottom. As livebait on light float-tackle they are deadly for bass and pollack and other species. They can also be used when ground-fishing from a boat for codling and other varieties. To hook a live prawn, insert the point of a suitable round-bend hook into the last-but-one segment before the tail from the underside of the animal, and bring the hook out of the back.

Rag-worms: a loose term used by fishermen to describe many marine annelids. Rag-worms are flattish, many-jointed, and have a 'beard' of feet along either flank. Many of the species have very sharp nippers that can give the bait-seeker an unpleasant tweak. Length, anything from three to eight inches. Colour can be red, greenish, or bronze. They are found on muddy beaches between tide marks, and even beyond low-tide mark. Many varieties swim well. Where rags are known to exist, random digging at about six inches depth will produce a fair haul. Good big rags are often discovered beneath rocks. The bait-picker should seize a rag-worm boldly behind the head if he doesn't wish to be bitten. Rags can be kept lively for a day or more in seaweed-filled boxes to which a proportion of damp sand has been added: the boxes should be of wood. Rags are deadly bait for all kinds of fishing from spinning to use with float tackle, from bottom fishing to drift-lining. Fish take them well only in areas where they are dug. For instance, on the South Coast, they are mainly ineffective for most species. To get the maximum wriggly effect, a good length of tail should be left trailing from the hook after the rest of the worm has been threaded on to the hook, and then the point caught back through the worm.

King-rags are magnificent creatures that resemble their smaller relatives but sometimes grow to eighteen inches. *Nereis virens* is the biggest and best of the tribe. Very often fragments only of these giant worms are used on the hook, where they prove nearly as effective as the smaller variety of rag-worm complete.

Razor fish: these bivalves live in a long, thin shell, shaped something like an old-fashioned cut-throat razor. The type most sought by anglers for bait is *Ensis siliqua*. The razor-fish can burrow fast, is hinged along one side, and opens at both ends of its shell. From one end come the siphons, or feeding and breathing tubes, and at the bottom extends the muscular foot. You spot razor-fish by looking for key-shaped holes in the sand. They are capable of taking cover with great speed, so the approach needs to be almost as cautious as that used when hunting lobworms on a dew-dappled lawn after dark. Razor-fish can be captured by putting salt on their tail, or perhaps head. Simply place some block salt into the burrow: this makes the 'fish' rise and gives the man with a spade a better chance of digging it out. Many anglers make up special razor-fish spears that consist of two long-shanked sea hooks straightened out and re-tempered, then mounted in the end of a wooden rod, with their barbs opposed to each other and facing outwards. This imple-ment is plunged quickly into the razor's burrow and the whole animal impaled on the barbs, is then carefully drawn out. Cut up, or used whole, the razor-fish catches all manner of flatfish, rays, etc., on the bottom, and bass just off the beach.

Sand-eels: are of four kinds round the coasts of Britain, but only two, the Greater and Lesser Sand-eel, really interest the fisherman. The Greater has a wedge-shaped lower jaw and can grow as long as a foot, and sometimes more. The lesser variety is more likely to be less than six inches long. Like the river eel, the sand-eel is a true fish, lacking only pelvic fins. Dorsal and anal fins extend much of the way along the body. In colouring, sand-eels are not unlike bleak, having a greenish back running into bright silver flanks. The creatures occur right inshore and also in deep water, swimming from surface to mid-water. In summer the young eels often swarm in sheltered spots. When left behind by the tide they bury themselves happily in the sand. They can, therefore, be caught when swimming freely or when taking cover. Netting sand eels is by no means easy: perhaps the only effective method is to use a small seine net, home-made from muslin.

Buried eels can either be dug up or scraped to the surface. There is no means of telling where they lie, except perhaps by the activity of gulls on a certain stretch of the beach. In dryish sand they can be effectively dug up: in tidal shallows and pools, by scraping with an old table knife. This is driven into the sand with its point slanting towards the user, and is then drawn back through the sand. Any eel encountered is brought to the surface by the blade.

Sand-eels are tricky things to keep alive. A perforated container, not metal, is needed and should be suspended in moving sea water. These eels are probably the best baits known for drift-lining or float-fishing for sea trout, pollack, bass, mackerel, flounders, etc. To bait with an eel either pass the hook down through the mouth, out at the gills, catching the point in the skin of the belly; or, the hook may be put through the skin of the back close to the point of balance.

Shrimps: smaller than the prawn, of course, practically translucent and lives in sandy places. A shrimping-net is the best way to collect these creatures. It should be pushed along the bottom, the sand being banged occasionally to put the shrimps up. The shrimps can be kept alive in wet weed in sacks. They make useful baits for float-fishing for flounders, etc.

Squids: these cephalopods are usually caught by trawlermen though sometimes they come into harbours during warm summer weather: they are attracted by lights and can be pulled out by means of a pole with foul-hooking triangles attached. An approach to trawl fishermen will usually guarantee a supply of squid. Small ones used whole or big squids cut up make excellent bait for a number of species including bass, conger, and cod. The squid should not be confused with the octopus or the cuttle-fish. Squids have ten arms, two of which are far longer than the others. The body is cone-shaped, and the whole animal rarely exceeds two feet in length. Squids are armed with the usual inky discharge of their kind. When being fished out of the water they should be given a chance to fire off their ink sac, as the fluid is extremely powerful in smell.

Cuttle-fish: grow to about a foot long, have flattened bodies, and a fin that runs round the entire body. They, too, have ten arms, with two longer than the rest. Cuttles are caught in trawls quite often, and live over sandy bottoms.

Octopus: the third member of the cephalopod group (all three make good bait when obtainable), has eight arms, lives amongst rocks, and is sometimes caught on a line and often in crab and lobster pots. There are two varieties in British waters. The Common Octopus has a double row of suckers on each arm: the Lesser Octopus has suckers in one row only.

Whelks: make fair bait for wrasse and bream, and also for cod, dogfish, and haddock. The bigger specimens are found beyond low-water mark and are often brought up in trawls. Arrangements for a supply can sometimes be made with local fishermen. They are also trapped in wicker baskets resembling lobster pots.

Winkles: found almost everywhere on muddy and rocky shores, these molluscs make fair bait for wrasse. Put them in water just off the boil for a few seconds only, and remove in classic fashion with a pin.

Other sea-fishing baits: dry bread surface-fished before a shoal of mullet will sometimes catch fish. Paste, as used in river fishing, and made up in pea-sized balls is also useful for mullet beneath a float. Pork fat catches mullet. Pork or bacon rind can be used on a baited spoon for bass, pollack, gurnard. A wet-fly is sometimes excellent.

Preserved baits such as peeler-crab can now be bought tinned, also lug and ragworm. Mussels, cockles, and lugs can be preserved in salt. When freshly gathered, place the bait in wooden boxes and cover liberally with coarse salt; a layer of bait, a layer of salt. After a day or two remove and put down again with fresh salt. Will keep several months after treatment.

Many odd names are given to bait in different localities. Squid is sometimes called 'quiddle'; dried black lug, 'tobacco bait'; 'sea loops' can be smoked out of rock crevices and resemble woodlice; 'rounder' is a West Country name for razor fish.

SEA FISH, Habits Of: sea fish are just as much subject to local and long-distance migrations as are freshwater fish. These movements are governed by spawning and feeding. In spring many species move to spawning grounds, then retire in the summer to feeding grounds for recovery, and finally, during the winter, move to the most congenial temperature belt. This movement is further complicated by the fact that all species do not have the same requirements. Some, such as the flounder, are deep-water spawners. Some fish seek warm water in winter: bass and mackerel are examples. Others, instance the cod, like cold water. Since the colder water is found in the deeps in summer and the shallows in winter the effect upon these species can be seen. It is possible, however, to draw up a rule-of-thumb guide as to what fishes the angler can expect to find at different phases of the year, and where.

Spring: the flat spot, generally, in the sea fisher's year when cold and warm water species are in transition. By May, pollack, bass and mullet are inshore, also flatfish: black bream come in range of the boat fisher.

Summer: June–September represents the best time for pollack, bass, mullet, flounders, plaice, dabs, wrasse, conger, gurnards, mackerel inshore: the offshore angler can expect rays, whiting, dog, brill, black bream, whiting, coalfish, haddock, rays, skate, turbot, sharks, tunny, tope during this period.

Winter inshore fishing brings flatfish, congers, codling, whiting, cod, haddock.

Recommended reading: *Salt-Water Angling* by Michael Kennedy, and *Sea Angling* by Derek Fletcher.

SEA TROUT: variously called sewin (Wales), phinock or finnock (Scotland), peal (West Country) and salmon trout (a fishmonger's term). Though many people would have it differently, the sea trout is *not* a separate species. It is basically and morphologically the same fish as the brown trout (*Salmo trutta*). The theory is that originally the *Salmonidae*, of which family trout are, of course, members, were sea fish but became land-locked, possibly as the result of an ice-age. Some of the family retain a sea memory and return to the rivers only to breed. The salmon and sea, or migratory, trout, are the prime examples. However, there are also what are sometimes called 'slob' or 'bull' trout which hang around in the brackish water of estuaries. These are brown trout that have only half made up their minds. True sea trout know exactly where they are going. The life pattern of the sea trout follows almost exactly that of the salmon, except for the fact that, once in the sea, sea trout almost certainly do not range so far afield.

Big sea trout (the British record is 22 lb. 8 oz. from the River Frome in Somerset) closely resemble salmon. A superficial difference is in the spot marking. Sea trout spots are somewhat like asterisks and are dotted about the body more freely below the lateral line. The fish often has a purple colouring, especially when seen in the water. But the only sure way of telling salmon from sea trout is by a scale-count. The salmon has 10–12 scales from lateral line to dorsal fin, the sea trout 16.

When hooked, the sea trout puts on an astonishing fight, being out of the water almost as much as in it. The time to fish for it is as dusk falls, and often in total darkness. It will be found, like salmon, resting in the pools as it makes its up-river ourney.

SEA TROUT FISHING: sea trout follow approximately the same life cycle as salmon; that is to say they leave the rivers as smolts to feed and grow in the sea, and return to the rivers to spawn. It is during the run up-river to the spawning grounds that the angler catches them—though it must be admitted that sea trout are sometimes caught on bait, fly and in nets around the coast and in estuaries when looking for river entrances.

For its weight, the sea trout is probably the most sporting fish that swims. It has double the tenacity of the brown trout, with the added fighting quality of leaping freely from the water. To land sixty per cent. of the sea trout one hooks is a fair performance.

The fish will take a number of offerings, including worms, spinning baits of the smaller sort, and flies of bright and gaudy pattern almost invariably fished wet. Sea trout will take during the day but the best time to try for them is at dusk.

Little need be said about worm fishing. At best it is an inartistic sport as far as sea trout are concerned. On the Hampshire Avon they can be taken by trotting down float tackle in the Avon manner. This requires the usual float-fishing skill and is not to be sneered at. They come fiercely at small Devon minnows, small spoons, and fly spoons, but the most satisfying way of fishing for sea trout is with a wet-fly or flies. As has been said, the sea trout behaves in much the same way as the salmon, travelling up-stream when a freshet of water comes down from the hills, and lying up when shortage of water or fatigue prompts him to rest in one of the recognized holding pools on the river. He usually rests out of the current, unlike the salmon.

Wet-flies—three on a cast is probably wise during daylight, but two will be found less dangerous after dark—are thrown in the orthodox manner, down and across, and are worked by hand coiling or bunching of the line to give them movement.

When night fishing make sure the net is ready for action. Many a sea trout has been lost in the last few seconds of the battle. They make delicious eating and have a flavour similar to that of salmon.

Recommended standard wet-fly patterns: Alexandra, Butcher, Bloody Butcher, Teal and Green, Teal, Blue and Silver, Teal and Black, Mallard and Claret, Peter Ross, Golden Olive, Grouse and Orange, Professor, Zulu.

SEAWEEDS: various zones of weed are found on the beach as one moves down from high- to low-water mark. Beyond low water in the perpetually covered zones are further species. On the beach the topmost level is occupied by channelled wrack (*Pelvetia canaliculata*), so called because its fronds are curled up at the sides like gutters or channels. Next comes flat wrack (*Fucus spiralis*) which somewhat resembles channelled wrack except that the fronds are level and smooth-edged. Further down again one finds bladder wrack (*Fucus vesiculosus*) and knotted wrack (*Aescophyllum nodosum*). Bladder wrack is

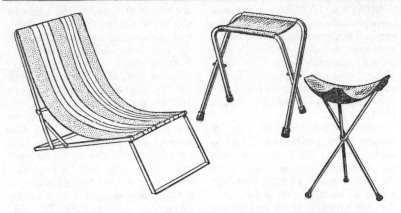

SEATS. *Three seats suitable for use when bank fishing.*

the well-known variety with the small air blisters which may be 'popped': knobbed or knotted wrack has thin stems swollen with large bladders.

In the lowest beach zone of all is found the notched or serrated wrack (*Fucus serratus*), which has jagged edges to its fronds. Exposed only by the lowest tides at springs is the kelp or oarweed (*Laminarie saccharina*). This is the long, crinkly brown weed which, after being detached from the rocks by a storm, is found by holiday makers and hung up to tell the weather. Another variety of kelp is the one that grows on a long stem with a head like a many-pronged fork (*Laminaria digitata*).

Bootlace weed, a long, thin, green weed growing many feet in length, is also found below low-water mark. This is a particular menace to the angler since it rises nearly vertically with the incoming tide and fouls his tackle at all levels.

SEATS: for coarse fishermen some kind of bank seat is invaluable. The main thing to remember is that this should be light and not too high; the angler must remain as invisible as possible. Perhaps the best all-round answer is the Sheffield seat-basket, or one of the metal framed canvas seat boxes with shoulder straps, now on the market.

SELF-COCKING FLOAT. *The right amount of small shot to weight the float, is contained in the hollow body of the float.*

SELF-COCKING FLOAT: a float which is in itself sufficiently weighted to stand upright in the water.

SENSES OF FISH: fish almost certainly have no brain in a thinking sense. They react to a given situation —danger, hunger, suspicion—in a purely instinctive way. A carp, which has the largest of brains among our freshwater fish, is probably slightly more stupid than a farmyard hen.

Hearing: fish certainly 'hear' or at least detect sounds and vibrations under water. They are probably insulated from sounds made above the surface in air. There is now even a line of thought that argues that fish can be attracted by underwater noise. The Heddon bait company of America has produced a 'sonic' or noise-making pike plug. Fish can also make noises on their own account.

Sight: fish vision is very keen under water, though restricted optically when looking through the surface. To a submerged fish the surface above his head looks like a mirror except for a fairly clear patch right in the centre. Through this he can see murkily to the outside world, and at a fixed angle. This patch is called by anglers 'the window'. Most freshwater fish are monocular, that is to say that each eye looks out on its own flank and without co-ordination with the other eye. Significantly enough, the predatory fish have mainly binocular vision: they can focus both eyes on an object. This plainly is necessary for grabbing a moving meal. Monocular fish, such as roach and bream, need to keep a sharp look-out on either flank in order to protect themselves from attack.

Feeling: fish are probably largely devoid of feeling as human beings know it. For instance they don't feel pain—as far as we can tell—when a hook penetrates their lip. There are numerous cases of fish being foul-hooked in the eye, of the loosened eye being put on the hook as bait, and of the same fish taking its own eye and being caught on it a few moments later. Fish certainly experience fear, or at least an urgent need for flight. Most of their nerve centres are distributed along the lateral line which runs midway down the flank. Through this they can detect vibrations in the water: it is thought that a pike spots its prey when still at long range through this lateral line mechanism. Fish almost certainly feel heat as a pain, being themselves cold-blooded. To hold them in the hand is no kindness to them and may even cause permanent damage, especially if the protective coating of slime is removed.

Touch: fish have an acute sense of touch. Several species, notably the bottom-feeders, use this in searching for food. Witness the barbules on the gudgeon and barbel and the cod family.

Smell and taste: both almost certainly play a part in the life and habits of fish, though it is hard to say where one ends and the other begins. It is now thought that salmon smell their way back to their home rivers by detecting in solution the infinitesimally small variations in water 'smell' of their native streams. Experiments in America have tended to substantiate this. Smell on dead baits, particularly formalin-preserved ones, seems to have an adverse affect on their powers of attraction. On the other hand, pike anglers are having increasing success with dead herring fished on snap tackle. This is believed to be because the pike detects by smell the oily scent of the herring. Eels seem capable of smelling their way to a dead bait, since most of their feeding is done at night.

SET: a permanent bend acquired by a rod either from use or because it has been incorrectly stored.

SEWIN: the name used in many parts of Wales for sea trout.

SCHELLY: *Coregonus clupeoides stigmatus*, a fish very similar to the powan found in Ullswater and Haweswater in the Lake District.

prominent British sport. Sharks are found in the warm-water channels round many parts of the south and west coasts and undoubtedly more and more shark-fishing centres will be opened up. The north coast of Cornwall is an obvious shark ground. In Newlyn the sharks are actually seen to come into the

SHARKS. *Three of the species most commonly found round the coasts of Britain, mainly in the western and south-western waters of Devon and Cornwall.* Top, *Porbeagle;* Centre, *Mako;* Bottom, *Thresher.*

The fins of the schelly are black and the upper half of the fish has numerous black dots. Powan fins are green and the back is deep purple. The schelly also has one more ray in the anal fin. The name is often pronounced as 'scheely'.

SHARKS: Since 1952 when more than 80 sharks were caught by rod-and-line anglers out of Looe, Cornwall, shark fishing has become a

harbour, probably to scavenge round the outfall from the pilchard factory. Shark-fishing off the West of Ireland is already well developed, Achill Island, County Mayo, being particularly well known (the biggest porbeagle on record—365 lb.—in British waters was caught there; unfortunately it was finished off with a Luger pistol and thus could not qualify for record status). Details of shark fishing tackle and technique are given under BIG-GAME FISHING. What follows here is a brief description of the main species among the British sharks.

The big-game sharks are the Blue Shark, the Porbeagle, the Thresher, and, lately, the Mako. Of these the biggest is the porbeagle (*Lamna cornubica*). In colour this fish is olive to khaki, has a deeper body than the other varieties, very long gill openings, and a tail whose lower lobe is long and keel-like. It also has very long teeth. A porbeagle of 271 lb. was caught from Looe in 1957.

The Blue Shark (*Carcharinus glaucus*) is the most common of the fish to give sport to the now flourishing Shark Fishing Club of Great Britain. This is a slimmer, smaller fish altogether, the record at the moment being 212 lb. The gill openings in this case are small and the fish has a long slim snout.

The Thresher (*Alopias vulpes*) is fairly rare in British waters and, like the porbeagle, grows to a great size. The record, taken off Dungeness, stands at 280 lb. This fish has an immensely long upper lobe to its tail. Both second dorsal and anal fins are noticeably small. The fish when hooked gives a most acrobatic and truly big-game performance, leaping yards out of the water.

The Basking shark, found off the west coasts of Scotland and Ireland, must also be mentioned. *Cetorhinus maximus* is a huge brute that is almost harmless to fish and man, being a plankton-eater. Though much has been written about hunting these sharks they are in fact pretty easily subdued. Their bulk is their only weapon. They are never fished for with rod and line. Commercially they are valuable for the oil extracted from their liver.

It remains to be added that among the minor members of the shark tribe to be found in British waters are the tope, the nursehound and spur dogfish.

SHEFFIELD STYLE: the accepted match-fishing style, using a light tip-action rod and gossamer tackle; fully described in the entry on CASTING.

SHOT, SPLIT-SHOT: small lead pellets, partially sliced through, which can be nipped on to line or cast to weight the tackle and cock the float. They correspond in size roughly to the various gradations of shotgun pellets. They are sold usually in a selection of sizes. Swan shot are very big, as are AA or BB. Dust shot are minute and are used only with the lightest of quill floats. Shot are also used to stop leger weights. They are best nipped on to the cast with a fine pair of long-nosed pliers.

SHOOTING LINE: refers to the manner in which the fly-fisherman gets line into the air when casting. He 'strips' line from the reel with his left hand and feeds it through the rod rings into the air, usually when making the back-cast. Several yards can be shot at the same time by the practised hand. Line is also shot during the final forward cast in order to make the fly fall softly on the water, and so avoid the line falling straight. The shooting is done in this case almost as the throw exhausts itself. The effect of adding another yard or so at the last moment prevents the line from jerking tight, and the fly from rebounding at the end of its gut or nylon cast.

SHRIMP, FRESHWATER: *Gammarus pulex*, a small crustacean with a rather flattened body found in running water. Almost transparent: a valuable item of trout and coarse fish food. Trout that take a lot of shrimp tend to have pinkish flesh.

SIDE-STRAIN: lateral strain applied horizontally to a running fish in an effort to turn it from water unfavourable to the angler.

SILICONES: used these days in flotants for fly and line. A dry-fly immersed in silicone-treated spirit will float for a remarkably long time if it is cleaned after catching a fish.

SILKWEED: greeny weed of cotton-wool like texture found on piles and particularly on weir sills. Undoubtedly eaten by fish of many species including chub, dace, roach and even barbel, especially in early summer. When fishing weir-pools, the angler will do well to try this bait. To get it on the hook simply drag the latter across the weir sill until enough adheres. Fish may take it for itself alone, or for the animal-culae that are found in the weed.

SILVER BREAM: see BREAM.

SIMPLE RAYS: fin rays that consist of one single spine, as opposed to the bifurcations of branched rays.

SINK-AND-DRAW: an old and trusted method of taking predatory fish with deadbait. The lure, a small dead fish, is fixed head-down with a lead weight in its mouth and is armed with hooks along its flank. When cast out the deadbait is allowed to plummet to the bottom and is then retrieved in a sink-and-draw motion that causes it to dive and swoop enticingly. Pike fall for this trick. Minnow used in this manner are deadly for perch. The tackle for perch fishing is sometimes described as 'drop minnow'. The old word for this type of spinning was 'trolling', not to be confused with 'trailing'—pulling a bait behind a boat.

When fishing sink-and-draw for pike the weight is sometimes put two or three feet up the trace in the direction of the rod. In this case, the bait is mounted facing up the line, so that it follows the lead towards the bottom in a wavering motion. This works extremely well when fishing a weed-covered bottom. The lead can be allowed to touch bottom, recovery being commenced directly this is felt. In this way, the bait itself seldom reaches the weed thus minimizing the risk of it being entangled therein. No spinning vanes are attached for this kind of fishing, the natural shape of the bait causing it to dart and wobble slightly. Sink-and-draw can also be carried out effectively with lobworms for perch.

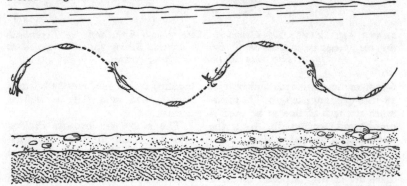

SINK-AND-DRAW. *An effective method of catching predatory fish. The undulating movement of the bait attracts the attention of a hungry fish.*

SIX-NINE TACKLE: a standardized method of describing heavy sea-fishing tackle. Six-nine is used sometimes for tarpon and sail-fish though it is not strictly in the big-game class. The specification, drawn up in the early days of big-game and international sea fishing by the Catalina Club of California and others, is for a rod of

ever, the two most common are: the Thornback (*Raia clavata*), and Common Skate (*Raia batis*). The sting-ray, often thought of as a skate, is in fact a member of a separate family, the *Trygonidae*, and is itself known as *Trygon pastinaca*. Skate are found over sandy ground in which rocks or even mud patches abound. They feed on small crus-

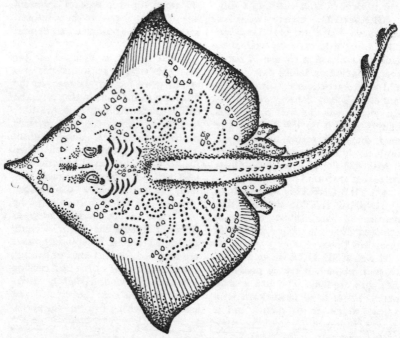

SKATE AND RAYS. *The Common Skate, shown here, and the Thornback are the species most common in British waters. Strong tackle is needed to raise these fish once they go to ground.*

6-foot minimum length and butt of 18-inch maximum length. The maximum strength of line to be used is nine-thread, or 27 lb. b.s.: the test-curve of the rod, 7 lb.

SKATES AND RAYS: family *Raiidae*, also (sting-ray) *Trygonidae*; there are at least a dozen different species that may be caught by the sea angler in British waters. How-

taceans, crabs, fish, especially small flatfish, and sand eels, as well as worms, etc.

The skates are broadly divided into long- and short-snouted varieties. Among the long-snouted are Common Skate—grey to purple on upper surface, smooth-skinned, with a row of spines down the tail. The snout of the female is longer than that of the male and the eye is smaller. It grows to a length of 7 feet at least and can be caught weighing up to 200 pounds in deep water. The Long-nosed Skate (*R. oxyrhynchus*)—reaches a length of about three feet, has the first dorsal larger than the second. It is greyish on both surfaces but has spots and streaks on the upper side. The Flapper Skate (*R. macrorhynchus*)—under-surface white with black spots, brown above and seldom growing much more than two feet in length. The White Skate (*R. alba*)—largest of the British skates, having been known to reach 500 lb., is distinguished by its pure-white underside. The Shagreen Skate (*R. fullonica*)—yellowish brown above and white below and seldom exceeding three feet.

The short-snouted tribe include: the Spotted Ray (*R. maculata*)—found on the South Coast of Britain and growing to about three feet, chocolate brown in colour with heavy spotting on the upper surface. The Starry Ray (*R. radiata*)—a deep-water ray that is very rare, having a brown under-surface without spots. The Cuckoo Ray (*R. naevus*)—this species has a pear-shaped body with the sides forming a continuous curve. The Painted Ray (*R. microcellata*)—is between two and three feet in length, grey above and blotched with white and brown. The Thornback—has a brownish upper side mottled with spots and a white under-surface. This skate comes closer inshore than most but seldom exceeds 30 lb. Thorny spines on the snout, body, and tail give it its name.

SKATE-FISHING: calls for neither fine tackle nor great finesse. The fish can be taken in some localities, though rarely from the beach. Usually a boat is necessary in which case the bait is legered or paternostered on a sandy bottom, or else drifted over the sea bed. Fresh fish baits kill best. Tackle needs to be strong stuff to stand up to the inevitable tug of war which a battle with a big skate is bound to become. Line of 40-lb. breaking strain, the last two or three feet being doubled and knotted, is needed. A strong, short rod with plenty of lifting power is essential. Trace wire to combat the rough backs and sharp spines of these fish should be of 30-lb. b.s. while hooks must be large enough to hold a big bait (say 10/0) and well tempered.

Many a hook has straightened out during a fight with a skate. When a skate is hooked its invariable tactic is to try and bury itself in the sand which, by movements of its 'wings', it can do surprisingly quickly. In which case only steady, brute pressure will move it, unless irritating tactics of plucking the line or sending an old weight down on a loop of Cuttyhunk will stir it into movement. In either case the angler must seize the initiative immediately the skate moves and keep it off the bottom, pumping it to the surface.

Skate can be mighty unpleasant things to handle. Sacking and a gaff should always be to hand since many blood-poisoning cases have resulted from cuts received from spines and from the razor-sharp surfaces of the claspers found in the male fish. With the sting-ray, particularly, great care must be shown. This fish, which has a long, serrated spine on the tail, though no fins thereon, is darker than the others and its belly is invariably white. But the sting, an ugly-looking spine, is in the tail. This can inflict bad wounds into which poison is injected. Primitive warriors used to tip their spears with sting-ray spines. A skate bite is difficult to recognize since there is nothing consistent about it. The big fish usually take quietly. Very often skate are foul-hooked. This is thought to be because they cover the bait with their bodies, the mouth being on the underside. A quick strike often drives the hook home into belly or wings.

SKELLY: a slang name for chub.

SLIDING-FLOAT: a float designed for use where the water to be fished is much deeper than the length of the rod. The line passes through two rings on the float. The float is free to move on the line up to the point at which a rubber stop is tied on to the line. For casting purposes the sliding-float rests on the top-most weight of the tackle. It then rises through the water until it meets the rubber stop. The latter, of course, is set at the exact depth to be fished. A taking fish immediately pulls the float against the rubber stop thus giving a normal reaction.

SLIPPING-CLUTCH: a device built into a fixed-spool reel that enables a running fish to take line. This clutch is the most misunderstood piece of apparatus in the whole of fishing. The point is that the angler cannot do any good by winding against a running fish, slipping clutch or not. The clutch should be adjusted to a setting at which a fish can take line without causing a break. In playing the angler must apply additional pressure to the spool with his fingers. Only when the fish permits does he recover line.

SLOB-TROUT: sometimes called bull trout, are brown trout that migrate only as far as the estuary. There is now no doubt that brown and sea trout are one and the same fish, except for the fact that the sea trout has the migratory instinct and changes its coat and method of life when it

begins its movement to the sea. Slob-trout are somewhere in between the full sea trout and the brown trout. Because of the richness of estuarine feeding, they usually grow to a good size: their flesh is pink.

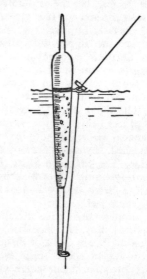

SLIDING-FLOAT. *The line is free to move through the float-rings to where a 'stop' is tied to the line.*

SMELT: caught along the South Coast on light tackle, a silvery greenish fish with a silver line along its flanks. The tail is forked and there are two dorsal fins, one of them really an adipose fin. Small fragments of worm or tiny ragworms are used on small hooks. Several hooks are used and the tackle is lightly shotted. The bite is a gentle one and a slight strike, provided it is made quickly is enough.

SMOLT: the term used to describe the young of both salmon and sea trout when they have grown sufficiently large to leave the river on their first migration to the sea. At this stage they have taken on their silver coats.

SMUTS, SMUTTING: smut is the term loosely given by trout fisherman to tiny flies of the *Diptera* (two-winged insects) family. The trout take these avidly on occasions, often ignoring more succulent insects. A smutting trout is difficult, if not impossible, to catch, simply because the makers of artificial flies cannot produce one sufficiently small.

SNAILS, Freshwater: are of many varieties, most of them of more interest to aquarists than anglers. However, some of the smaller varieties are avidly eaten by fish, particularly trout. Unfortunately, they are difficult to put on the hook or to imitate. There seems some reason to suppose that fish mistake hempseed for one of the fresh-water molluscs, possibly the pea-shell cockle.

SNAP-TACKLE: a tackle designed in the first instance by Alfred Jardine, a great pike angler of the later years of the last century, designed for holding livebait and for giving the pike fisherman the chance to strike almost the instant the pike begins its run. The tackle is mounted on wire, and the upper triangle slides along this mount. The tackle is adjusted to the size of the livebait so that the top triangle, which has a specially shaped point for the job, can be stuck through the ridge of the bait's back in front of the dorsal fin. The flattened third hook of the end triangle is then laid inside the gill-opening of the bait.

SNATCH, To: an illegal method of taking fish by foul-hooking with a hand-line and large triangles. Used by salmon poachers against fish resting in well-known lies.

SNECKED HOOKS: hooks with an off-set point, sometimes favoured by game-anglers.

SNOOD: sea-fishing term for the hook-link of pasternoster or leger gear when made of flax line or nylon rather than of wire or plastic.

SOLE: *Solea vulgaris,* family *Pleuronectidae.* There are four varieties to be found round British coasts, but *vulgaris* is the one usually caught. The others are: sand sole (brownish with small black dots); the solenette, often caught in shrimping nets, which looks like a small common sole, and seldom exceeds four inches; and the thickback, or variegated, sole (reddish brown with six or so dark bands running between the fins).

A bunch of small ragworms is perhaps the best bait, though mussel and shrimp both work. Dried soleskin makes excellent pollock bait when wrapped round a long-shanked hook. It is fished near the surface. Lemon sole is purely a fishmonger's term. A common sole of specimen size scales in the region of one-and-a-half pounds.

SNAP-TACKLE. *A wire-mounted tackle equipped with treble hooks for mounting livebait and used in pike-fishing.*

SOLESKIN: dried soleskin cut into slips and put on a long-shanked hook makes a deadly trailing lure for many sea fish.

SONAGHAN: local name for a beautiful and hard-fighting Irish trout.

SPHAGNUM: or bog-moss—the foundation material of many peat bogs. Extremely useful to anglers for the storage of worms to be used as bait.

SPAWNING: the all-round angler is fortunate in the fact that the so-called coarse fish and the salmon and trout groups have their spawning periods at different times of the year. The coarse fish spawn approximately, and accordingly to latitude and locality, from February to mid-June, and the *Salmonidae* from September until February and even March. Between these two families comes the grayling which is biologically and morphologically a member of the salmon group, but chooses to spawn with the coarse fish. How do the different species go about reproducing their kind?

Nature is careful to give fish every chance of propagating their species. The enemies in the underwater world are so numerous that some form of natural 'insurance policy' has to be devised. Thus the smaller fish, having small body capacity in which to house spawn, lay few eggs and then guard them fiercely: the bigger species deposit many hundreds and even thousands of eggs on the principle that some must get through.

As instances of the small fish, the stickleback builds a nest in which the eggs are laid and fertilized, the male standing guard over them to keep away predators. The bitterling places its eggs, by means of a long oviduct extending from the female, into the open shell of a freshwater mussel, where the young fish remain until sufficiently developed to hold their own with some, at least, of the predators surrounding them.

Perhaps the best co-operative effort of male and female is seen in the salmon and trout groups. Here the spawning fish make their way to gravel shallows. The salmon and sea trout have travelled many miles upstream from the sea to do this. River trout make local migrations to friendly shallows to lay their eggs. Fish of these groups can often be seen working side by side to dig out shallow trenches in the gravel spawning beds, known as 'redds'. The female does most of the work with her belly and tail fin, the male sometimes assisting. The female lays her eggs, a few at a time, over a period of days, one of the accompanying males swimming in to shed his milt and fertilize the eggs. The period in which fertilization can take place is an extremely limited one, extending from half a minute with brown trout to five minutes in the case of carp. Once the eggs are laid and fertilized the female scoops gravel over them to hide and protect them and moves off to fresh spawning or feeding grounds. Her job is then done and she assumes no further responsibility for what may come. Floods, insect predators, fish, all claim their toll of fertilized and developing eggs. However, sufficient survive. After two or three months the alevins, or young fish, emerge. To see them through their first few weeks of life they are equipped with a yolk sac filled with nourishment.

The coarse fish, particularly the cyprinid group, are far more casual in their spawning methods, and consequently they lay many more eggs to make up for their haphazard way of breeding. Perch lay their eggs in long sticky strings that attach themselves to water plants, where the males find them and fertilize them. Perch eggs hatch in from eight to ten days according to water temperature. Perch fry in the early days can be spotted by their attempts to reach the surface in shoals where they seek air to fill their swim bladders: if they fail in finding this through detergent film or other forms of pollution, they perish.

Pike lay many thousands of sticky eggs, the females frequently devouring the smaller males who have recently fertilized their ova. Pike fry once hatched cling vertically to water plants. After about three weeks the fry assume a horizontal position and begin their predatory life, seeking water-fleas, larvae and other small water creatures. A few weeks more and the pike is fully launched on its life of eat or be eaten, attacking anything of its own size and even larger, and frequently trying to swallow its shoal fellows.

Most of the cyprinid family follow the pattern of the pike during their first few hours of existence. On hatching, the carp, for example, leaves its egg case and sinks head-first to the bottom. There, or on the way there, it attaches itself with its mouth to a water plant. Then the fry rests until it is strong enough to reach the surface where it goes through the complicated and laborious process of filling its swim bladder. Because of the warm time at which the eggs hatch, carp quickly reach a true fish-like shape and are recognizable for what they are after a month or so of growth.

Apart from the salmon the most fascinating of all spawning stories is probably that of the eel which migrates from the local duck-pond to the nearest river and so to the sea where it eventually finds its way by some far-from-blind instinct to the centre of the South Atlantic Ocean. There, in the region of the Sargasso Sea, it spawns. Eventually the young jelly-like fry are carried by the Gulf Stream to all the coasts which that current touches. The young eels, known now as elver, make their way up the rivers, and across land to lakes and ponds to begin the story all over again.

SPEAR, Butt: a screw-in device fitted, usually to fly rods, in place of a button or butt cap. When not in use, the rod can be stuck

SPEAR, BUTT. *A screw-on butt fitting which enables a rod to be stood upright in the ground.*

upright in the bank. This is invaluable when the angler is sitting waiting for a rise. The danger in laying a rod down on the bank is that sooner or later you are certain to tread on it.

SPEY-CAST: an intricate fly-cast developed for use on the River Spey where frequently there are obstacles at the back of the caster. The essence of the Spey-cast is that the line doesn't pass behind the angler.

SPINNER: term meaning the perfect fly, the imago of the ephemerid group of insects: also one who fishes by spinning; a spinning bait; even a spinning rod.

SPINNING: a method of taking predatory fish by presenting them with a moving imitation of their small live prey. Spinning is a branch of angling that produces many specialists. Properly, it is but part of the all-round angler's armament.

The tackle is described in detail

under RODS and REELS. Here we are concerned with the theory of the business.

Almost all freshwater fish can at times be taken on a spinner. There are records of bream, barbel, roach, rudd and even carp being caught on spinning bait. The true quarries of the spinner are, however, perch, pike, chub, and, of course, trout, sea trout and salmon, and several sea fish such as flounders and bass. All these are fish that live practically entirely by major predation.

To achieve the maximum attraction the spinning lure must obviously simulate the kind of living food its quarry best likes to seek. All fish, and particularly predatory fish, are faced with the same economic problem. How to catch as much food as they need for survival and health without expending too much energy in so doing. Plainly, the more energy they waste in the chase, the more they have to catch and eat to recharge their batteries. It follows, then, that the easy-to-see, easy-to-detect, easy-to-catch meal, fished at the most convenient depth, will be the one the predator goes for first. On top of this the lure should be as attractive as possible in shape, size and actual species (if deadbait is used), or simulated species, if an imitation is employed.

The problems to be solved then are (1), to find the predatory fish at the right depth and in the right spot; (2), to present a spinning bait in its most attractive form.

To solve the first, an acute eye for water is needed. The spinner must be able to visualize the effect of currents on the lurking fish and realize that physical features of rivers are not confined to its banks and visible aspects. Underwater topography has an equally pronounced effect upon the feeding habits of fish. Predatory fish do not care to waste energy. They will, therefore, be found where food exists in sufficient quantity to make hunting it worthwhile. They will also hide in spots where they have to exert themselves comparatively little in holding their place against the current. It follows that shelter from the force of the stream, and natural cover in the form of weed beds, are two factors influencing the lies of predatory river fish.

In still waters, pike and perch may be more difficult to locate. Temperature has a pronounced effect upon the behaviour of predators, and, indeed, on all fish both in still and running water. In very cold spells, lake fish will tend to congregate in the depths where, strangely enough, the water is at its warmest. After three weeks of heavy frost, pike and perch should be sought in the deepest holes of a lake or reservoir.

Now for the question of presentation. All fishing rules exist to be broken. One can make only generalizations, and stress that experience may well prove the opposite to be true on certain occasions. For instance: it is fairly safe to say that big pike like big spinning baits—especially in the Irish loughs. Nevertheless, the Lough Conn record of 53 lb. fell for a small spoon.

Here are some general spinning principles:

Salmon: salmon are said not to feed in fresh water. Just the same they take flies and spinning baits, notably plugs of various sorts, small Devon and Wye minnows, wagtails, phantoms, spoons, quill minnows, and prawns. Generally speaking, the lure has to be shown to the fish. That is to say it must be flashed in front of its nose, as if to goad it, and, if necessary, several times. Accurate casting and retrieving is essential, and, of course, close knowledge of the salmon's lie.

Sea trout: these migratory trout generally fall for a fast, bright spin with a small bait, probably a minnow. They'll be found in recognized holding pools, as will salmon. In the evening, spinning the tail of the pool will often produce fish.

Brown trout: normal spinning principles apply. Judge the most likely holding water and spin it carefully with smallish, fast-moving baits. The brown trout does not mind a darting chase.

Pike: pike, without doubt, like crippled, slow-moving, hesitant, or unusual fish. They also, being lazy brutes, like a good feed for their money. Pike baits should be selected either to make a well-defined vibration which gives the impression of a fair-sized fish moving with difficulty (either wounded or sick): or, to provide plenty of flash; or to produce an impression of apparent size. Fast, even spinning is to be deplored. The retrieve should be jerky and even faltering with changes of depth and occasional halts punctuated with lively spurts.

Perch: these fish don't mind chasing. They appear to like to attack their prey by damaging the tail. Small bright baits work best. Artificial minnows and small spoons are fine.

Chub: small plugs and spoons fished in likely lies sometimes lure the really big specimens.

Note: at the start of the coarse angling season, when fish are re-recovering from spawning, many species not normally known for taking meat meals are seen to be attacking fry. Under these conditions, particularly when fry are noticed scattering in the shallows, a tiny tear-drop, or fly-, spoon spun

amid the shoals can provide an unexpected taker.

Apart from varying the speed of retrieve, life can be given to a spinning bait by raising and lowering the rod top, and by moving the rod laterally.

SPINNING BAITS: these all have the same purpose—to imitate when drawn through the water some small fish appetizing to predators. They divide roughly into artificials and those lures using deadbait. The artificials include:

Spoons: brightish baits with a spoon-shaped blade. The blade either spins round a central rigid axis or else flutters freely from its front end.

Plugs: solid, torpedo-shaped, non-rotating baits armed with one or more triangles and designed to imitate wounded fish limping through the water. Deadly when fished in spurts and dashes for pike.

Devon minnows: small gold, silver or blue metal torpedo baits with spinning vanes at the nose. Usually there is a single triangle at the tail attached to a wire 'flight' running through the centre of the minnow's body. Above the tail triangle is a bead which acts as a bearing surface on which the body can rotate. Not much use for pike. Good for salmon, trout, sea trout, perch and bass.

Rubber plugs: these are mainly French in origin. They closely imitate small fish. The 'Plucky' is a notable example, also the 'Vivif' baits marketed by a British firm.

Deadbaits: usually are mounted on wobbling or spinning 'flights'. The wobbling flight has a bar which is stuck into the middle of the fish to give the body twist. Spinning flights have rotating vanes at their head: the 'Archer' flight is a famous example. The baits used with these can be either freshly caught, bought from the fishmonger, or else preserved in formalin. The great advantage is that they do look like the real thing and give the attacking fish a soft and lifelike texture on which to bite. Deadbaits can also be bought encased in a cellulose or plastic solution. A further variation is the 'Scarab' bait in which the deadbait is placed in a transparent sheath equipped with spinning vanes.

SPLIT-CANE: a method of rod-making in which the finest bamboo cane is taken, split with fractional accuracy into long strips of carefully calculated section, and then stuck together with (these days) synthetic resin glues. Such rods are usually hexagonal. They are occasionally built hollow for lightness. They may even, for heavy duty, have a thin steel core inside the cane —a refinement that generally adds little beyond weight to the rod. Split-cane rods when made by craftsmen are without doubt the finest weapons an angler can use. Unfortunately the numbers of such craftsmen are rapidly falling. Before long, split-cane—unless manufactured abroad, as in Japan—is likely to fall out of general use. Fibreglass will probably replace at least the cheaper split-cane rods.

SPLIT-RINGS: small split metal rings used for connecting swivels to traces, hooks to spinning lures, etc.

SPOONS: these spinning baits are said to have originated at a tea party held by an ornamental lake at which the hostess let fall a small silver teaspoon into the water. This was immediately gobbled by an outsize pike. Though there is almost certainly no truth in the story, perfectly good spinning baits can be made from the business end of a common-or-garden tablespoon. The device is probably much older than the tea party in question. South Sea islanders have known about the value of wobbling and revolving lures for hundreds of years.

The principle of any spoon is the same, namely that it revolves or flutters when drawn through the water, giving an impression of bulk. Because the rotating action of the bait transmits twist, or 'kink', to the line, swivels must be used on the trace. These, unless of the ball-bearing type, or assisted by an anti-kink device in the form of a vane or weight, will still permit twist. The function of all such devices is that they provide resistance to kink well below the central axis of the swivel. To put kink into the line, therefore, the bait not only has to turn the swivel but also swing the anti-kink weight or vane through 360 degrees, which it is unable to do against the pressure of the water.

The simplest type of spoon is one attached to the line or trace by a split-ring or swivel at its front end. A split-ring holds a triangle hook at the rear. When drawn through the water the spoon flutters and rotates.

However, the more deadly patterns give an impression of size by being attached at the front end only to a central wire or bar. This bar carries the nose-swivel and rear hooks. The spoon itself whirls in a wide arc about this bar so that it looks far bulkier than it really is. Notable examples are the Horton Evans 'Vibro' and the old-established kidney bar spoon. The Colorado spoon, which is centrally mounted about a wire axis, spins by virtue of two vanes at its front end. Because of its shape and the area of these vanes, the Colorado when drawn through the water also appears larger than it is.

For chub and trout, small spoons,

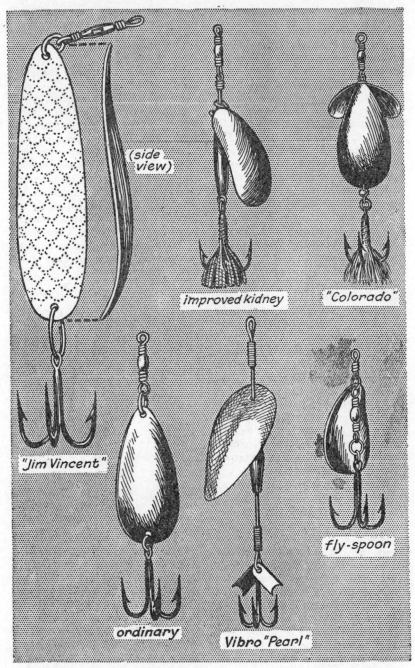

(side view)

improved kidney

"Colorado"

"Jim Vincent"

ordinary

Vibro "Pearl"

fly-spoon

SPOONS. *A selection of some of the spoons used by spinning enthusiasts.*

frequently bring results. These, sometimes known as tear-drop spoons, or, more commonly, fly spoons, are minute affairs attached at the front end to a swivel. Many small Continental patterns are now on the market. Some of the best are those combining feathers or an actual fly with a small spoon or spoons. The Continentals are also adept at producing small spoons with plenty of body weight for casting and holding their place in the stream. Do-it-yourself spoon makers should note that sectional density is an essential. No spoon made of flimsy material will react properly when drawn through the water.

SPUR-DOG: a member of the shark family, grey in colour and something like a tope. It gets its name from two spurs in front of the dorsal fins. These are poisonous and highly dangerous.

STAR-DRAG: adjustable tension device often built into big sea multiplying reels. Tension is varied by means of a star-shaped nut.

STEEPLE-CAST: a fly-cast designed to miss tall obstacles to the rear of the caster. It is made like the normal backcast of the overhead throw except the the line is thrown upward behind the fisherman.

STEWART TACKLE: two- or three-hook worm tackle, the hooks, generally round-bend patterns, being mounted one above the other on the cast. Where three hooks are used, the middle hook usually faces in the opposite direction to the other two. The tackle is designed for holding large lobworms so that a fish attacking them at any point has an equal chance of being hooked. The snag is that the tackle has three times as many chances of becoming caught on weed as the single hook. On balance, the added hooking power justifies the risk. Stewart

tackle can be easily made up by whipping eyed hooks to a suitable piece of nylon.

STICKBAIT: a slang name for caddis larvae.

STICKLEBACKS: small spined fish that rarely occur in fertile fishing waters. There are two varieties, the ten-spined (*Pygosteus pungitius*) and the three-spined (*Gasterosteus aculeatus*), both of the *Gasterosteidae* family. During the breeding season the male takes on a splendid red colouring. Males are extremely aggressive, particularly in the neighbourhood of their nests. Care should be taken when keeping sticklebacks as aquarium occupants. They attack other species readily.

STEWART TAĆKLE. *Three-hook mount for use when baiting with lobworm to make the bait more secure.*

STOMACH CONTENTS OF TROUT: these are worth examining. In fact, it often pays to slit open the first takeable fish of the day, and place its stomach in a saucer of water. The various insects in the stomach will then separate and float on the surface. Identification may tell you on what the trout are feeding and guide you to the right artificial. A marrow spoon is sometimes used to achieve the same effect. It is poked down the trout's throat and turned round in the top of the stomach to scoop up contents.

STONE-FLY: the largest member of the *Perlidae* family, found in rough moorland streams mainly. The larvae crawls out of the water to hatch. Most effective as a bait when fished in May as a 'creeper', i.e., in larval form.

STREAMER FLIES: flies consisting mainly of a large back-swept 'wing' made of hair or long cock's hackle. They are all fry-imitating and are used for trailing for predatory fish, also for wet-fly fishing proper, notably for sea trout and lake trout.

STRET-PEGGING: another name for 'laying-on' with float tackle.

STRIKE: the act of pulling the hook home, on indication of a bite or take, into the fish's mouth. Usually this is performed by a sharp wrist action. The quicker the bite, the sharper the strike needed. Quick-biting fish include sea-trout, barbel, roach, dace, bleak, trout. Slow-biting: bream, tench, carp, gudgeon, perch, pike. However, here as practically everywhere in angling, there are no set rules about striking. Trout in may-fly time on the Gloucester Coln, for example, take the artificial in an almost leisurely manner. On an Exmoor brook the rise to fly is a lightning splash and one must strike almost as one sees the fish coming up through the water. Experience only can tell you how and when to strike. Here are some guiding principles:

Barbel: strike when a heavy tug is felt. Strike firmly because the fish are likely to be found in strong water where the line may have a great deal of 'belly' in it.

Bream: bream generally lift the bait. With a float, wait until it lies flat and begins to glide away. Then strike gently but firmly.

Carp: once a carp runs, give it stick to put the hook home.

Chub: these fish have big mouths and the bite is usually decisive. Strike at once.

Dace: quick biters, strike quickly.

Eel: give it time to take the bait.

Grayling: quick biters, strike quickly.

Gudgeon: let these little fish take the bait. Strike at once if the float goes well under.

Perch: perch play with the bait. Ignore the first few bobs of the float. Strike when it goes away.

Pike: when swallowing livebait, the pike has to take, turn and pouch the fish. When using snap-tackle, let the fish complete its first run, tighten, and then strike sideways away from the direction of the run.

Roach, Rudd: strike on indication.

Tench: let the float slide away after initial hesitations.

Trout, salmon and sea-trout: these normally will be seen or felt to take the fly or lure.

STURGEON: *Acipenser sturio*, family *Acipenseridae*. The only survivor of a group of fishes that flourished millions of years ago. Occasional visitors come into British coastal waters and rivers, probably journeying from the Baltic area. There are five rows of bony scales running the length of the body, and the upper lobe of the tail is elongated like that of some of the sharks. There are four barbules at the underside of the head. The fish has a long snout and the mouth can be extended telescopically for bottom feeding. Breeds in fresh water. Chiefly sought in Asia for its roe—caviare. All sturgeons captured in British waters must be reported and are the property of the Crown.

SUN-GLASSES: the spectacles of this type that are most useful to the angler are those fitted with polarized lenses. These lenses cut out reflection and make it possible, frequently, to see to the bottom of a river or lake. This is especially useful to the salmon and trout angler. The effectiveness of polarization depends largely on the angle at which the glasses are worn. This is important when normal lenses are being worn in addition. Adjustment usually can provide the right answer.

SURFACE FISHING: strictly speaking this term would include dry-fly fishing, yet that is so much an art in itself that I prefer to take surface fishing as meaning bait angling at the surface. Two freshwater species notably are tempted by surface baits. These are the carp and rudd. Carp will suck down crusts floating on top of the water. When this is seen to happen it is time for the angler to cast out crust on fixed-spool tackle. Rudd feed on or near the surface, so that a slowly sinking, unweighted, unscoured maggot often proves deadly. Chub, too, are surface feeders where insects are concerned. The means of taking them with a live insect, such as a caterpillar suspended on the surface, is called 'dapping'. Margin-fishing for carp is a technique that must be included in surface angling. This method is used at night when a crust is lowered to the surface from a rested rod, just under the angler's own bank. Care should be taken to fish on the bank towards which the wind is blowing, as scraps will naturally drift in that direction. Other species besides carp are sometimes hooked thus, notably roach.

SWIM: the length of river fished at any one time by any one angler. In competition fishing, individual swims should be at least ten yards apart.

SWIMMING THE STREAM: causing float tackle to take the bait along the course of the chosen swim. The essence of this technique is to present the bait naturally. The swim first should be judiciously groundbaited to attract and hold the fish in it. Moreover, the swim should have been carefully plumbed along its course before starting to fish. A ledge, hole, or shelf will frequently reveal where the fish may be expected to congregate. Despite the need to keep the bait moving smoothly along the swim, bites often can be achieved by checking the tackle slightly to allow the bait to swing up off the bottom. The tackle should always precede the float in its progress downstream. Ideally, a centre-pin reel should be used. Swimming can be done from a fixed-spool reel provided the angler is ready to catch the line with his finger at the first sign of a bite. If no free-running or fixed-spool reel is available, line must be fed from the reel by hand to keep the float moving.

SWIM-FEEDER: perforated cylinder, usually of celluloid, that can be packed with light groundbait.

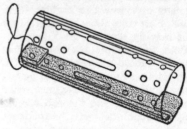

SWIM-FEEDER. *Weighted and perforated transparent cylinder used for ground-baiting.*

The feeder slips down the line, acting as a leger weight. The action of the stream washes the groundbait out through the perforations, thus feeding the swim close to the hook bait.

SWING-TIP: a recent legering innovation that has become popular with Midlands and North Country anglers. It consists of a slender nylon tip about nine inches long which forms a false top to the rod. This is stiff at the tip end and floppy at the lower extremity. It carries at the stiff end a normal top rod ring, and, somewhere about halfway along, a normal intermediate ring. The floppy part is bound to the rod top itself, and the line is then threaded through the rings on the rod and also the rings on the swing tip. When the rod is set in its rest, the tip hangs down loosely below the rod proper. Any movement of the line by a taking fish immediately swings the tip, thus giving a sensitive indication of bites.

SWIVEL: device to prevent rotary action of the bait in the water from twisting or kinking the line. This action may be imparted by spinning, trailing, by force of the current, or by the actions of a livebait. When spinning and trailing, even the use of several swivels may not guarantee that the line will not kink. They usually need assistance in the form of an anti-kink weight or vane: these hang down below the line so that the bait has first to turn the anti-kink device through 360 degrees before it can impart a twist to the

SWIVEL. *A metal link to prevent line becoming twisted. The buckle-swivel (right) is a type used by sea anglers to attach trace to line.*

line. This it invariably fails to do. However, the disadvantage of such devices is that they give the angler two masses to cast instead of one. The simplest answer is to use ball-bearing swivels. These rotate freely enough to work on their own. They are comparatively expensive but well worth the additional cost.

T

TACKLE: the term includes everything used in the catching and landing of fish. To enumerate the items in one section would be to complicate matters unduly. Tackle suitable for each species will be found under the heading of the fish concerned.

TAILER: an alternative device to the net or gaff for landing salmon. A wire slip-loop attached to a metal arm is tightened over the 'wrist' just in front of the fish's tail.

TAXIDERMY: the art of setting up, or stuffing, fish and other creatures to make them appear lifelike. Though essentially a job for the professional taxidermist, quite good results can be achieved by an amateur with skilful fingers. I have mounted my own fish with some success for quite a while now. Here is my method briefly described; others will probably introduce their own improvements.

For example, take a specimen perch and proceed as follows:

(1) Trace an outline of the fish on white card. This will be needed later as reference for the original shape of the specimen.

(2) Take colour references in artist's water-colours of fins, flanks, eyes, etc.

(3) Dry the fish. Apply a coating of flour paste to one side of a sheet of stout brown paper, and on it lay the fish—'show side' down. This protects the scales from damage.

(4) When the paste has dried start skinning the fish by making a slit along the upper, or 'non-show', side, from just in front of the tail root to just behind the gill-cover.

(5) With the fingers or a blunt fruit-knife, start to ease the flesh away from the skin through the slit.

(6) Carry on upwards and downwards until fin roots are met: cut through these with a pair of scissors.

(7) Continue to skin down the far side of the fish until the entire carcase is free.

(8) Cut through the backbone just behind the skull and in front of the tail, and then lift out the carcase. (In the case of a very large fish, such as a pike, it may be necessary to take out the carcase in sections.)

(9) Clean off any surplus flesh that remains clinging to the skin.

(10) Now comes the fiddling, messy part of the operation—the removal of all remaining flesh from the head, tail root, inside of skull, gills, mouth (cut out the tongue), eyes, etc. My advice is that you should not attempt to remove the flesh from under the cheeks. You will probably do better, at first anyway, by letting these shrink as the skin dries: build them up afterwards with putty or plaster.

(11) A preservative must now be applied. I use a 50/50 mixture of burnt alum and saltpetre, shaking it generously into the head and gill cavities and also into the tail root and eye sockets. Also I rub it gently into the skin.

(12) From this stage onwards the skin is going to dry out. If left on its own it would shrivel, distort and become shapeless: it must, therefore, be set.

(13) To set the fish I fill it with silver sand, but first I paste or lay tissue paper inside the skin to

receive and hold the sand. This prevents the sand from clogging with the preservative.

(14) Take the white card on which the outline was traced and place it on a board of suitable size (this board will be needed later to assist the turning over of the specimen). Trim the brown paper adhering to the fish to within the latter's outline and place the fish, slit uppermost, to fit precisely over the outline drawn on the card. Now begin to feed in the silver sand through the slit. Fill the skin until it assumes the outline made on the card. Err on the generous side with this filling.

(15) When filling is completed, lay tissue inside to cover the slit and sew up the slit with needle and thread.

(16) The fish has now to be turned over so that the 'show' side will be uppermost. To do this, lay another board over the fish and, holding the fish between the two boards, turn it over and take away the board that is now uppermost. Now soak off the brown paper; for this I use methylated spirit. Peel off the paper and carefully wipe away any loosened paste that may be adhering to the scales.

(17) With a suitable implement, such as a knife-blade or a wooden spoon, pat the fish where necessary in order to make it assume its rounded shape correctly. The silver sand inside the skin will, of course, yield to this treatment and will retain whatever shape you give to it.

(18) The fins must now be set. These should have been loosened with water before the skinning began, in order to free the rays. Provided that there is now no risk of the fin rays sticking, spread them gently and place them on thick card cut to shape. The fins can either be held in position for setting between two layers of card held with clips, or be held down between the cards by small weights. The latter method works well for the dorsal fin.

All you can do now is go away and pray. Your fish will probably take two months to dry out, maybe more. During this process it will sweat a certain amount and may even gather a light coating of fuzzy mould. Wipe this off with spirit whenever it appears. A weekly check-up should be sufficient.

Provided the skin feels quite hard at the end of two or three months you can get ready to empty the sand out. For this, turn the fish over again, making sure that it is well supported throughout its length. Snip the thread closing the slit, pull out the tissue paper covering the latter and begin to spoon the sand out. When you have got most of it clear you can probably turn the fish back again when the remaining sand can be shaken out.

You should now have a rigid shell that will permanently hold its shape without the insertion of any extra stuffing.

Colour references now come into play, for the skin will have lost all its natural colouring in the drying process. For repainting, which needs to be done gradually and with great care, I use artist's water colours or photographic inks. Rebuild shrunken portions such as the eye sockets, cheeks, top of the skull, and isthmus (the 'neck' of the fish), using plaster or putty. If putty, remember that water colour will not take on it: you'll have to repaint this part with oil paint. Eyes can be bought from professional taxidermists. For large fish I have made very effective eyes from the type of torch bulb that has a flattened top. If the fish has been set with its mouth open you'll need to add a putty imitation of a tongue.

Note that I haven't yet advised the taking off of the cardboard backing from the fins. During the painting and filling process, it's as well to keep the mounts there for protection. The fins will be rigid but will split fairly easily.

The time has come to think about a mounting by which the fish can be fixed to the back wall of whatever showcase you're going to use. Mounts can be made out of wire quite simply. They may need packing into position inside the fish with a bit of cotton wool. Once the mount is in place, stick brown paper over the slit through which the mount protrudes. This will help hold it fast.

Soak the card protectors off the fins next. Take your time over this. Sponge off any paste adhering to the fins carefully, and add colouring where necessary.

The water colours may have given the specimen a disappointingly flat appearance. Now is the time to bring it to life with a coating or two of finest copal varnish. This will immediately give it life and lustre.

You will, no doubt, have your own ideas about the sort of case in which to place your fish. I have made them out of five-ply and even hardboard. Some people prefer the old-fashioned —and usually quite inaccurate— decorations, such as bunches of coarse grass through which the fish peers as it never peered in nature. My own inclination these days is to paint the inside of the case pale green, with maybe a trail or two of darker green weed painted on in the background. The pebbly bottom can be imitated by sticking washed pebbles or sand to brown paper, and then sticking this to the bottom of the case, and varnishing the result.

You may not get a professional finish for your first few efforts. The betting is that you will produce something presentable and will have saved yourself £10 or so in the process.

TEMPERATURE: water temperature affects the feeding habits of fish as well as their local movements. The metabolism of most species undergoes a violent adjustment when temperature alters radically. Generally speaking, the colder it is the less most species want to feed, at least until they become adjusted to the cold. This is particularly true in lakes where most of the cyprinids cease to feed altogether as winter comes; they go into a state of at least partial hibernation. The predators on the other hand still feed well, especially the pike. Weeks of boiling sun can be equally damaging, robbing the water of oxygen and putting most fish off the feed. All species have a definite temperature range within which they will feed.

In the sea, temperature change is chiefly responsible for causing the various species to shift feeding grounds. For example, a mild spring brings the bass and mullet inshore early. If the shallows become too warm during weeks of summer sun, the flatfish along the shore will tend to move out into the deeps. All in all, the best that can be said is that the individual angler must study the habits of fish in the waters he frequents and note their reactions to temperature changes. A word of warning must be given. It is the water, *not the air*, temperature that matters. A sudden snap of cold does not mean that the water is immediately cold: it will probably have retained the heat stored up in it by the preceding mild spell.

TENCH: *Tinca tinca*, family *Cyprinidae*. A fish of great beauty and power, varying in colour from dark green to yellow: usually, however, dark bronze. The fins of the tench are round and paddle-shaped. The eye is a startling red. The tail has an almost straight trailing edge and is broad and blunt. Altogether the fish cannot be mistaken for anything else. Tench occur in many slow-flowing rivers and a great number of lakes. The Norfolk Broads are perhaps the most celebrated tench waters together with the slow deep the mud when a pond dries up during summer and survive until winter comes have been substantiated on many occasions. Tench, like carp and rudd, are mainly summer quarry.

A specimen tench is a five-pounder. The British record, from the Leicester Canal in 1950, stands at 8½ lb. One scaling 9 lb. 9¾ oz. was taken at Wraysbury, Bucks., in 1959 but it proved unacceptable for

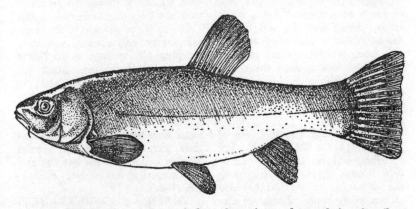

TENCH. *Inhabitant of lakes and slow, deep rivers, the tench is primarily a warm weather quarry. Comparatively few are caught after October.*

drains and rivers of Fenland. Nevertheless there is many a local pond that supports tench of up to two pounds in weight. The tench puts on weight rapidly, being almost omnivorous. Vegetation, larvae, bloodworms, fish eggs all go into the capacious mouth of the tench.

Tench are shy and must be approached with care. They live a sluggish existence until hooked, and then all lethargy departs in a hurry. A two-pound tench puts up a surprising fight. Anything over three pounds provides a battle. Like carp, tench are immensely tenacious of life. They can live out of water, especially if wrapped in wet sacking or newspaper, for many hours. The stories that tench can bury themselves in record purposes because it was diseased. In fact, it died within a few weeks of being captured. There is an old tale that the tench is a doctor fish, curing the sick of other species by contact with the slime of its body. Apart from the wild scientific inaccuracy of this belief, no one who understands the fierce competition of the underwater world could think for an instant that any one species was out to do any other species a good turn—even if fish were capable of any kind of thinking process. About the only good that tench do the rest of the inhabitants is in clearing up refuse that might otherwise sour the water. Tench are good to eat either baked or poached in cider, though few coarse anglers will consider this an ethical practice.

TENCH-FISHING: dawn and dusk in the summer are the times to be fishing for tench, though the fish will also feed sporadically through the day. They will often be found in the neighbourhood of lilies from which they like to suck snail eggs, etc. Gear needs to be light though powerful, and nothing less than a good Avon rod should be considered if three-pounders and upwards are expected. Line, obviously, should suit the rod, but I would advise a minimum of 5-lb. b.s. when weed beds are present. In heavily weeded water the angler might be wise to go as high as 10-lb. b.s. Hooks should be large — No. 10 to No. 6 — and I prefer 'Model Perfects'.

Baits for tench are, in order of preference: bread flake, bread-paste, maggots, redworm, lobworm, brandling. Worms should rank higher in the list but for the fact that they also attract every other species in the water. In any case it is wise to seek local advice on baits, for tench in any given water usually show marked preferences, taking bread flake but refusing paste, for example. It always pays to groundbait for tench, and frequently it pays to rake the bottom. I discovered this more or less by accident when cutting out swims in weed-beds. Fishing in such newly made openings only an hour after completion of dragging operations I have taken good bags of fish. The reason, I believe, is that the raking has stirred up bottom food including bloodworm, of which the tench are especially fond.

Tench may be caught by conventional float-fishing with the bait on the bottom, by float-leger or by straight legering. When fish are shy in still-water I prefer the type of weightless legering developed for carp, where the bait is sufficiently large to make casting possible and no other form of weight is used. When float-fishing the bite is indicated by a series of tremblings, risings and eventual moving off of the float. This is possibly because the tench stands on its nose to take the bait, maintaining its position with powerful tail movements that cause the float to tremble. In any case, the strike should not be made until the float goes under and away.

In the warm months when tench are mainly 'on', evening and early morning fishing pays best. Tench can undoubtedly be caught by margin-fishing at night and by surface-fishing with crust, as for carp, during the day.

TERYLENE: this excellent man-made fibre makes up into first-class lines, including fly lines. Its virtues are that it does not rot like silk and has comparatively little, if any, stretch in it.

THAMES CONSERVANCY: the Thames has no River Board but is administered by a Conservancy. This body does not charge any licence fees to anglers nor does it have a full-time fishery officer. The advantages and disadvantages of this situation from the angler's viewpoint are hotly debated. A copy of the Conservancy's Fishery by-laws can be obtained (price one shilling) from its offices, 2 Norfolk Street, London, W.C.2. (See Appendix.)

THERMOCLINE: this is the shallow layer of temperature change that exists in all deep-water lakes between the upper stratum of warm water (the epilimnion) and the lower block of cold water (the hypolimnion). The thermocline itself is a narrow stratum within which the temperature is subject to rapid change. In summer and autumn the fish, generally speaking, will be feeding on that area of bottom covered by the warm water layer.

Imagine now the effect of a strong wind blowing from south to north across, say, a big reservoir. Because the layers will not mix readily without considerable and prolonged heating or cooling, the effect of the wind will be to push the warm upper layer to the windward side of the reservoir. This will pile the warm water up at this end. The thermocline will, therefore, tilt from south to north to make way for the additional warm water blowing towards the north end. Thus, at the windward side, there will be an area of bottom far greater than usual covered by friendly warm water in which the fish may feel disposed to feed. The lesson to be learned from all this scientific jargon is that: when a strong wind is blowing across a large deep-water lake, put up with the discomfort and go and fish with it in your face. That way you will probably catch some unexpectedly large fish. Bill Penney caught his record 3 lb. 14 oz. roach in this fashion.

The effect of winter on deep-water lakes also needs examination. The autumn gales and first frosts start to chill the epilimnion so that the surface layer sinks to the bottom, warmer water moving up to replace it. This goes on until all the water is cooled to 39.2 degrees Fahrenheit, at which point water is at its heaviest. No further cooling can cause the surface water to sink, therefore. Once the lake has reached a universal 39.2, then, further cooling can only produce super-cooled water, even down to freezing point, at the surface, the warmer stuff remaining in the deeps. Lesson for anglers: when this condition has been reached, seek species still likely to be feeding, such as perch and pike, in the really deep holes. Perch have been caught in depths of thirty and

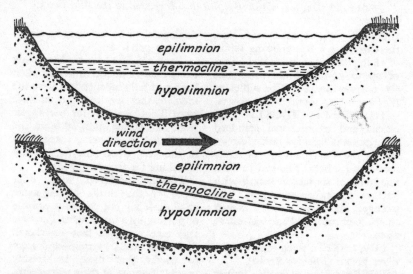

THERMOCLINE. *On a calm day (top) the thermocline layer is parallel with the surface. When a wind springs up (bottom) the epilimnion, or warm water layer, becomes of greater depth on the side towards which the wind is blowing.*

forty feet in some lakes, simply because this was where the warmest water was to be found.

THREAD-LINE: an outdated term for the fixed-spool reel. It is outdated because these reels are now built with alternative spool to take line of up to 15-lb. breaking strain. In the case of sea fixed-spools considerably stronger line may be used.

THREADS (in description of sea-fishing lines): the strength of sea lines is usually expressed according to the number of threads from which they are woven. Each flax thread has, when wet, a breaking

very widely distributed round the British Isles, at times coming right inshore on to the beach in its search for food. The tope is a long, slim, torpedo-shaped fish varying in colour from grey to fawn. It has very powerful serrated teeth and a sandpaper skin. It does a great deal of damage to inshore fishermen's nets, tearing big holes in them when on the feed. As with pike, the big fish are almost invariably the females. Weights run from about 20 to 40 lb. in the majority of cases, though the record tope (female) is 73 lb. 3 oz. and male, 65 lb. The male can be

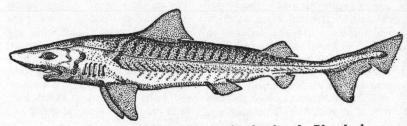

TOPE. *A slim, torpedo-shaped fish that is related to the Blue shark.*

strain of 3 lb. A six-thread line, therefore, has a wet breaking strain of 18 lb. For big-game fishing, lines of up to 54-thread are used, but six- or nine-thread will be sufficient for most fishing round British coasts.

THREE-SIX TACKLE: an official and international standard description of light sea tackle, drawn up by the Catalina Club of California and others. The rod to be a minimum of six feet in length with butt of 12 inches maximum: the strongest line used must not exceed 18 lb. (6-thread) and the test-curve 2¼ lb.

TINPLATE: a slang term for the silver bream (*Blicca bjoernka*).

TOPE: *Galeus vulgaris,* family *carcharinidae.* A small shark of the same family as the blue shark and

distinguished by the claspers alongside the pelvic fins.

Tope are live-bearers, the young being about a pound in weight when born and fully independent from the moment they are launched on their own. Tope are 'on' for the angler from late spring until autumn, the bigger fish often being taken early in the year when ripe females are searching for spawning beds.

TOPE-FISHING: tope offer some of the thrills of big-game angling. They are certainly capable of putting up a lively fight. The tope will take any fish bait—mackerel, flatfish, whiting, herring—and seem to prefer that these be freshly caught. Because of their sharp teeth, strong wire traces are essential for tope fishing. Piano wire does nicely when equipped with swivels, the reel line (about 20-lb. b.s.) being doubled up for the last three or four feet and knotted to give added resistance to the tope's rough skin. Hooks should be about 1¼ in. in gape and the rod as light as is consistent with the line mentioned.

When boat fishing for tope it is better to risk losing a few fish rather than to handicap them right out of the fight by using unnecessarily heavy tackle. A baiting needle is needed to run the hook into the bait where the point is to protrude halfway down the belly of the fish, the wire trace emerging somewhere close to the vent to be attached to the reel line.

Legering and paternostering will both catch tope. When fishing from a boat the bait should be about 12 feet from the 4–6-oz. lead necessary to get the tackle down and hold it on the bottom. When the right amount of line has been fed over the side, a matchstick can be tied with a clove-hitch to the line to prevent the lead sliding down to the bait.

A number of good tope have been caught in recent years from South Coast beaches, particularly those in the Lymington area of Hampshire. The bite of a tope is a shy affair when compared with the tactics of the hooked fish. Very often the bite commences with little more than a faint tremor felt on the line. If the fish feels a check it will usually drop the bait. Once it believes that there is nothing to be afraid of it will make a powerful run, stripping many yards of line from the reel. If the line goes slack after initial interest has been shown, do not relax. The rush may come at any second.

Paternoster gear from the shore works well, the hooks being baited with fresh fish. The top of the flood tide at night, particularly when there is a strong moon, often produces fine fish. When surf or tides are strong, a gaff is essential for getting the tope up the beach quickly.

TORGOCH: a species of Welsh char found in one or two lakes, notably at Llanberis.

TRACE: that part of the tackle which comes between reel-line and hook. The word more properly applies to spinning tackle.

TRICHOPTERA: the scientific name for the family of sege-flies. The word comes from the Greek and means 'hairy-winged'. The flies that emerge from caddis larvae are sedge-flies.

TROLLING: this is frequently confused with 'trailing' which means to tow a bait behind a moving boat. Trolling, properly, is deadbait fishing for pike, perch, or other predators by sink-and-draw methods. A dead fish is attached with a weight in its mouth to the end of the line and armed with triangle hooks along its flanks. This is then cast out into likely pike holes and allowed to dart to the bottom, being checked throughout its descent to give it life and movement. Little time should be wasted on one spot. Two or three casts are usually sufficient to detect the presence of the quarry.

TROUT: *Salmo trutta*, the brown trout. This is the great game fish of British waters. Many still believe that there are endless species of native trout. In fact, there is only one. The vast differences in colouring and spotting that you find from water to water are purely a matter of environmental adaptation. Even the sea trout is basically the same animal as the brown trout. The only trout in Britain that is of a different strain is the rainbow (*Salmo irideus*) and this occurs only where it has been introduced by anglers. It seldom breeds in Britain, although two notable exceptions which, for some reason have never been explained, are the River Chess, Buckinghamshire, and the Dove, Derbyshire.

The brown trout is a beautifully symmetrical creature, being well streamlined with the front spine of its dorsal fin set almost exactly at the point of balance. The tail is something like that of the salmon though it is not quite so spade-ended and has a small indentation

spots and they will be a quite definite brown. It is believed that these adjustments of colour to background are made through the optical mechanism of the fish. I have seen a trout of startling yellow standing out like a neon sign on a chalk stream where every one of its fellows was suitably camouflaged. When caught this trout proved to be badly damaged in one eye. Flank covering differs enormously also, from olive green to nearly black.

The closed season for trout very

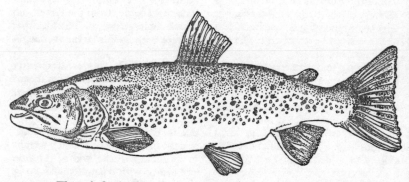

TROUT. *There is basically only one type of trout native to Britain, namely* Salmo trutta, *the brown trout. The sea-trout is the same fish with a migratory instinct.*

to its trailing edge. The trout has the adipose fin as proof of its membership of the salmon group of fishes. Small brown trout are frequently confused with salmon parr. The sure give-away of the trout is the maxillary or upper jawbone which extends well beyond the centre of the eye: that of the parr finishes in line with the pupil of the eye.

All trout have spots and it is largely these which give it the title 'brown'. However, the spots vary enormously. Catch a four-ounce brook trout on Exmoor and its spots will be bright red and the size of shirt buttons. A trout from the Kennet in Berkshire will have fewer

closely matches that for the salmon. Trout are winter breeders and they recover fully from spawning only as early spring comes. They lay their eggs on gravel shallows of small streams, quiet glides, and headwaters just as do salmon. The young trout alevin newly hatched has a yolk sac attached to support it through the first week or so of life.

Brown trout can and do grow to enormous size. As with most other species food supply alone inhibits or encourages their growth. On a moorland beck a good trout may be reckoned at half-a-pound. A chalk stream would have to produce at least a two-pounder before it was considered a good fish. Every season during the may-fly a chalk river gives up its quota of four-, five-, and six-pounders. The Scottish lochs hold some huge fish. The record from Loch Awe, taken in 1886, weighed 39 lb. 8 oz. The River Dungloe surrendered a 21 lb. 7 oz. fish to Mr. C. Gallagher as recently as 1946.

A quite mistaken impression has got around that trout are fastidious aristocrats that live exclusively on flies. Aristocrats, yes. Their sporting quality and their appearance wins them that title. As to fastidiousness in diet, however, they will feed on anything from offal to bread, to worms, to snails, crayfish, larvae, and perhaps, finally, a fly or two. They are also highly predatory and make no exception for the young of their own species.

Again, fly-fishermen are often heard to talk scathingly of 'cannibal' trout as if they were a separate species. In fact, all trout are cannibal, though, when a meat eater gets to a certain size—say three pounds and upwards—it develops a distaste for practically every other form of food. With a wicked-looking hook to its lower jaw it lurks in its hold in some well-known pool causing slaughter amongs smaller relations. Then, is the time to get rid of the pirate and put him in a glass case—by fair means or, if necessary, by foul.

The brown trout is a well-muscled fish who likes streamy well-aerated water. Once the trout is hooked, the muscle developed by life in such streams comes into its own. He is a formidable fighter, never 'in the bag' until in the net. On occasions he will jump mightily, though not nearly so much as his relatives, the rainbow and sea trout.

Though icthyologists are satisfied that there is only one basic kind of brown trout, local names still exist and are implicitly believed in. Here are some of them.

Salmo trutta: Sea trout, sometimes called sewin (Wales), peal (West Country), finnock (Scotland).

Salmo fario: name, once given to ordinary river brown trout.

Salmo ferox: Great Lake Trout. Actually a big brown trout found in some of the Scottish lochs and Irish loughs. Grows to great size. Usually caught by trailing a dead bait or spinner.

Salmo stomachicus: Gillaroo, a big trout found in some Irish loughs. Reddish in colour. Has thick stomach walls somewhat resembling a gizzard.

Salmo levenensis: Loch Leven trout of incredible beauty having magnificent spot pattern.

Salmo irideus: separate species, the Rainbow trout.

TROUT-FISHING: trout are cannibal; they are also very nearly omnivorous. They will eat offal, carrion, bread, worms, maggots, larvae, small fish, snails, and each other. Luckily, they occasionally eat flies. It is this last fact that makes trout fishing the most artistic of all forms of angling.

Trout require clean, well-aerated water. This means that, though a hundred years or so ago they were found in practically every river, today they are confined to comparatively few streams. These streams are divided into two categories, (1) slow and clear; (2) fast and clear. The former are generally lowland rivers, and the latter come dashing out of the mountains and off the moors. It is these two different types of water that give rise to the two main methods of catching trout—at least with a fly. Thus the style of the slow river is the dry-, or floating, fly, and that of the dashing brook the wet-, or sunken, fly.

Dry-fly fishing was perfected on the chalk streams of Hampshire. These immensely rich rivers filter slowly, crystal clear, out of the chalk hills. The fish in them are large because of the abundant food, and much of that food supply is aquatic fly life of one sort or another.

Of this fly life the most important section is occupied by the ephemerid flies—the Olive, Pale Watery, Iron Blue, Blue-Winged Olive, and, of course, May-fly. These insects rise as larvae from the bottom silt to the surface to hatch. Having broken out of their larval skin, the flies sit more or less helpless for a short time on the water. Later, as 'spinners', the females return to the water to lay their eggs: they then die and fall on to the water. At all these times, when the flies are touching the surface, the trout take them for food. Thus originated the idea of presenting the trout with an imitation of these flies in one of their several stages of development: in other words with a dry-fly. Naturally the ephemerids are not the only flies found on such streams. There

are the sedges—the flies that come from caddis larvae—and alder (*sialidae*), and gnats (*diptera*), besides land insects blown on to the surface. All these can be imitated by the fly-tyer.

Now the slow-stream trout usually lies just below the surface. He has much to choose from, and he has time in which to choose it. Moreover, he is in a first-class position to detect a fraud. It follows from this that the angler must often spot the exact fly that the fish is selecting from the several varieties floating down to him; he must then present it so that it falls in range, for, because of the limitation of his 'window', the trout will not otherwise see it; he must also present it softly or else the trout will become scared; he must present it naturally so that the fly does not move sideways across the water causing a V-shaped ripple ('drag'). Moreover, since the water is clear and the trout is lying facing upstream, it follows that the accurate cast of the dry-fly fisherman must be made from below the trout: hence the description of the conventional dry-fly cast as 'upstream and across'.

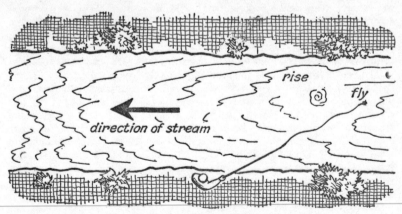

TROUT-FISHING. *The dry-fly fisherman makes his cast 'upstream and across'.*

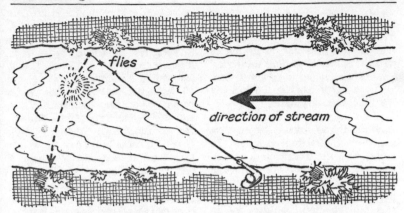

TROUT-FISHING. *The wet-fly man casts 'downstream and across'.*

To be a consistently successful dry-fly angler it is much more important to be able to present your fly well than to be an expert entomologist, recognizing every fly on the water.

Let's look at a dry-fly angler in action. First, he spots a feeding fish, that is to say a trout regularly taking fly at the surface. He tries to see what it is feeding on, or at least what fly is 'on the water'. Having tied on his imitation he stalks the fish, keeping out of sight and moving softly. Probably he kneels to cast, downstream of the trout. He begins to get out line by false-casting, keeping the gut and line out of the trout's vision. When enough line is in the air he drops his fly lightly on the water about two feet above the trout's nose. The fish is taken in, rises with a swirl, is hooked and begins to fight. The supreme satisfaction of dry-fly fishing, apart from the joy of casting, is that the battle takes place in view of the angler from start to finish.

Now for another form of dry-fly fishing: nymph fishing. This again was perfected on the chalk streams, and by the late G. E. M. Skues.

We have seen that trout feed freely on larvae of aquatic flies, 'nymphs' as the angler calls them. When nymphs are moving up to hatch the trout may prefer to take them to the emerged fly. On such occasions, the trout can be seen swimming about restlessly without apparently feeding, though now and again a 'bulge' may be seen at the surface as one swallows a nymph just sub-surface.

Chalk stream fishermen are extremely conventional and when Skues suggested that an imitation of a nymph fished sunken should be tried on these trout, he met with the accusation that this was tantamount to wet-fly fishing, which the chalk stream man scathingly referred to as 'chuck and chance it'. However, nymph fishing is far from that, since an individual fish must be spotted, intercepted on his submarine feeding beat and presented with the sunken imitation cast upstream. To time the strike in this form of fishing is no mean art in itself.

A further variation of dry-fly work is that practised on some of the rough streams. Rarely is there a rise or hatch of fly on such becks. However, trout can often be tempted up to the surface provided the angler knows where the fish will be lying. This technique is really a combination of wet- and dry-fly fishing in that the angler is 'fishing the water' rather than casting to an actual fish, but is using a floating fly. Usually the fisherman will wade.

Wet-, or sunken-, fly fishing, is done mainly on streams which have stretches of fast, broken water. In such rivers, the trout cannot remain suspended just below the surface in mid-current watching for surface-borne titbits. Generally they are sheltering behind boulders or in depressions in the stream bed. They have limited vision of objects on the surface because of the broken water. The stream is moving at such a pace that they have little time in which to make their decision whether to rise or not. Moreover the nature of the water is such that most of the insects that alight on it, or hatch on it, are soon smashed under the surface. Once submerged they are seen quite easily by the trout and at a fair distance.

It must be added that these rough streams are usually acid ones that naturally support a poor supply of trout food, particularly of fly life: the power of the water and the recurrence of spates also makes the odds against a large fly population considerable. All this adds up to a single fact: that the trout are much more likely than are their chalk stream cousins to grab at anything that is offered. This does not mean that such fish are completely indiscriminate: it does mean, however, that there is little to be gained from the 'exact imitation' school of thought in fly-tying.

Wet-flies are tied to sink. To this end a soft hackle from a hen bird rather than a cock is used. They are tied with a narrow, or stream-lined, entry that aids the sinking. If they have wings, these are brief, swept-back affairs that do nothing to keep the fly afloat. Many such flies are relations of dry-flies, and are tied with basically the same sort of materials and bear the same names. There are, for example, wet and dry versions of March Brown, Hare's Ear, Red Spinner, Black Gnat—to name but a few. Now it is very hard to say precisely what a fish mistakes these wet-flies for. There are three main alternatives: (1) hatching aquatic flies; (2) drowned land or aquatic insects; (3) fry of fish. In fact, they probably at different times take them for all three. There are certainly flies in group three which are deliberately tied to imitate fry.

Unlike dry-fly fishing, three wet flies are normally fished on a cast, and sometimes four. These are known as (a) point fly; (b) first dropper; (c) second dropper; (d) bob fly. The latter is kept dancing just on the surface, and, though it is sometimes taken by trout, it more often serves as a guide to the angler that a fish has taken one of his submerged offerings. The bob fly, whether fished with two or three flies below it on the cast, should, of course, be a dry pattern to keep it afloat.

The object in using multiple flies (three flies is often referred to as a 'leash') is twofold: to cover more water, and to give the impression of a hatch of insects rising to the surface. Of the two, the former is certainly the more important. The triple use of flies has perhaps given rise to the calumny that wet-fly fishing is 'chuck and chance it'. True, the dry-fly man is throwing to one identified trout while the wet-fly man is prospecting, but the point is that his is highly skilled prospecting.

The very fact that he does not know exactly where his fish are justifies the use of several flies. However, he must have a very good idea of where they are likely to be lying in the stream bed, and herein lies half the skill of the good sunken-fly angler. He must be able to read water. He must spot likely trout holds, such as boulders on the bottom, and also depressions. He must be able to tell where trout will be waiting for food and cast so that his flies will work naturally to these spots in the river.

The other part of his skill lies in spotting the take and striking to it. This is by no means easy when a fish is darting at a fly which is perhaps a foot beneath the surface. The indications may be a flash of the trout's turning flank, a 'bulge' at the surface, the disappearance of an inch or two of gut, or of the bob, or simply a tug. If the latter, the fish will almost certainly be off before it is hooked. Now look at a wet-fly angler at work.

His rod is likely to be longer and of softer action than the floating-fly fisher. He needs a rod with soft action down to the butt in order to take the strain of lifting yards of sunken line. A largely tip-actioned rod might snap at the strain, or at least work uneasily. His line can be level rather than tapered, since precise casting and careful putting down of the fly are not so necessary. His cast can be level, too.

The angler walks down the bank looking for fishable spots. He casts to all the likely ones throwing his flies downstream and across, as opposed to the dry-fly man's upstream and across. He lets the current wash the flies down past the lie of the trout and then, when he judges that he has shown the flies to any fish urking there, retrieves the cast, usually by coiling or bunching the line in a special fashion in his left hand. The flies are frequently taken when they are being worked in this way against the current.

There is, however, a variation to the normal method, used often when water is low and clear. This is fishing the wet-fly upstream, a technique that calls for wading, a short line, and exceptional skill in spotting and reacting to the take of the fish. This style comes somewhere between nymphing and upstream worming, with which I shall deal later.

Trout are also caught on the fly in still water, in fact many of the biggest trout come from Scottish lochs and Irish loughs, as well as from some of the English reservoirs such as Blagdon and Chew Magna, both near Bristol. Lake trout are a different proposition as far as locating the fish goes. These usually swim on a circular course, feeding as they go. The course will generally be dictated by currents, but not by easily discernible ones. The currents in the case of still water are caused by temperature changes or by wind acting on the surface water.

Dry-fly technique is much as practised on a river, except for the fact that allowance does not usually have to be made, at least to any great extent, for drag. Fish are spotted feeding either from the shore or from a boat and cast over in the normal fashion. In the case of a travelling fish, a succession of rises should be spotted, the interval between each judged, and the cast made at a predicted interval ahead of the last rise and in the direction of travel. Lake trout usually take the fly down with them, and the strike needs often to be slower than that of the river angler. The method of spotting the rise pattern and casting

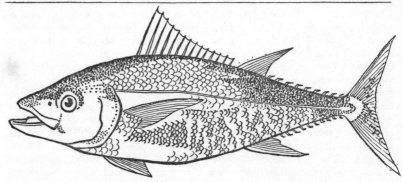

TUNNY. *Related to the mackerel, this large fish migrates to British waters during the summer months, and feeds mainly upon herring, mackerel and pilchards. The British record stands at 851 lb.*

ahead is that used in fishing the spent gnat in the evenings during may-fly time on the Irish loughs.

Wet-fly fishing on still waters is generally done from a boat, the boat being taken upwind and then allowed to drift down broadside over the fish, the anglers in it sitting one at bow and one at stern and casting a shortish line ahead of the drift. The flies are allowed to sink for a second, and are then worked back towards the boat with the bob fly just touching the surface. The flies used are very large and often of sea-trout size. The really big fish, when in taking mood, sometimes hook themselves.

There are other methods of taking trout, of course, most of them perfectly legitimate on many waters. The most obvious is perhaps spinning or trailing. Trout being predatory will take anything that looks like a small fish. Spoons, big flies, Devons, and all the small, bright baits will be taken on occasions when cast normally or pulled slowly behind a boat. On the really big inland waters trailing, or trolling as it is called locally, is often the only effective way of covering and searching an area.

Trout, as has been said, will take all manner of baits, and though fishing snobs are inclined to decry the use of baits, many enlightened fly-fishermen recognize their place, and, indeed, two of the most respected and ancient methods of catching trout involve baits. These are fishing the stone-fly creeper and dapping.

The creeper is the larvae of the stone-fly, found on rough rivers and hatching out in May. When put live on the hook it is deadly for trout, but great skill is needed both in collecting the creeper and in fishing it. It is best found under stones in the shallows in the early morning, and should be fished much in the same way as the upstream worm, of which something shortly. Dapping is done with the live may-fly on the Irish loughs. The flies are put gently on the hook, and allowed to blow out on a fine line from a long rod. The big trout are frequently deceived, but the method seems to be losing in popularity since it is relatively dull and extremely exacting in its call for stamina and concentration.

Among other baits that trout will swallow are live minnows, crayfish, shrimps, and, of course, worms of all descriptions. If you want a trout for the pot and the rules of the water allow you to use these methods, there is no ethical reason at all why you should not do so.

One form of worm fishing is seldom frowned upon, at least on rough wadable streams, for, apart from being extremely skilful, it is the only method that will take fish on many a bright summer day when the water is dead low and gin-clear. Upstream worming requires a long-ish rod and light line. A roach rod with nylon monofilament is a good combination, although, of course, a fly rod may be used. The business end of the tackle should be two- or three-hook Stewart tackle to which is fixed a lively redworm. The angler moves upstream swinging the worm out ahead of him and allowing the current to wash it back in a natural fashion past likely lies. Trout under these conditions are often found at the edge of the stream.

Recommended reading: *Trout Fishing* by H. D. Turing, *Still-Water Fly-Fishing* by T. C. Ivens. *Trout in Troubled Waters* by F. E. Tudor.

TUNNY: *Thunnus thynnus*, family *Scombridae*. The blue fin or short-finned tunny is the fish that big-game anglers catch off Scarborough as it follows the herring shoals, Dark blue above and with silver flanks, it is really a gigantic mackerel in general shape; how giant can be judged from the fact that it probably grows to 1,500 lb. or more, the British record standing at 851 lb. Its relative, the long-finned tunny (*Orcynus germo*) is occasionally taken off the west coast though this fish really belongs to the Mediterranean.

Tunny fishing from Scarborough started in 1929. The season lasts from the end of July until the early part of October. Details of fishing technique will be found under BIG-GAME FISHING.

TUP'S INDISPENSABLE: a famous dry-fly tied to imitate a Pale Watery ephemerid. The name is worthy of a note. The inventor took the wool for the body from the scrotum of a tup, or ram.

TURLE KNOT: the most common knot for attaching fly to cast. See KNOTS.

TWAITE SHAD: *Alosa finta*, family *Clupeidae*. Silver fish with markedly forked tail that comes into some rivers and travels quite far upstream to spawn. The Severn has a notable run of shad. The fish fights well and can be taken on worm, spinner or sunken fly. Maximum length about 20 in. and 3 lb. in weight. Average length 12-16 in.

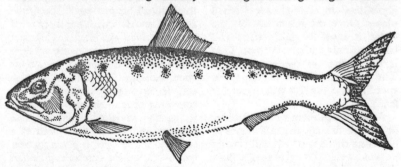

TWAITE SHAD. *The Twaite has a more streamlined body and is smaller than its relative, the Allis Shad. The row of spots varies in number.*

U V

UMBAR: an Old English word for grayling.

UPSTREAM WORMING: a highly skilful means of catching brook trout in low-water conditions of high summer. In such weather the water becomes over-heated and shallow and the fish are disinclined to take fly at the surface. This is the moment when a worm may tempt them. A longish rod is necessary, as the bait has to be swung out ahead with an underhand lob. I advise a roach rod, but any trout rod of nine feet or more will do. Fly-line can be used with a two-yard level 3X nylon cast, but I prefer ordinary monofilament reel line. The business end of the tackle should be light two-hook Stewart tackle, and the bait a small redworm.

The angler wades upstream cautiously, swinging the bait out ahead of him into likely holding places. He fishes where he would otherwise put a fly; in other words he needs an eye for water. Trout will be found sheltering behind boulders, along the edges of the stream, in smooth glides, and in all their accustomed places. Once the worm has hit the water it must be allowed to roll back naturally with the current. That is the essence of the whole affair. The slightest check or unnatural speeding and the fish will detect the fraud.

As when upstream wet-fly fishing, or nymph fishing, the skill comes in detecting the take which will usually be underwater. You may see the flash of the trout's flank as it turns over to take the worm; rarely a 'bulge' may be spotted at the surface; but perhaps the best method is to watch the nylon cast where it enters the water. Any sudden shifting sideways or tugging will indicate a fish, and the strike should come immediately. On some moorland brooks worm fishing is forbidden. So make sure from your ticket or licence that upstream worming is in order.

UP-TRACE SPINNER: spinning tackle in which the rotating vane, usually of celluloid, is displaced from the lure by quite a distance. It is, in fact, placed 'up-trace'.

VENDACE: a rare member of the salmon family. *Coregonus vandesius* occurs in two small lochs near the town of Lochmaben, Dumfriesshire. The vendace rarely exceeds eight inches, looks like a dace in colouring, but, of course, has an adipose fin. It also occurs in a slightly different form—there are differences in fin construction—in Cumberland, both in Derwentwater and Bassenthwaite. There is a legend—highly unlikely to be true—that Mary Queen of Scots introduced the fish to Lochmaben. Probably the French courtiers with her discovered and identified the fish, having met it first in France, the name vendace being a corruption of the French for dace, *vandoise*. The fish is good to eat, is seen in numbers only at spawning time in the autumn, when it shoals in the shallows. The Cumberland version is treated as a separate species and is given its own name—*Coregonus vandesius gracilior*.

VENTRAL FINS: the paired belly fins of a fish; known also as pelvic fins.

WADERS: rubber thigh boots, essential for many forms of fly-fishing and for beach fishing. For rocky streams, the waders should be metal-studded. Brogues and gaiters are an expensive alternative. To keep the feet warm in rubber boots two pairs of socks should be worn, the outer pair of oiled wool. Cut-out instep socks made of newspaper also help.

WADING: on many trout and salmon rivers, particularly those of hill and moor country, wading will be necessary if not essential. Banks are often overgrown and the normal back-cast of the fly-fisherman will become caught up. By wading, fish can be reached that would otherwise be unapproachable. By contrast, on gentle streams, especially chalk streams, wading will usually be forbidden (1), because it causes too much disturbance and stirs up the bottom silt; (2), because the banks are usually well keepered and free from obstruction.

In rough water wading can be dangerous. It pays always to have studs fixed to the sole of the rubber or leather waders. In very powerful rivers where a tumble into an unsuspected deep can prove bad trouble, a wading staff is advisable. This can sometimes be combined with landing-net, the whole being attached to the body by a lanyard, so that the angler can let go of the net if he needs his left hand free. Frequently when wading, it is necessary to free both hands, as when unhooking the fish. The best thing in that case is to stick the rod butt down the top of one wader. Rope-soled sandals give excellent grip in warm weather, provided the angler doesn't mind paddling.

WAGTAIL: a type of spinning lure having a rubber or leather body mounted on a wire flight. Its virtue is that it gives the attacking predator something soft to bite on, thus persuading it to hold on for the second necessary to enable the angler to drive the hooks home.

WALTON, IZAAK: 1593-1683, author of *The Compleat Angler* written in 1653, and biographies of Dr. John Donne, Sir Henry Wotton, Mr. Richard Hooker, Mr. George Hooker, etc. Born in Stafford, he settled in London and set up as an ironmonger where he remained in business until after the Royalist Defeat at Marston Moor. Most anglers talk about Walton and his famous book as if they knew it intimately, and as though it were a Bible of fishing lore. In fact, it's very doubtful whether more than one-tenth of the entire fishing public has ever read it. As to it being a compendium of fishing wisdom, it is, in fact—as one would expect of Walton's day and age—a strange mixture of instinctive know-how and fabulously inaccurate old wives' tales.

This is not the point, however: *The Compleat Angler* has deserved immortality for its charm, style and fascinating reflection of early rural England. The book was added to by Walton throughout his life. By 1676 the original thirteen chapters had grown to twenty-one and a second part on fly-fishing had been added by a brother angler, Charles Cotton.

Recently some doubt has been cast on the originality of Walton's work. An earlier book, from which much of Walton's information is now said to have been taken, has been unearthed. No angler should be shocked or surprised at this, and certainly no angling writer.

During the past fifty years there have, perhaps, been ten writers who have contributed anything new to the sum total of fishing knowledge. The remainder, sometimes excellently and sometimes deplorably, have simply rearranged existing information and flavoured it with their own personality or experience. If Walton was doing the same, he at least had the distinction of being one of the first. All anglers should read his work. Its charm is never-ending.

WASP GRUBS: useful bait for almost any fish that will take a gentle. They should be baked before use in order to toughen the skin and prevent them hatching.

WATERHEN: another name for the moorhen or common gallinule. Certain feathers are useful to fly-tyers. Too many of these birds on the water are aggravating, especially to trout fishermen. Their splashy take-off frequently puts down feeding fish. They also make a meal off healthy weed. If you do have to shoot some, be consoled by the fact that when skinned they are quite tolerable eating.

WATER PLANTS: fish life depends in the beginning on the presence of plants for its existence. The whole elaborate structure of aquatic life is built upon the fact that the sunlight penetrating water encourages both elementary forms of life and plant growth. The plants provide shelter for the animalculae and larger organisms on which the fish feed: in some cases they provide food itself: in all cases they aerate the water by giving off oxygen during the dark hours. Without this oxygenization, the population of any water, especially a still one, would have to be considerably smaller, since atmospheric oxygen does not dissolve readily in water.

The smallest of the plant groups produced by sunlight are the phyoplankton and nannoplankton (net-passing plankton), including the algae. In Windermere alone 67 species of microscopic plants have been traced and there are probably many more. The angler, however, is more familiar with the larger plants which he can see round or on the water, and also with the weeds that foul his line and hide his bait as it sinks to the bottom. Round the edge of lake or river he will find first the reeds—sedge, the green reed with the rapier-like leaves; branched bur-reed, with broad leaves and spiked burs like the heads of mediaeval maces; yellow flag, or wild iris; reed-mace, commonly and mistakenly called the bulrush; flowering rush with a multi-blossomed pink flower.

At the edge of the water also grow water mint, with its bluish purple flower and broad leaves; water pepper with exceptionally broad leaves and tall branching flower having five or six pink blossoms radiating on fine stalks from the centre of a three-spiked leaf; water plaintain, having long thin leaves and producing a tightly bunched elongated pink flower; water parsnip, a variation of what is commonly called cow parsley.

Out of the water, but still rooted in the bottom silt, grow: mare's tail, a straight-growing plant with spiked leaves sprouting outwards in groups from the central stem, the whole effect being something like a

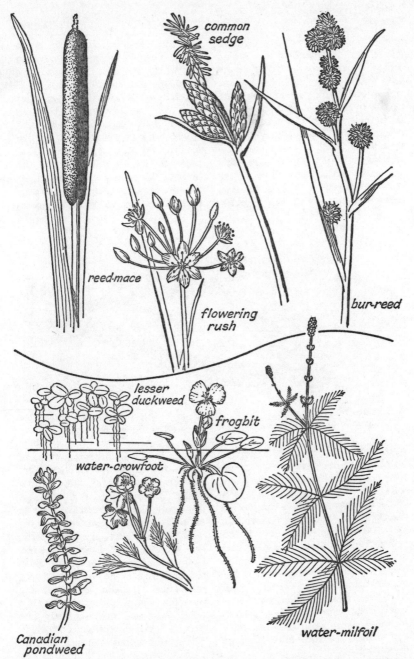

WATER PLANTS. *A selection of the plants seen in British lakes and rivers.*

miniature conifer; arrowhead, whose leaves are described in the name but which produces a white flower with three petals; frogbit, a plant with a small white flower that floats and derives its nourishment direct from the water; bladderwort, a less common plant that has finely divided leaves and small bladders along its submarine fronds which act as traps for small water animals such as fleas (bladderwort is thus a true carnivore, just as is a pike or perch);

and the hair-like roots hang down into the water. When a layman uses the word 'stagnant' to describe a pond he usually means that it is covered in duckweed. Water lilies need no description; they often shelter fish, especially carp and tench, both of whom seem to like feeding off the animalculae that populate the flat undersides of the leaves. Water fern is sometimes found completely carpeting the surface. This has an emerald green,

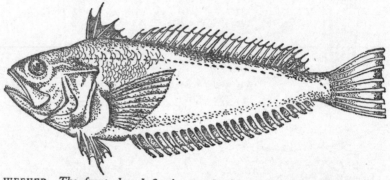

WEEVER. *The front dorsal fin is armed with sharp, poisonous spines and should be handled with extreme care. This is the Lesser Weever.*

water crowfoot, often called water buttercup, which takes its name from the fact that its underwater foliage is fine and spiked and each leaf somewhat resembles the foot of the bird in question (crowfoot's leaves above the surface are broad and rather like those of the normal field buttercup); Canadian pondweed, one of those that torment the angler, for, although bottom-rooted, the long trailing strands with their small leaves growing outward from the single stem break loose in winter and drift in to the shore in huge quantities.

Duckweed usually grows in dense patches; a few types flower. The green leaves appear at the surface

sponge-like leaf. Shining pondweed is another menace with its broad flat leaves growing on long trailing stalks. Unless cleared regularly this can easily block a stream, at least as far as fishing is concerned.

WEEVER: there are two species, the Greater and Lesser Weever, both of the family *Trachinidae*. Both are brownish in colour having two dorsal fins, the front one consisting of a few sharp spines, the rear fin being long and many-spined. The first fin is armed with poison glands. When the spines cause a wound, poison flows into the puncture. The result on a human being is quite alarming and may even be very dangerous. Any fish suspected of being a weever should be handled with the greatest possible respect. Arms and legs stung by weevers quickly swell up to nearly twice their size and hospital treatment is usually necessary. Unfortunately the lesser weever delights in burying itself in the sand where unlucky bathers' feet sometimes find it. The greater weever is very similar in appearance, though rarer. Its tail has blue lines on it.

WHEAT: excellent bait for roach and some other species. The grain is usually swollen in hot water before use. This process is known as creeding.

WHERE TO FISH, Freshwater: Only brief notes, obviously, can be given on the principal rivers and still waters. Detailed information can usually be obtained from the appropriate RIVER BOARD or angling clubs in the area concerned.

England. *Arun (Sussex):* good coarse fishing, also smallish run of very big sea trout. Fishing centres: Pulborough, Amberley, Arundel. Best tributary, Rother: good coarse fishing, especially chub.

Avon (Bristol): good coarse fishing, some trout in higher reaches. Fishing centres all the way along its course.

Avon (Hants): the finest mixed fishery in Britain and probably in the world. Everything grows to great size including brown trout, pike (the record at the time of going to press, 37½ lb., came from the Avon), chub, roach and barbel. Salmon and sea trout run freely but are mostly preserved. Several angling societies sell day tickets. The Royalty Fishery at Christchurch is justly renowned for its barbel, chub, roach and salmon.

Bure (Norfolk): first-class Broadland coarse fish river with trout in

upper reaches. Day tickets obtainable in some reaches.

Brue (Somerset): good coarse fishing from Highbridge to Glastonbury. Trout in upper waters.

Coquet (Northumberland): a late salmon and sea trout river, good for brown trout. Tickets obtainable in most places.

Dart (Devon): salmon, sea trout and brown trout. Mostly preserved. Tickets available through Dart Angling Association.

Eden (Cumberland): salmon, sea trout in lower and middle reaches, chub and grayling in parts. Upper reaches fish late. Many associations issue tickets.

English Lake District: mixed fishing for trout and coarse fish. Fish are of no great account as far as size is concerned, though beauty of surroundings probably compensates. Hotels will inform.

Esk, Border: salmon and sea trout river with brown trout in upper waters. Sea trout run well from June to August. Salmon in spring and October.

Exe (Somerset and Devon): grayling and coarse fish in lower reaches; higher up, salmon and trout. Mostly preserved but some ticket and many hotel waters. Main tributary, Barle: a beautiful moorland river mostly preserved by hotels. Trout small but game.

Fowey (Cornwall): trout. seatrout and salmon. Lostwithiel best centre. Some ticket water.

Frome (Dorset): chalk stream with run of big sea trout and some salmon. The record sea trout, 22 lb., was caught here. Mostly preserved but some day permits from Dorchester.

Grand Union Canal: mixed coarse fishery along its entire length. Let to angling societies some of which give day tickets. London Anglers'

Association has much. Day tickets from societies at Southall, Tring, Fenny Stratford and Weedon, among other centres.

Hull (Yorkshire): mainly famous for its tributary, the Driffield Beck, which is a true chalk stream, strictly preserved.

Isle of Wight: chiefly sea fishing but some fair freshwater. Enquire from River Board.

Itchen (Hampshire): one of the most famous of the chalk streams. Almost entirely preserved.

Kennet, also *Kennet and Avon Canal:* one of the best mixed fisheries in the land. Mostly preserved. Some day tickets issued by societies having canal stretches.

Lea (Herts): fair coarse fishing on upper stretches of Walton's favourite river.

London reservoirs: Metropolitan Water Board reservoirs provide excellent coarse fishing for specimen fish. Apply Room 113, New River Head, Rosebery Avenue, London, E.C.1.

Lune (Lancs): salmon, sea trout and trout; tickets obtainable on several stretches.

Medway (Kent): good coarse fishing, sometimes excellent. Day tickets obtainable on many reaches.

Nene (Northants): good coarse fish river with bream and pike notable. Day tickets obtainable.

Norfolk Broads: Barton, Heigham Sounds, Hickling, Horning, Horsey, Ormesby, Salhouse, and Wroxham Broads all have excellent coarse fishing, mainly free. Some are disturbed by boat traffic, especially in the summer months. Where a charge is made for fishing it usually is collected on the banks. Pike fishing is exceptionally good. For rivers see: *Bure, Thurne, Waveney, Yare.*

Ouse, Great: excellent coarse fishing almost throughout its length.

Tickets usually available. Some notable chub fishing. Excellent tributaries include: Nar, Cam, Ivel.

Ouse (Sussex): coarse fish, but quite exceptional run of big sea trout.

Ouse (Yorks): coarse fish water with ticket and free water in places. Has barbel and, in tributaries, good trout. Tributaries are too numerous to name. Among the most famous are: Wharfe, Nidd, Swale.

Parret (Somerset): fine coarse fish water with trout in some tributaries. Day tickets obtainable.

Ribble (Lancs): some good coarse fishing between Great Mitton and Preston. Salmon, sea trout, and brown trout, also grayling in higher waters. Tributary, Hodder, has good game fishing throughout.

Rother (Kent): trout and coarse fish in upper reaches. Good chub.

Severn: good salmon river. Excellent coarse fishing in upper waters, some controlled by Birmingham Anglers' Association, but much free.

Stour (Dorset): trout, salmon and coarse fish. Excellent water. Day tickets obtainable in some places.

Stour (Suffolk): excellent coarse fishing, dace, perch, roach all specimen size. Suffers from water extraction badly. Much preserved.

Tamar (Cornwall): salmon, sea trout and trout. Tickets can be obtained at Launceston.

Taw (Devon): salmon, sea trout, trout, also roach and dace at Barnstaple. Mostly preserved by land-owners and hotels.

Tees (Yorks and Durham): salmon, trout, grayling and coarse fish. Day tickets in places.

Teign (Devon): salmon, sea trout, and brown trout. Mostly preserved.

Test (Hants): England's most famous trout river and chalk stream. Fishing entirely preserved.

Thames: good coarse fishery, particularly in middle and upper reaches. Entirely free below Staines. No licence necessary. Some trout but very wily. Barbel good down to Kingston. Bream excellent in Goring and Pangbourne areas. Tributaries offer fair to excellent fishing. These include Mole, Wey, Loddon, Kennet, Cherwell, Evenlode, Windrush, and Gloucester Colne.

Thurne (Norfolk): Popular Broadland river, yields roach, perch, bream, pike.

Torridge (Devon): salmon, sea trout and trout. Mostly preserved.

Trent (Notts): the longest river system in the country, and once its best mixed fishery. Coarse fishing fair in many districts still. Mostly association water but day tickets available in many places. Notable tributaries: Soar, Wreake, Derwent, Dove, Churnet, Sowe, Penk.

Tyne (Northumberland): once a fine salmon river but grossly polluted. Now improving for coarse and game fish.

Waveney (Norfolk and Suffolk): first-class coarse fishing with bream exceptional. Is connected to Oulton Broad.

Welland (Lincs): favourite coarse fishing and especially match fishing river. Day tickets obtainable.

Witham (Lincs): same as for Welland. Note that the drains and artificial rivers, eaus and leams of the Fen district all give exceptional coarse fishing.

Wye (Monmouth and Hereford, Brecon and Radnor): exceptionally fine salmon and coarse fish river, especially for chub. Coarse fishing tickets obtainable in many places. Salmon mainly preserved. Notable tributaries: Lugg, Arrow, Ithon.

Yare (Norfolk): another Broadland river with first-class roach fishing in middle reaches.

Wales: The principality is mainly a game-fish country with brown and sea trout (called in Wales, 'sewin') and salmon abounding. A great deal of very cheap trout and sea trout fishing is to be had, especially in middle and North Wales. Many of the South Wales streams suffer from industrial pollution. Of recent years there has been a strong move towards coarse fishing in mid- and South Wales. Here are some notes on the main rivers.

Clwyd (Flint and Denbigh): game fish river. Tickets can be obtained in some areas from hotels or tackle merchants.

Conway (Caernarvon): game fish; day tickets obtainable in several stretches.

Dee (Denbigh): a famous Welsh salmon river. Grayling and coarse fish almost throughout its length. Tickets obtainable at many places.

Dovey (Merioneth and Montgomery): excellent sea trout river with small May-to-October run of salmon. Tickets obtainable in many places. Good brown trout fishing in many of the tributaries, free or nearly so.

Dysynni (Merioneth): good game fish river with day tickets obtainable.

Mawddach (Merioneth): game fish river preserved mostly, but with day tickets obtainable on some stretches.

Teifi (Cardigan): salmon and sea trout river, sea trout starting in July. April and May best for salmon. Much of the river can be fished on day tickets.

Towy (Carmarthen): salmon, sea trout and some brown trout. Mostly preserved but day tickets obtainable in many places.

Usk (Monmouth): fine salmon river, mostly preserved, also excellent for brown trout. Trout fishing tickets are obtainable in some stretches.

Scotland: salmon is the great quarry of Scottish angling with, of course, sea trout and brown trout. Fishing for the latter is thought of in a poor light compared with that for salmon—the only creature dignified by the name 'fish'. Coarse fishing is not touched by the inhabitants. Just the same, for Sassenachs there is some excellent coarse fishing to be had. The record Scottish pike from Loch Lomond weighed 47 lb., and there are certainly many bigger ones. In 1956 the chub record was beaten by two pounds by a sea trout angler on the River Annan. Permission to fish for coarse fish is usually readily given. Now, for some principal rivers.

Annan (Dumfries): late salmon river with good sea trout and chub. Tickets can be had in many centres.

Ayr (Ayrshire): brown trout good, also salmon and some sea trout. Permission can be obtained on some stretches.

Clyde (Renfrew and Lanark): polluted for salmon in lower reaches but good brown trout fishing above for both wet- and dry-fly. Tickets obtainable in most places. Its best-known tributary, the Leven, has run of salmon and sea trout, being connected with Loch Lomond.

Dee (Aberdeenshire): a very famous river for salmon, also has sea and brown trout. Mostly preserved.

Deveron (Aberdeen): good game fish river with tickets obtainable in some places.

Forth (Stirling and Perth): good game fishing with tickets available in many places. Trouting good in upper reaches and connecting lochs, especially Loch Leven, probably the most famous trout fishing lake in Scotland.

Ness (Inverness): drains Loch Ness, famous for salmon and sea trout. Permits can be had.

Thurso (Caithness): One of the best early salmon rivers in Scotland. Hotels have much water but permission obtainable in some places. Good trouting on lochs.

Halladale (Sutherland): very good early salmon river; nearly all preserved.

Spey (Moray and Banff): famous salmon fishery, almost entirely preserved.

Tay (Perth): Scotland's most famous salmon river with tributaries that also produce fine salmon fishing in their own right. Mostly preserved, but trout fishing in surrounding lochs and streams often free or nearly so.

Tweed (Roxburgh, Berwickshire): a great salmon river with best sport usually in spring. Very big sea trout. Much of salmon fishing preserved, but trout and grayling tickets obtainable in many places.

The Scottish Tourist Board's publication *Scotland for Fishing,* issued yearly, gives detailed information about all waters in Scotland.

Ireland: the problem in Ireland is rather where *not* to fish. There is an acre of water to every 35 acres of land. Many of the stream and lake beds are limestone and the size of the fish in most of the waters could be legendary if it were not actual. Undoubtedly much of the water has barely been explored: certainly not for coarse fishing, which is an anathema to the Irish just as it is to the Scots. Nonetheless, the record pike (53 lb.) came from Loch Conn. Bream have been caught in Belturbet, County Cavan, up to 15 lb., and there are certainly bigger ones. Three- and four-pound rudd (which the Irish call roach) are not exceptional. Perch are numerous but tend to run disappointingly small (a two-pounder is looked upon as a very good fish). Tench are being introduced, carp exist already in some waters, while chub and dace—species thought previously not to be found in Ireland—are in plentiful supply, in very large size, in the River Blackwater, in the Fermoy area.

The possibilities for coarse fishermen are endless. They are endless, also, for trout fishermen. The Irish do not call a trout a good fish until it tops the 3-lb. mark, and there are plenty of these and even bigger fish landed regularly from the famous loughs such as Sheelin, County Cavan, and Mask, County Mayo. All the Western loughs—Conn, Corrib, Cong, Mask, Derg, etc., produce very big trout and excellent sport on wet- and dry-fly.

Hitherto, information on fishing in Ireland was rather scanty. The Irish did not seem to appreciate that the visiting angler might not wish to fish in the accepted local manner. For example, many English trout fishermen prefer rivers to lakes. Unless sufficient reconnaissance is done, local guidance, with the best will in the world, might take the visitor straight to the nearest lake whereas there may be an excellent trout river in the neighbourhood.

In recent years two guides have been issued by the Irish Tourist Board. They are *The Angler's Guide* (10s. 6d.) and *Ireland for Coarse Fishing*, a free booklet.

WHERE TO FISH, Sea Angling: the following is a brief summary of some of the main sea fishing stations in Britain. More detailed information should be sought in *Where to Fish*, published by *The Field*, and in *Sea Angling* by Derek Fletcher (Faber and Faber).

Aberdeen: surprisingly little rod fishing done here although the area abounds in good sport. Mackerel come into the Dee estuary and travel quite far up river where they can be taken on spinner. High and steep cliffs make shore fishing difficult although there are spots where a precarious descent can be made. Boat fishing affords sport for cod and codling, mackerel, whiting, haddock and flatfish.

Aberdovey: first-class all-round sport both in the estuary and in the surf along the beaches. Bait can be found locally including rag and lug worms, peeler crab, mussels, etc. Bass, codling, whiting, plaice and mackerel.

Aberystwyth: boat and rock fishing for skate, for whiting, bass, etc. Mullet sometimes come into the river mouths here.

Ballycotton: the Irish village that has become the Mecca of sea anglers in recent years. The best fishing, anyway for giant skate, halibut, etc., is from a boat. Smaller species such as bass and wrasse can be caught from the rocks. Eastern Ledge is the famous offshore pollack fishing mark.

Barnstaple: good bass and mackerel fishing in the Taw and Torridge estuaries. Surf-fishing for bass can be good at Saunton Sands and Woolacombe. Ilfracombe pier offers fair all-round fishing with occasional conger.

Bexhill: fair all-round fishing from boats: goodish bass from shore.

Blackpool: boat and pier fishing, the latter improving steadily as the autumn advances. Codling, tope, whiting, dabs are all taken. Tope fishing has recently been developed.

Bognor: excellent all-round sport from pier (there is a special angling extension), sandy beaches in all directions, and from boat. Bass, black bream (May and June), conger, tope, and bull-huss are all to be had on well-known local marks.

Bournemouth: first-class all-round sea fishing from pier, boat and beach. In summer time the best angling is to be had at night due to the daytime crowding of the beaches. Ragworm is dug plentifully at Sandbanks. Hengistbury, Durley Chine and Southbourne are all favoured locations for beach fishing.

Bridlington: fine fishing all year through from shore, pier and boats. North Pier can be fished in winter only. Tope, cod, and codling are notable.

Bridport: fishing from boat and shore is good. Seatown, Cogden, Burton Rocks and Eype are all well-known fishing stations. Boat fishing some five miles offshore provides really big skate, conger, pollack, etc.

Brighton: out of the holiday season fishing here is good for flatfish, mullet, mackerel and bass. Some of the best flat-fishing is to be had from November onwards.

Brixham: excellent sea fishing with bass, mackerel, and pollack coming high on the list. Bass fishing is at its best late in the season. Live prawn is a favoured local bait. Plenty of bait available locally. Probably one of the finest all-round sea fishing spots in Britain.

Broadstairs: good fishing from June onwards for tope, bass, and from September onwards for cod, skate, and bull-huss.

Cardiff: good all-round sea fishing in this area. Cardiff Dock foreshore (a dock permit is necessary) provides excellent conger fishing, also bass and whiting. Penarth, Ranny Beach, St. Mary's Well Bay can all be recommended.

Christchurch: fine sea fishing from boat and beach. Big tope caught in the bay during the summer, the best taken by trailing a mackerel. All other usual species in abundance from boat. Highcliffe beach east of

Christchurch is a useful spot for the beach angler.

Clacton: Good fishing for bass, soles, eels and whiting. Best times April to June and September to November. Later in the year, boat anglers get into big skate, ray and dogfish.

Cromer: flatfish and whiting, also codling are taken from the pier and along the beaches of this Norfolk resort.

Dartmouth: one of the finest sea fishing stations in the West. Sheltered fishing inside the estuary and well up the River Dart, of which the first few miles are predominantly salt. Number of well-known bass and pollack marks offshore. Dartmouth and Kingswear pontoons can be fished on a permit issued by British Railways. They are ideally sheltered stations in rough weather and provide good bass catches. Kingswear also produces fine pollack.

Deal: beach fishing here throughout the year. Eight miles of sandy beach to the north of the town gives fine flatfishing. Big skate fall to boat anglers and the Goodwins offer big tope chances.

Dover: Eastern Arm, Admiralty Pier and Prince of Wales pier regularly produce specimen catches. Whiting, conger, cod, bass, plaice, soles, pollack are all 'on'. A shilling day permit is necessary to fish all but the upper level of Admiralty Pier. It can be had from the pier gate office.

Eastbourne: soft crabs lure specimen bass near Beachy Head. Boats take bass, bream, dog, conger, pollack, etc. Excellent all-round sport.

Exmouth: good estuary and foreshore fishing for bass, mackerel, etc. Notable flounders are landed every season, usually taken by baited spoon. Best bass fishing is in the estuary from boats using a drifting sand-eel.

Falmouth: fair fishing in the harbour for pollack and bass. Good offshore fishing for pollack, mackerel, bass, whiting, etc.

Felixstowe: a notable bass fishing centre, the record fish of 18 lb. 2 oz. came from here. Boat, pier and beach fishing all available. Visitors invited to join the local club as holiday members.

Folkestone: fair fishing to be had from the harbour pier, particularly at the lighthouse end. From the beaches the best sport is obtained two hours either side of full tide. Pollack in the harbour are taken largely on float tackle.

Fowey: pollack, bass, mackerel all to be caught in early summer. August is usually a poorish month owing to abundance of natural food. Shark found offshore in the same waters fished by anglers out of Looe. The estuary gives bass fishing for several miles upstream.

Great Yarmouth: harbour, piers and beaches all afford sport. Best fishing is from beginning of autumn until the New Year. Cod have been taken over 20 lb.

Hastings: boat, pier and beach fishing of good standard. All species are caught, including tope about a mile offshore.

Herne Bay: fishing is good here almost throughout the season. In the early spring the nearly mile-long pier provides dabs, plaice, and skate. Bass come in during June, as do the tope. There is excellent beach fishing at Reculver Towers.

Hythe: best fishing from the beaches during the autumn. Codling, bass, conger, flatfish are all landed. Sometimes mackerel in the summer.

Isle of Man: perhaps the best sea fishing centre in the British Isles.

Many of the biggest fish are caught from boats, including conger, tope, shark, pollack, cod, hake, skate, bull-huss. Pier and breakwater fishing of a high order can be obtained at Port St. Mary, Ramsey, Peel, Douglas, and Port Erin among other centres. In Castletown harbour, grey mullet feed freely. Beach fishing is being developed with success.

Jersey: first-class sea fishing of all kinds from the many jetties and harbour walls. One of the favourite spots is the three-quarters-of-a-mile-long St. Catherine's breakwater, also Elizabeth Castle breakwater, outside St. Helier's port. July to October gives the best sport for bass and pollack.

Kingsbridge: this South Devon town is a good centre, particularly for bass fishing. Excellent sport will be found in the River Avon estuary at Bantham and Bigbury. Sand-eel and prawn are favourite baits. Salcombe, not far away, has first-class fishing of all sorts both in and outside the harbour.

Littlehampton: fine boat fishing out of Littlehampton for all the usual species, including black bream (in June), bass, skate, conger, pollack and tope.

Lizard: an enthusiast's centre, much of the best fishing being from rocks that require tenacity and fitness to reach and climb. Pollack and bass are the local speciality with mackerel and wrasse a close second.

Llandudno: Bass and flatfish from the Black Rocks neighbourhood on the west shore; best sport being from half tide to full. Fair all-round fishing from the pier. Large skate are caught from boats in the bay.

Looe: a popular sea fishing centre that has gained tremendous publicity through the activities of the Shark Fishing Club of Great Britain

Offshore in boats, specimen fish of many species are caught, particularly pollack, bass, and mackerel, Sport from harbour and rocks, especially for bass.

Lymington: a beach angler's and surf-caster's centre. Barton, Milford, Hurst Castle, Pennington Marsh all provide fine beach fishing from sand and shingle.

Margate: bass fishing off the rocks round Foreness. Boats get fair bags of flatfish, whiting and dogfish. Tope two to four miles offshore.

Milford Haven: excellent and largely unexplored boat and rock fishing round the shores leading to this fishing port. Tope, bass, whiting, mackerel, pollack all good.

Minehead: fair to good bass fishing from the middle of August until the end of September. Fishing allowed from the harbour wall. Best sea fishing from the beach at the golf course end, also for bass from Greenaleigh beach behind North Hill.

Morecambe: fair fishing which improves as the winter approaches. Tope are caught from boats. Permits are needed for Heysham Harbour, and there is a charge for fishing the West-End and Central piers. Flatfish and bass are caught from beaches. In winter, codling and whiting are taken.

Newhaven: excellent all-round fishing from beach, jetties and boat. Bass from shore: mullet from July to September on bread-paste.

Newquay (Cornwall): first-class all-round sea fishing for fish of specimen size. The pollack record was broken here in 1957. Big bass are taken from the beaches, while boat fishing affords a chance for almost everything, including the possibility of sharks. Pollack, wrasse, pouting, skate, conger, dogfish are all to be caught.

Paignton: Bass are taken from the beaches either by ground-fishing or spinning. Mackerel come right in close to the pier and are caught on float tackle as well as by other methods. Pollack, conger, whiting, flatfish are all to be had here. Prawns, caught in beach pools, are popular bait.

Plymouth: excellent shore and harbour fishing for bass, mackerel, mullet, flounders, pollack, etc. Sutton Harbour (pollack), Victoria Wharves (pollack, mackerel, flounders), Hoe Lake backwater (mullet), Mouthstone Point (wrasse, bass, mackerel), Season Point (ditto) are all well-known fishing stations. Boat fishing in the Sound is good: boats can be hired from West Hoe Pier and Barbican.

Poole: good boat fishing from here. Mullet, flounders, and bass are all taken. Flounders give the best sport in winter. Brownsea Island is profitable for bass. Shell Bay beach can be recommended for bass fishing.

Porthcawl: miles of sandy beach that give good bass fishing. A stone jetty commands good bottom over shingle. At high water there is fair fishing from the rocks towards Rest Bay: strong tackle is needed here, however. Whiting and codling come in during winter.

Portland: the finest mullet centre in the country. From the long shingle spit known as Chesil Beach all kinds of fish can be caught—codling and bass among them. Bread-paste is used locally when boat fishing for mullet.

Ramsgate: fine all-round centre. Specimen conger, flounder, cod, tope, bass, and whiting can all be expected. Boat and pier fishing.

Ryde, I.O.W.: flounder, plaice, mullet from pier. School bass come in from May onwards. One mile offshore, boat fishers can expect black bream, pout, skate, tope.

Scarborough: expensive tunny fishing. Boat, shore and pier fishing for usual species. Codling, pouting and wrasse, also mackerel, pollack, plaice and dabs give good summer sport.

Seaton: summer and early autumn provide mackerel, whiting, most flatfish, conger, skate, dogfish, with bass in the mouth of the River Axe. Boat fishing is most profitable.

Sidmouth: trolling finds big pollack here. Good bass fishing from the shore, particularly during May and June. Evening conger fishing from boats often produces good

flounders, mullet and bass are taken from the latter. Boats take flounders from May to July.

Sunderland: codling are caught in great numbers here mainly through the autumn and winter. Roker and Seaburn beaches give good all-round sport.

Torquay: good fishing from April to November. Shore stations include Meadfoot, Beacon Cove, Princess Pier. Boat fishers get into tope, turbot, brill, conger and skate.

Worthing: fishing from pier and beach for flounders, and bass. Lancing Pipe gives fine fishing for big bass to boat anglers. These fish

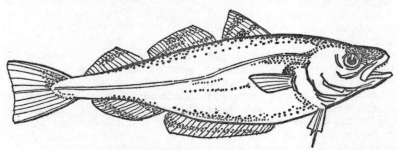

WHITING. *This relative of the cod family may be distinguished from the Pout Whiting by its more slender body and the lack of a barbule beneath the mouth.*

hauls. Skate fishing one mile offshore can be excellent: occasional skate are landed from the beach.

Southampton: king ragworm dug from the shore at low tide accounts for enormous flounder catches on occasions. Flounder are fished for off the mouth of the River Test at Redbridge right round to Calshot. Hythe Pier is good for flounders. Permits can be obtained to fish the docks from Dock House at Old Docks. Good deep-water stations here for flounder, bass, mullet, whiting, etc.

Southend: boat fishing and also angling from the famous one-and-a-half-mile-long pier. Garfish and

can be taken by spinning or on live wrasse. Ragworm can be dug locally.

WHITING: *Gadus merlangus,* family *Gadidae.* The record whiting is 6 lb. and anything which is over a pound-and-a-half can be reckoned as a good fish. The whiting is a member of the cod family, but has no barbule beneath its chin and is easily recognized by the dark spot just in front of the pectoral fin. Whiting are winter fish, moving into the shore as the first frosts touch the water. The fish caught inshore during the summer are mainly immature.

The whiting is a shoal fish that scours the sandy bottoms for it meals. In feeding it is somewhat capricious so the angler after whiting should take a variety of baits, including among them: fish strips, mussels and lugworm. Whiting fishing is not particularly skilful. If the fish are there they will usually take. Moreover they require little striking, frequently hooking themselves. The bite is shown in a series of quick tugs. Light tackle should be used where conditions permit, to give the maximum sport. Paternoster is the usual gear either from a boat or from pier or beach. The hooks should be baited with various offerings until it is found which one the whiting are taking.

WINDOW: this term refers to the area of upward vision of a fish, and is usually used in conjunction with trout fishing. The point is that fish have a fixed angle of upward vision. This, in the case of a trout, is about 48 degrees on either side of the vertical. Within this angle the fish can see through the surface to the outside world, even though indistinctly. The area of surface included in the window is roughly oval with its main axis parallel to the line of the trout's body. All round this window the surface appears like a mirror. The fish sees nothing through it. He simply gets back a reflection of the bottom and his surroundings. To underwater vision none of this applies. The fish can see very clearly and at great range anything floating towards him submerged. Moreover, the depth at which the fish lies has no effect upon the angle of his vision through the window in the mirror. Thus, the deeper he is in the stream, the bigger will be his window.

Compare the effect of shining a fixed-angle torch beam on a wall at six inches and then at three feet.

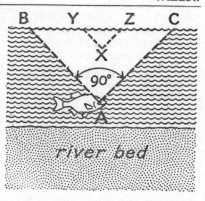

WINDOW. *The vision of a fish through the surface is confined within an angle of 90 degrees. Thus, a fish at A can see through a greater surface area than can one at X.*

At three feet the circle of light has widened out considerably although the angle of the beam remains unaltered: thus with the trout's window. But depth makes the trout's view through the window more uncertain, especially if the surface is ruffled.

One other factor must be considered, and that is the angle of refraction of light rays entering the water. True, the trout's upward angle through the window may be fixed at 48 degrees on either side of the vertical, and from this it may seem that a fisherman, to be noticed, would have to come within range of this angle, However refraction of surface light, from air to water, is such that the angle is distorted until it is bent at the surface to a mere ten or fifteen degrees to the horizontal. Obviously, then, the fisherman on the bank must keep pretty low if he does not want to come into the trout's window, particularly when it is remembered that a glimpse of his rod, or even of his hat, is sufficient sometimes to put the trout down.

From all this, certain deductions can be made. (1), a trout can see a floating fly only when it comes within the window. The closer he is lying to the surface, the more accurate must be the cast; (2), a sunken fly, or even part of a half-submerged fly, is spotted without trouble and at long range; (3), when a dry-fly is floating properly it is unlikely that even the hackle points penetrate the surface film. What the trout sees in this case is probably a blurred outline of the fly which is sufficiently near the real thing to cause him to rise, and also the dents made on the surface by the hackle points: these, although far more numerous than the dents caused by the six legs of an ephemerid fly, say, are in many cases sufficient to make the fish rise to the artificial.

The effect of the surrounding mirror can be seen by the human eye —which differs considerably in construction from that of the trout— when looking upward through the bottom of an aquarium.

The reason, incidentally, why deep-lying fish such as grayling so frequently miss the fly on the rise, is that they see it indistinctly through the window in the first place.

WITCH: a flatfish very similar in appearance to the sole, and occasionally caught in deep water over mud by the angler who is plaice fishing with worm bait. The lateral line is straight and the eyes are placed on the right side of the head.

WORMS: earthworms will take practically any fish that swims from the *Salmonidae* to the humble gudgeon. The two most common and useful varieties are the lobworm and the brandling. The first is the sort you find on lawns after dark, and in flower beds when you're digging: the second kind favour piles of moist leaves and the compost heap. Brandlings smell, have striped skins, and give off a yellow juice when broken.

There is quite a lot to the preparation of worms for fishing. They are tougher on the hook if scoured for a few days before use by being made to work their way through florist's moss. This can be achieved by turning the tin containing them upside down every twelve hours or so: they will always wriggle their way back to the bottom.

Purely of academic interest are the following facts: there are probably about fifty species of worm in British soil: worms have a complete set of male and female reproductive organs but cannot fertilize themselves—they need another worm; eggs are laid in a band that encircles the body. This is later shed, slips off the worm's body and becomes a self-contained cocoon.

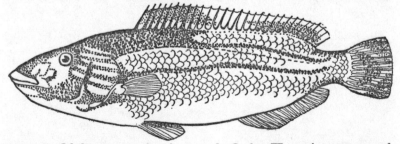

WRASSE. *Of the seven species of wrasse the Cuckoo Wrasse is most commonly seen in British waters. It favours rocky coastlines in the south and west.*

233

Worms can be stalked after dark on a wet lawn. Though they cannot see, they are very sensitive to vibrations. A stealthy approach is essential. When spotted, the worm must be grabbed quickly before it draws itself back into its hole.

WRASSE: there are seven varieties of the family *Labridae* found round British coasts. These are: the Rainbow wrasse (*Coris julis*), Ballan wrasse (*Labrus maculatus*), Rock cock wrasse (*Centrolabrus exoletus*), Cuckoo wrasse (*Labru mixtus*), Scale-rayed wrasse (*Acantholabrus palloni*), Corkwing wrasse (*Crenilabrus melops*) and Gold-sinny wrasse (*Ctenolabrus rupestris*). All have large scales, spiny dorsals, and thick lips. In colouring, most of the species are almost tropical.

The three most common varieties as far as the angler is concerned are the Ballan, Cuckoo, and Corkwing, and these will be found off rocky coasts, especially in the south and west. The Cuckoo wrasse is a magnificent creature with blue and orange stripes that, unfortunately, do not last long in brilliance when taken from the water. The Ballan, the biggest of the tribe, is tan and light blue. The Corkwing is somewhat perch-coloured having the rudiments of stripes on the upper half of the body. The Rock cock has a black spot near the gill.

The great thing about wrasse as far as the angler is concerned is that they are most obliging and will continue to give sport throughout a blazing, calm summer's day when few other species will look at the bait: in this they are rather like the bleak, ruffe, and gudgeon of the freshwater man. Float-fishing for wrasse can prove good sport, large baits being used, and almost anything, including garden worms, serving on the hook. A quick bob of the float usually means a small wrasse, and a quick strike is needed to hook him; bigger fish take the float in much the same manner as a perch and the angler can wait until it slides away. A light rod, something of the order of an Avon rod, or a longish spinner will serve, together with a drum reel loaded with 5–6-lb. breaking strain line. When fishing from the rocks a net with a long handle is a 'must'.

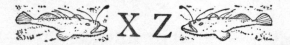

X Z

XANTHOCHROISM: the term that describes the colour variations in fishes by which they are able to alter their natural pigmentation to gold. The goldfish, golden tench, and golden orfe are examples. The colour-producing cells, or chromatophores, of fish are situated in a layer of tissues beneath the outer skin.

ZANDER: *Lucioperca lucioperca,* usually called pike-perch. Found in European waters and recently introduced into a few English lakes. Pike-like in shape but having marked perch characteristics, especially in the dorsal fins and flank marks. Average length about 18 in. Excellent eating and gives good sport.

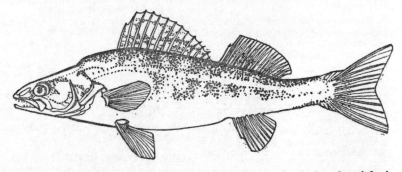

ZANDER. *Otherwise known as the pike-perch, the zander is found mainly in European waters. It possesses some of the characteristics of both species.*

Appendix

IN this appendix I reproduce extracts from the bye-laws of many of our principal River Boards. I have selected sections that, read together, will give a reasonably full picture of the regulations imposed on anglers throughout the country. Since these extracts are necessarily vastly abridged, it is advisable for anyone fishing a strange river to check on the full regulations in force. The bye-laws relevant to rod and line fishing are usually reproduced on the back of the River Board licence which the angler must obtain (Thames and a few other rivers excepted) before starting to fish.

AVON AND DORSET RIVER BOARD

Close Season For Trout. The period between the thirtieth day of September and the first day of April.

Minimum Sizes

Gudgeon	4 in.	Bream	8 in.
Roach	8 ,,	Barbel	16 ,,
Perch	8 ,,	Tench	9 ,,
Dace	8 ,,	Trout	10 ,,
Rudd	8 ,,	Grayling	12 ,,
Carp	12 ,,		

The minimum size shall be ascertained by measuring from the tip of the snout to the fork or cleft of the tail.

BRISTOL AVON RIVER BOARD

Close Seasons

Salmon, between the 31st October and the 1st February.

Trout, except in certain Bristol Waterworks Reservoirs: the period between the 30th September and the 19th March. In the Bristol Waterworks Reservoirs: the period between the 15th October and the 19th March.

Freshwater fish and eels: the period between 14th March and the 16th June.

It should be noted that the above dates are exclusive; for example, the freshwater fish close season commences on the 15th March and ends on the 15th June.

Minimum Sizes

Pike	22 in.	Perch	9 in.
Bream	12 ,,	Grayling	8 ,,
Carp	12 ,,	Roach	8 ,,
Chub	12 ,,	Rudd	8 ,,
Tench	10 ,,	Dace	7 ,,
Trout	9 ,,		

The size shall be ascertained by measuring from the tip of the snout to the fork or cleft of the tail.

EAST SUFFOLK AND NORFOLK RIVER BOARD

Minimum Sizes. Pike, 24 in.; Trout, Bream, Chub or Grayling 10 in.; Carp Tench, Perch, Roach, Rudd or Dace 8 in.

The length in each case to be measured from the nose to the fork of the tail.

Removal of Fish. No person shall take or remove or carry away in any day more than 4 trout (excluding migratory trout) or more than 2 freshwater fish of each kind.

GREAT OUSE RIVER BOARD

Use of Lure and Bait. No person shall use in connection with rod and line fishing: (a) Any lure or bait which is trailed from a moving boat; or (b) Any gorge bait for pike fishing; or (c) Any lure or bait for trout fishing between the thirty-first day of March and the sixteenth day of June, in any year, except artificial fly and preserved or artificial minnow.

Minimum Sizes

Pike	24 in.	Barbel	18 in.
Trout	11 ,,	Grayling	12 ,,
Tench	12 ,,	Carp	12 ,,
Chub	14 ,,	Bream	12 ,,
Roach	8 ,,	Rudd	8 ,,
Perch	8 ,,	Dace	7 ,,

The size shall be ascertained by measuring from the tip of the snout to the extremity of the tail.

Fishing For Eels During Annual Close Season For Freshwater Fish. Fishing for eels by means of rod and line during the annual close season for freshwater fish shall be permitted provided that no hook or other metal appliance is attached to the line.

Close Season For Trout. (Rod and

Line.) The period between the thirtieth day of September and the first day of April.

Close Season For Pike. The period between the fourteenth day of March and the first day of October.

KENT RIVER BOARD

Close Season For Salmon and Trout. (*Rod and Line.*) The period between the thirtieth day of September and the first day of April following, except in the waters of the Darwell and Great Sanders Reservoirs of the Hastings Corporation where the close season shall be the period between the fifteenth day of October and the first day of April following.

Minimum Sizes			
Barbel	16 in.	Gudgeon	5 in.
Bleak	4 „	Perch	9 „
Bream	12 „	Pike	18 „
Carp	12 „	Roach	8 „
Chub	12 „	Rudd	8 „
Dace	7 „	Tench	10 „
Grayling	12 „	Trout	10 „

The size shall be ascertained by measuring from the tip of the snout to the tip of the tail.

No salmon, trout or freshwater fish, nor any spawn thereof, may be introduced from any source into any waters within the River Board Area without the previous consent in writing of the River Board.

LANCASHIRE RIVER BOARD

Close Seasons

Trout (other than Brown Trout) Rods. The annual trout close season for rod and line for migratory trout shall be the period between 31st October and 1st May.

Brown Trout Rods. The annual trout close season for rod and line for brown trout shall be: (1) in that part of the River Board Area comprising the former Kent, Bela, Winster, Leven and Duddon Fishery District including the Catchment Areas of Leighton Beck and the Rivers Bela, Kent, Gilpin, Winster, Bea, Rothay, Brathay, Leven, Crake and Duddon and Haverigg Pool with their tributaries and, in the River Wyre and its tributaries, the period between the 30th September and the 3rd March; (2) in the remainder of the River Board Area the period between the 30th September and the 15th March following.

Char Rods. The period between 30th September and the 3rd March.

Worm Fishing. (a) No person shall, excepting as hereinafter provided, use in fishing for salmon and trout a worm baited on more than a single hook and such hook shall not exceed 1½-in. in length overall, nor ½-in. in width of gape and the weight or weights used to sink the hook shall not in any case exceed ½ oz. in the aggregate; provided that in fishing for trout a tackle of two or three hooks may be so used if tied upon a single strand of gut and if each of such hooks does not exceed ¼-in. in length and is not more than ¼-in. in width of gape. (b) No person shall use any worm in fishing in non-tidal waters for salmon or migratory trout during the month of October in each year.

Baiting. Between the 14th March and the 16th June in any year the use of maggots as hook bait and the use of any lure or bait other than one which is on or attached to a hook or line are prohibited.

Provided that this byelaw shall not apply to lakes, ponds and canals.

Size Limits

Migratory Trout	10 in.
Non-Migratory Trout	8 „
Tench, Bream, Grayling	9 „
Roach and Perch	7 „
Dace and Rudd	6 „
Gudgeon	4 „

The size shall be ascertained by measuring from the tip of the snout to the fork or cleft of the tail.

Angling For Eels during Annual Close Season for Freshwater Fish. It shall be lawful to fish for eels with rod and line during the annual close season for freshwater fish.

NENE RIVER BOARD

Fishery Byelaws.

No person shall at one time fish with more than two rods and lines.

No person shall use any gorge bait tackle in connection with fishing for pike.

Fishing for eels with rod and line shall be permitted during the annual close season for freshwater fish provided that no hook of a gape of less than ½-in. is used

No person shall take or kill or attempt to take or kill any salmon, trout, freshwater fish or eels in any of the rivers, streams, drains, lakes, ponds, waters and watercourses under the control or jurisdiction of or in the area of the Nene River Board by means of any instrument or mode of fishing except a rod and line or a landing net or gaff used as auxiliary to angling with a rod and line.

Minimum Sizes

Pike	28 in.
Chub and Carp	15 „
Bream and Tench	14 „
Trout and Grayling	12 „
Roach, Rudd and Perch	9 „
Dace	7 „

The size of such fish shall be ascertained by measuring from the tip of the snout to the extremity of the tail when the mouth is shut.

No person shall take or remove or carry away from any waters within the jurisdiction of the River Board more than 5 freshwater fish in any one day.

Provided that for the purpose of this byelaw no account shall be taken of roach, rudd or dace of not less than 5 in. in length and not exceeding 20 in any one day taken as live bait for fishing for pike within the Nene River Board Area.

The annual close season for Pike shall be the period between the fourteenth day of March and the first day of October. The annual close season for trout shall be the period between the thirtieth day of September and the first day of March.

SEVERN RIVER BOARD
Close Seasons

Salmon. The period between the fourteenth day of September and the second day of February.

Trout. The period between the fifteenth day of September and the fifteenth day of March.

Freshwater Fish. The period between the fourteenth day of March and the sixteenth day of June.

Minimum sizes of fish and districts in which they are prescribed.

Gudgeon 4 in. Perch 8 in. Rudd 8 in. Tench 9 in. Bream 10 in. Roach 8 in. Dace 8 in. Chub 9 in. Carp 9 in.

All waters within the River Board Area except: (1) the waters of the River Severn (including its tributaries) above or upstream of its confluence with the River Vyrnwy, and (2) the waters of the River Teme (including its tributaries) above or upstream of Stanford Bridge.

Minimum sizes of Trout and Grayling and districts in which they are prescribed.

The waters of the River Servern below or downstream of Shrewsbury Weir—10 in.

The waters of the River Severn (in-

cluding its tributaries) above or upstream of Morfodion Railway Bridge: the waters of the River Vyrnwy (including its tributaries) above or upstream of Dolanog Weir: the waters of the River Banwy (including its tributaries) above or upstream of Dolanog Weir: the waters of the River Banwy (including its tributaries) above or upstream of its confluence with the Afon Gam: the waters of the River Tanat (including its tributaries) above or upstream of its confluence with the River Rhaiadar—7 in.

All other waters within the Severn River Board Area—9 in.

The size shall be ascertained by measuring from the tip of the snout to the tip of the tail.

Uses of Lures or Baits With Rod And Line. (a) No person shall use in connection with fishing with rod and line for salmon any float carrying or supporting any lure or bait. (b) No person shall during the annual close season for freshwater fish use in connection with fishing with rod and line any float carrying or supporting any lure or bait, or use as a lure or bait, cereal or maggots.

Angling For Eels During Freshwater Fish Close Season. It shall be lawful to fish with rod and line for eels during the close season for freshwater fish.

Trailing or Trolling. The trailing or trolling of Natural or Artificial spinning baits from boats in motion is prohibited.

Spinning For Trout During Freshwater Fish Close Season. Spinning for trout during the close season for freshwater fish is hereby prohibited.

SOMERSET RIVER BOARD
Close Seasons

Salmon. The period between the first day of October and the sixteenth day of February.

Migratory Trout. The period between the fourteenth day of September and the third day of March.

Non-Migratory Trout. In the Blagdon Reservoir and the Barrow Reservoirs of the Bristol Waterworks Company and the Durleigh and Ashford Reservoirs of the Bridgwater Corporation; the period between the fifteenth day of October and the nineteenth day of March.

Freshwater Fish. The period between the fourteenth day of March and the sixteenth day of June.

Use of Gaff. It shall not be lawful to use a gaff in connection with fishing with rod and line for salmon or migratory trout except during the period between the twenty-ninth day of April and the second day of October.

Prohibited Modes Of Fishing. No person shall use in fishing for salmon, trout or freshwater fish more than two rods and lines at the same time. No person shall use any gorge bait in fishing with rod and line.

Minimum Sizes

Bream	14 in.	Roach	9 in.
Carp	14 „	Trout	7 „
Chub	12 „	Rudd	8 „
Tench	12 „	Dace	7 „
Perch	9 „	Pike	22 „
Grayling	10 „		

The size shall be ascertained by measuring from the tip of the snout to the fork or cleft of the tail.

Limitation on Number of Fish Taken. No person shall take or remove in any one day more than 6 freshwater fish irrespective of species nor more than 2 of any one species.

THAMES CONSERVANCY

Fishing in The River Thames Between Teddington and Cricklade.

General Information.

Fishing in the river below Staines is open to the public.

Above Staines the fisheries are privately owned, but in some parts fishing is not objected to by the owners. In certain places the owners either do not allow fishing or require their permission to be first obtained. In one or two cases they make a charge.

No licence is required from the Conservators to fish in the river within their jurisdiction (i.e. between Teddington, Middlesex and Cricklade, Wiltshire).

The Close Season for coarse fish is from the 15th March to the 15th June (both dates inclusive), and for trout from the 11th September to the 31st March (both dates inclusive). Between the 1st April and the 15th June persons fishing for trout must do so with a rod and line and with an artificial fly or spinning or live bait.

Minimum sizes. Any of the following fish which are caught of less length than that specified must be returned to the river with as little injury as possible:—

Barbel	16 in.	Lamperns or	
Bleak	4 „	Lampreys	7 in.
Bream	12 „	Perch	9 „
Carp	12 „	Pike or Jack	18 „
Chub	12 „	Roach	8 „

Dace	7 in.	Rudd	8 in.
Flounders	7 „	Smelts	6 „
Grayling	12 „	Tench	10 „
Gudgeon	5 „	Trout	16 „

The size shall be measured from the tip of the snout to the tip of the tail.

Night fishing is not allowed above Staines or from a boat below Staines.

TRENT RIVER BOARD

Immature Fish. For the purpose of the Salmon and Freshwater Fisheries Act, 1923, the following kinds of fish of the sizes less than those respectively specified as hereunder shall be deemed to be immature:—

Pike	20 in.	Tench	9 in.
Barbel	15 „	Carp	9 „
Trout	9 „	Roach	8 „
Grayling	8 „	Rudd	8 „
Bream	10 „	Perch	8 „
Chub	9 „	Dace	8 „

The size shall be ascertained by measuring from the tip of the snout to the extremity of the tail fin.

Fishing for Pike. No person shall use any gorge bait in connection with fishing with rod and line for pike.

WYE RIVER BOARD

Close Season for Salmon (Rod and Line) (a) In the River Wye below Llanwrthwl Bridge the period between the thirtieth day of September and the twenty-sixth day of January and (b) In all other waters of the River Wye and in all tributaries of it the period between the twenty-fifth day of October and the twenty-sixth day of January.

Use of Float with Lure or Bait. No person shall use in fishing for Salmon with rod and line any float carrying or supporting any lure or bait.

Use of Worm as Bait. No person shall use in fishing for Salmon with rod and line any worm as bait between the thirty-first day of August in any year and the fifteenth day of April in the following year.

Use of Maggots as Bait. No person shall use as bait between the fourteenth day of March and the sixteenth day of June next following in any year any maggot, grub or larvae, whether natural or artificial when fishing with rod and line.

Taking of Undersized Trout. In that part of the Wye River Board Area which lies below Rhayader Bridge no pers n shall take any trout less than 7 in. in length measured from the tip of the snout to the fork or cleft of the tail.

Angling For Eels during Freshwater Fish Close Season. It shall be lawful to fish with rod and line for eels during the annual close season for freshwater fish.

The open season for: (a) fishing for Trout with rod and line is from 1st March to 30th September following inclusive; (b) fishing for Freshwater Fish with rod and line is from 1st January to 14th March, and 16th June to 31st December following inclusive; and also from 15th March to 15th June following in any privately owned fishery where salmon and trout are specially preserved, PROVIDED the Angler has a valid WRITTEN Permit to fish from the owner or occupier; (c) fishing for Eels, with rod and line, is from 1st January to 31st December inclusive.

Undersized or immature fish may not be taken as follows: *Salmon* less than 12 in. long from tip of snout to fork or cleft of tail; *Trout* less than 7 in. long from tip of snout to fork or cleft of tail from water below Rhayader Bridge.

YORKSHIRE OUSE RIVER BOARD

Weekly Close Time for Salmon and Migratory Trout; shall be the period between the hour of twelve noon on Saturday and the hour of six o'clock on the following Monday morning.

Close Season For Migratory Trout (Rod and Line). The period between the thirty-first day of October and the third day of April.

Close Season for Freshwater Fish. The period between the twenty-seventh day of February and the first day of June.

Use of Gaff. No person shall use a gaff in connection with fishing with rod and line for salmon or migratory trout except between the thirty-first day of March and the first day of October.

Minimum Sizes

Trout	9 in.	Tench	9 in.
Barbel	12 „	Dace	7 „
Bream	9 „	Perch	7 „
Chub	9 „	Roach	7 „
Grayling	7 „	Rudd	7 „

The size shall be ascertained by measuring from the tip of the snout to the fork or cleft of the tail.

Limitation upon the number of Freshwater Fish taken in any one day. No person shall kill, take or remove or carry away from any waters within the River Board Area more than 10 freshwater fish in any one day.

For the purpose of this byelaw "freshwater fish" shall be deemed to be pike, barbel, bream, chub, tench, dace, perch, roach and rudd.

Introduction of Fish or Spawn from other Waters. No person shall introduce any live fish nor any spawn thereof from any source into any waters within the River Board Area or transfer any fish or spawn thereof from one water to another without the consent in writing of the River Board.

Use of Electrical Apparatus for taking Fish. No person shall use in connection with the taking or attempted taking of salmon, trout or freshwater fish, or so as to kill or injure or attempt to kill or injure any salmon, trout or freshwater fish, any instrument or device which passes an electric current through or into the water of any fishery without the written permission of the River Board.